Land-Grant Universities
and
Their Continuing Challenge

LAND-GRANT UNIVERSITIES

and

THEIR CONTINUING CHALLENGE

EDITED BY

G. LESTER ANDERSON

MICHIGAN STATE UNIVERSITY PRESS
1976

Copyright © 1976
Michigan State University Press
Library of Congress Card Catalog Number: 75–44530
ISBN: 0–87013–198–2
Manufactured in the United States of America

★
★
★
★
★

Contents

Acknowledgments

THIS book was made possible by the Office of Gifts and Endowments of The Pennsylvania State University with undesignated gifts to the university from alumni. The possibility of such a book had been discussed by the administrators at the Center for the Study of Higher Education at the university, but it did not seem to be possible until the monies from the alumni were made available. A special thank you is due Mr. Charles Lupton, Executive Director of Gifts and Endowments, for his support for the volume.

A number of persons not listed among the authors, as is always the case, made much more than routine efforts to help bring forth what we hope will be a significant contribution to the continued growth of the land-grant idea. First among these was Janet Novotny Bacon, Editor at the Center for the Study of Higher Education, who did much of the heavy editing of first and second draft material. Thanks are also due Mrs. Carol J. Kersavage, who assisted particularly in the agriculture chapter; Mrs. Betty Meek, secretary to the volume editor; and the many Center typists who patiently typed and retyped the numerous drafts of the various manuscripts: Sara Alterio, Kathy Bell, Joan Irwin, Connie Jones, Kathy Kelligher, Diann McVey, Colleen Shaeffer, and Janet Zettle.

Finally, thanks are due to Dr. Garven Hudgins, Ms. Valerie Ventre, and Ms. Ione Phillips of the National Association of State Universities and Land-Grant Colleges, who encouraged us to carry the idea through to publication and provided much of the material to be found in the appendix.

G. Lester Anderson
University Park, Pa.
September 1975

Chapter 1

LAND-GRANT UNIVERSITIES
AND THEIR CONTINUING CHALLENGE

G. LESTER ANDERSON

The Land-Grant University Idea

THE United States Office of Education ceased collecting statistics on the land-grant colleges or universities in 1963—101 years after passage of the Morrill Act which established these colleges. What did this decision signify? Did it mean that the land-grant universities were no longer a viable or distinctive segment of the American system of higher education? Did it mean that the federal government no longer found it important to recognize a special class of colleges and universities which it had been instrumental in establishing? No answer is clear but it is a fact that land-grant colleges and universities today bear only a modest resemblance to what they were seventy-five or even fifty years ago.

This is so despite the fact that the concept and function of the land-grant university have not significantly changed in this century. The diminishing of their uniqueness is due to the adoption by other institutions of the basic concepts of the land-grant idea: democratization of education; applied or mission-oriented research conducted to benefit the people of the states; and service rendered directly to these people through extension agents, short courses, and continuing education. At the same time, the land-grant universities were developing and expanding even in those states where there was another public university. This created land-grant universities which were coequal with other public and private institutions.

Clearly the land-grant universities and the non-land-grant but public universities no longer constitute in any major sense two distinctive categories. But the idea of the land-grant university does and should persist. The values that have infused these institutions for over a century continue to be emphasized and constitute a system that merits consideration as the future of higher education in this nation is planned.

To assess the land-grant institutions quantitatively, some figures are relevant. There are seventy-two land-grant universities in the fifty states and three territories. They enrolled approximately 1.6 million students in 1974–75, which is approximately 16 percent of the 10.2 million students in higher education that year. If non-land-grant state universities now accept a share of higher education responsibilities that at one time were more or less an exclusive responsibility of the land-grant institutions, and, at the same time, if the land-grant institutions have become in a number of respects indistinguishable from the non-land-grant state universities, then the figures are as follows: 3.1 million students were enrolled in the 130 institutions which form the National Association of State Universities and Land-Grant Colleges in 1974–75. This represents more than 30 percent of American higher education enrollments for that year. Graduate and professional education (exclusive of teaching and nursing) are more or less exclusively the mission of universities both public and private. In terms of this mission the state universities and land-grant colleges award 64 percent of the doctorates conferred in any given year and approximately 36 percent of all bachelor's and first professional degrees. What, then, is the challenge of the future for the land-grant concept?

First, the land-grant idea was a product of two significant constituencies of the American body politic. It did not come solely from Justin Morrill or any other one person. The definitive act known as the Morrill Act, passed by the national Congress in 1862 and signed in the midst of the Civil War by President Lincoln, represented the culmination of political activity over a period of many years. David Madsen gives a lucid account of the history of the land-grant college in a subsequent chapter. The constituencies that brought it about were the organized industrial and agricultural interests of the nation, particularly of the Northeast. What we must recognize is that the land-grant idea represents *a political ideal*—an ideal which was accomplished at the national level by the grassroots constituency. Over time, the land-grant universities have represented a national commitment and a commitment by the Congress and the president of the United States.

Second, the creation of land-grant institutions is the most significant single representation of the *democratization* of higher education —a social phenomenon that has been ongoing not only since the nation's founding but in reality since its beginnings in the 1600s. One of the most persistent trends in all of American higher education has been an ever broadening concept of who should be educated. The nation has moved from a base of educating elitist males, to educating women, to educating members of the middle and lower classes—the sons and daughters of farmers and working people—and now to educating minority ethnic and racial groups. The nation has recently expanded the institutional bases for democratization with the rather fantastic development of community colleges. And when institutions such as the City University of New York move to "open admissions," the base has again been broadened. But the norm for land-grant institutions has always been to work from a concept of open admissions. From their very beginnings, they sought those who previously were presumed to be ineligible for college. Land-grant institutions were never elitist, however the elite might be classified, in terms of wealth or power or social class or intellectual promise. Two chapters in this book, "Land-Grant Universities and the Black Presence" by Samuel Proctor and "External Degree Programs: The Current Educational Frontier" by Kenneth Mortimer and Mark Johnson address the topic of continued democratization of the land-grant university.

A third feature of the land-grant idea has been that the work of scholars—and particularly their research—may be and at times should be deliberately planned toward *utilitarian* ends. One of the glories of the "university qua university" is that it is a manifestation of the intellect as revealed in scholarly work and research. Such activity normally profits most when it is not mission-oriented. But such knowledge and understanding, as Bacon once said, is always presumed to be ultimately useful.

Land-grant institutions undertook to develop an agricultural and engineering technology through organization, an assignment of resources, and the use of scholars, primarily scientists. The commitment of the scientist and later of the social scientist in terms of mission has probably nowhere been better represented than in the agricultural experiment stations. This development to its current status is presented in the chapter "Colleges of Agriculture Revisited." Suffice it to say here that a science of agriculture was created and that it has had revolutionary consequence in the production of food and fiber, in making agricultural labor nearly obsolete, and in reducing the family farm as it was known up to as late as World War II to nearly marginal status and in some instances to a status which is counterproductive. Science was also harnessed to produce the technologies that permeate the developed sectors of the world in almost every aspect of their functioning—industrial production, transportation, communication, distribution of goods and services, work in the home, care of the ill, war, population control, music, art, and architecture.

Strangely, however, the land-grant universities did not *systematically* go beyond their original mandates to cultivate agriculture and the mechanic arts in the organization of mission-oriented research to a high level. Nowhere have applications of the social sciences or the humanities through research and development activities been made on a scale comparable to that of science in agriculture, in technology, and in engineering, or more recently in the health professions. Perhaps this development cannot be attained. But the concept should be explored. Such is done in the following chapters: "Liberal Learning and the Land-Grant System: Futures and Optatives" by Maxwell Goldberg, "Social and Behavioral Sciences in the 1970s" by Renee C. and Robert S. Friedman, and "Land-Grant University Services and Urban Policy" by David Nichols.

A fourth significance of the land-grant concept is complementary to the concept of democratization and the concept of mission-oriented research. It is that the *fruits of research should be taken to the people.* Here again, the colleges of agriculture developed this concept to a high art. It is paradoxical that the colleges of agriculture are now being challenged through writings and court actions as having neglected rural America in favor of what is called agribusiness. The truth is that never were the fruits of research so developed and disseminated to the people as by colleges of agriculture.

The ultimate consequences of the dissemination of the scientific bases of agricultural production, its processing and marketing, were probably not anticipated in the development of agribusiness. But the forces which brought forth the current highly efficient complex known as agribusiness should not be chided. Rather, problems which emerge from efficiency should be considered. The concept of carrying research productivity to the people has been broadened far beyond agriculture in recent years. The function is typically called continuing education. It represents a significant educational service, particularly by land-grant institutions but not confined to them, to a constituency not represented by the conventional college student. The processes of continuing education are well understood and are increasingly being well developed when they are utilized by the professions and professionals, particularly for physicians and other members of the health-related professions, for teachers, and for business and industrial managers.

These four functions or hallmarks of the land-grant institution continue. The problems to which they are applied have and will continue to change, as will the milieu in which the land-grant university exists.

The question is: Will the land-grant institutions need to change their concepts of mission or goals in order to remain viable?

Goals and Governance of Land-Grant Universities: An Assessment

It is not self-serving for land-grant universities to assert that they have been splendid instruments for bringing education, research, and service to the people. There seems to be no need for major reform in either their goals or governance. There are some, however, who are asking for innovation. While innovation has been a cliché for higher education in the seventies, it is essentially meaningless in regard to intended connotations. Change for the sake of change is simply organizational foolishness. An innovative act in and of itself can be with or without significance. But the land-grant universities have never been static, and it must be assumed there will be continuing change. The chapters of this volume which follow are abundant in their suggestions for constructive innovation or change. This section will discuss those changes anticipated in goals or mission.

Powerful forces are continuously at work in the American body politic, in American business and industrial life, and in American culture. We must anticipate great value shifts, despite seemingly current conservative moods. Western culture continues to be a restless thing, and the American social streams are in turn moderately turbulent. These forces and the fact that universities and the institutions of higher education in their entirety constitute a social system in their own right make universities a social dynamic at once responsive to other social dynamics while retaining or maintaining a considerable autonomy within the system. It is in this complex of interactions that we presume to reassess the goals or mission of higher education with particular reference to the land-grant segment.

The now rather trite concepts of teaching, research, and service continue to be valid. The goal of the land-grant universities to be of service to the people in terms of these concepts also continues to be valid. What seems to be called for, however, is a *further extension* of these goals. Using the totality of the universities' resources, new modes of teaching, particularly new areas of applied research and service, must be created to make this extension meaningful and substantial. This means that the social sciences and humanities should be utilized in as appropriate a manner as the sciences have been by the agricultural and engineering components of the university. This seems to be a relatively simple idea. If it actually were, however, it would have been acted upon. Such is not the case; the challenge remains and is the challenge of this book.

To know the essence of the land-grant concepts of teaching, research, and service, we return particularly to look at agriculture and its related endeavor—home economics. Agriculture manifests an unequivocal commitment to mission (a systematic assignment of resources and an organizational pattern for their use) that is unrivaled by any other unit of the university. Agriculture is unique among the operational units into which the university is customarily divided. Agriculture deals with production but also, and without a rift in continuity, with processing and marketing. Historically, it has dealt with the system that carries out agricultural production and distribution not as a business or industrial complex but as a "community." The use of the word community in this association is accurate; that is, agriculture has dealt with the farm family as a means of production and as an end in itself. As Liberty Hyde Bailey often said, "We are preserving and enhancing the pastoral way of life." And so the grange, the 4-H clubs, the attention to the family as a unit—its child-rearing patterns and its recreation, its management of money and its nutrition, its house and garden—were not simply important; they were intrinsic to the colleges of agriculture and home economics. This totality of consideration is now somewhat attenuated. Pre-World War II agricultural production units, largely familial in character, have in some respects become obsolete. The farm family has in a considerable measure lost its characteristics as such—it has become one with other patterns of American family life. Thus, while the historic pattern, as represented in the university by agricultural education, research, and service, fails in some respects to serve as a model for a university commitment and structure for interaction with urban life. The idea which agriculture has represented over the last century remains to be more fully developed in terms of totality of life in the United States—urban as well as rural—and in terms of a fuller application of the sciences, social sciences, and humanities.

Another sphere of university activity which we must perceive and come to understand more meaningfully is science. This statement, on the surface, may seem foolish since science and its uses have become so pervasive and hence so commonplace. The growth, organization, and institutionalization of science have been the most powerful human development of the last hundred years. This development has occurred largely, although not exclusively, in the university. In the university it became the most powerful agent of change and the most powerful component of the university's constituencies. The basic sciences represent man's thinking of the very highest order. The ultimate developments of science lead to knowledge of "laws" of nature or of the universe.

In application, the fruits of science are the technologies that have profoundly changed modes of life. To name but a few: life saving and life giving by those who care for our health; structures which defy the most violent of nature's stresses; modes of transportation that move man and his materials faster than the speed of sound; the transmission of images and sound from any one spot on earth to another with the speed of light; aerospace systems combining technologies into a complex that have made it possible for men to walk on the moon and for most of us to see and hear them there; technologies for genetic control, for weed, insect and disease control, and for control of nutriments and moisture that fantastically increase the production of food from the soil.

Have there been outcomes from either the social sciences or the humanities that can compare? Might there be? The questions are puzzling and subtle. Achievements of philosophers and artists represent at their highest levels of critical acclaim without question the work of those whom we call geniuses—they represent, as does science, the highest reaches of the human mind. The social scientists, however, have less to represent of their work that can be called comparable. Nonetheless, through the world religions, the lives of men have been affected as profoundly as they have been by science. Through the processes of government—be it democratic or authoritarian—the lives of men pursued individually and in states and nations have been profoundly affected. Perhaps, then, science appears so spectacular in its effects because they are so recent.

However, much of contemporary life and culture has been little influenced since the days of the Greeks or Romans by man's learning and the fruits of his humanistic and social science scholarship. Do we know how to teach better than Socrates knew? Have there been significantly more scholarly or more analytical treatises on how to govern than Plato's *Republic?* And have such treatises as have been produced, also produced better governments? Have fundamental insights into the motives of men as expressed by Shakespeare or Goethe or our nearer contemporaries, Joyce or Tolstoy or Faulkner, caused men significantly to alter their ways of life? Have the psychologists who study motivation done better than Euripides and Homer? Perhaps nothing should be expected here.

It seems that economic theory should be able to bring greater control over the fluctuations in the economy than is now possible. Likewise, economic theory might lead to practices which could lessen the gap between underdeveloped and highly developed nations, a gap which now apparently widens year by year. So it would seem that the disciplines of psychology and sociology might find greater application to a variety of human interactions, for example, in government, or in the maintenance of peace, or in the governance of universities.

As for the arts and the humanities, which presume to relate to the quality of life in an ethical, spiritual, and esthetic sense, or at least in a value-laden sense—they affect few of us in any profound way. The masters are not easy to know. If, as Matthew Arnold said, culture is "the best that has been thought and said by men," it may only be known by long, disciplined study in which we know both individual writers and the intellectual and technical milieu in which they create. Perhaps here again nothing can be done. This pursuit must always remain elitist in terms of its being a quality effort to master a body of knowledge. But the arts and humanities must become non elitist by enriching the personal lives of Americans and establishing the amenities of life. At present, large segments of the university are oriented to teach only the elitist mode of the humanities. Serious curriculum reform in content and modes of instruction would seem to be required to enable the humanities to enrich human life. One step in this direction would be, as we make the excellent contemporary artist a teacher-performer in his specialty, to also give him full faith, credence, and confidence in the community of scholars. This is not always done. The graduate must come to know that the artist is not an entertainer but an interpreter of reality to the same degree as is the scientist or critic. The artist probes the value systems of a culture.

What we are asking for with this book is a reordering of goals, or at least an extension of them, to improve cities as we improved rural life, by applying social sciences to social interactions (family, city, class, or race) and humanities to the enrichment of the lives of all at the level of meaning and purpose.

This proposition raises questions: What should Federal City College, established in Washington, D.C. as a land-grant university some half dozen years ago, ultimately be? What might graduate schools of social welfare (operational in fifty universities, more or less) or of justice and criminology (John Jay College of City University) ultimately attain through wide application of the social sciences? What might happen if the universities of the land were as hospitable to creative artists as they are to critics and historians? Might it be possible to amend the original Morrill Act, or supplement it as has been done frequently in the interests of agriculture, to specify that the land-grant university shall deal with urbanism or the diffusion of the human arts or shall provide urban and social interaction research centers on the scale of the agricultural experiment stations in each of the fifty states? Could we also create modes analogous to the cooperative extension services and expand and fortify continuing education so that we could apply the fruits of the research in the social sciences and the humanities in urban and social interaction?

These questions may be the products of fantasy. They may represent such a simplistic concept of knowledge put to use as to be meaningless. Again, they may not. At least we invite an assessment of the goals of the land-grant universities in more contemporary terms. The chapters which follow have provided a substantial base from which this assessment can be continued.

Chapter 2

WHAT'S AHEAD
FOR THE LAND-GRANT COLLEGES?

RALPH K. HUITT

THE Morrill Act of 1862, a remarkable exercise of social vision passed and signed during a fratricidal war, had three main purposes.

The first was to develop manpower capable of meeting the needs of a swiftly developing industrial nation, the United States. America had an industrial labor force, growing every year, which was wholly adequate to do the common tasks. What was not in supply, however, was the leadership which only engineers and technicians could give. For this leadership, experts had to be imported from Europe. Furthermore, American agriculture was already on that disastrous sequence of ruin and move. Someone had to learn how to farm right and teach it to others. So one dimension of the act was public service —the performance of research and teaching in order to serve the nation's needs.

The second was to open up postsecondary education to young people who otherwise would have no access to it. In truth, few young people even went to high school; except for Massachusetts, high schools were rare across the country. So many of the land-grant colleges had to be high schools before they could be colleges. The University of Minnesota, for instance, granted its first baccalaureate degree eight years after opening its doors. The act speaks of educating the "industrial classes," by which Morrill meant all those young people who were not served by the traditional universities which trained the children of the elite to be lawyers, doctors, teachers, and preachers. So more nearly equal access to higher education is another dimension of the act.

The third was to see to it that young people received a truly good education.

The purposes of the act, to educate a new kind of student to perform a new kind of service, is fairly common knowledge. What is not is the purpose that this new student should receive a *"liberal and practical education"* (emphasis supplied). The act states that clearly, and the purpose shines through the entire law. Morrill did not mean these not-wealthy young people to be short-changed with a mere vocational or technological education. The Bankhead-Jones Act, which provides permanent authorization (though not funding) of further monies to the land-grant colleges, lists the courses of study for which the funds can be spent. There is a broad array of the social sciences and humanities among them. The third dimension of the Morrill Act is high quality education.

It is in terms of these three purposes of the Morrill Act, therefore, that we look toward the future of the land-grant colleges. A fourth dimension will be added: the relationship of the institutions to the government of the United States, which provided this original assistance and much more.

Two comments should first be made. There is little that can be said about the land-grant colleges that is unique to them. Most of the great agricultural colleges, with their combination of research, extension, and instruction, are at land-grant institutions (perhaps no more than three at other public universities are equal to them). But in most other ways the land-grant institutions are like other principal state universities; indeed, many are both. And they have been successful in creating scientific disciplines out of folklore. Allan Nevins has said that the "public university created the modern university." Yes; so much so that the great private universities are much more like them than unalike.

Public Service

The universities of America are great reservoirs of knowledge and skills which are relevant to the problems our society faces. The multiplicity of the linked-together problems of the large city—crime, education, transportation, health, poverty, discrimination, segregation—all have stimulated research and service projects in the universities. So have the related problems of environment—energy, inflation, depression. But what is lacking, in most cases, is a mechanism by which the science and technology of the universities can be transferred to the public problem-solvers who need it. The university system is not a gigantic computer which can be asked a question which can be answered by the information stored in it. The sources of knowledge about energy are scattered even more widely than the agencies of control in the national government; they are scattered among many departments on a campus, and there are many universities.

But in one area—the food problem—there is a mechanism. It is the partnership of the land-grant colleges and the government of the United States, especially the U.S. Department of Agriculture. Permanently authorized funds support the state experiment stations, which do research on agricultural production, and the cooperative extension service, which carries new technology to American farmers. The resident instruction on the campus completes the classic triad of research, extension, and instruction, which are conceived to be the responsibilities of the public university. The role American agricultural schools should play in the world food crisis turns on an understanding of the nature of the problem.[1]

By 1973, the United States had moved from the elevators and warehouses bulging with food and grain (the situation in 1971) to a situation where the newspaper headlines screamed daily of shortages and inflated prices. What had happened?

During the last two decades, the world had, in effect, three major food reserves:

(1) sizable grain stocks carried over by major exporting countries;

(2) millions of acres of United States cropland held out of production;

(3) available but only partly used agricultural technology.

Two decades ago, the world had just over 2.5 billion people. In 1973, the world had nearly 3.9 billion mouths to feed, up more than 50 percent in two decades. Meanwhile, the world's grain reserves had been declining, especially since 1973. Grain reserves are a critical

[1]What follows immediately is an adaptation of an analysis by agricultural scientists at Iowa State University, published by the National Association of State Universities and Land-Grant Colleges as "New Circumstances: Facing America's Ability to Meet Expanding Domestic and Foreign Demand for Food and Fiber" (1973).

measure of the world's food production needs, because 51 percent of man's food energy over the world comes from grain eaten directly.

On June 30, 1973 (the end of the trading year), grain stocks of the four major exporting countries (United States, Canada, Australia, Argentina) stood at 105 million metric tons, down some 18 percent from the 1955–64 average. The decline in grain reserves was caused by increased world demand and short crops in major producing countries.

Growing world demand for grains has two roots: (1) world population, which grows at the rate of about two percent a year, and (2) rising incomes in the developed parts of the world which are expressed in demand for higher quality diets, especially for meat. As a result, world cattle and hog numbers increased sharply in the last three years. In addition, long-sought foreign markets in Russia and China were opened by President Nixon's visits.

Unfavorable weather reduced 1972 grain production in many countries. Meanwhile, import demand was up in western Europe, Japan, and other countries. Russia decided to maintain its five-year plan for increased livestock production and bought large amounts of wheat and corn from the U.S.

The year 1972 revealed the precarious balance between world grain supplies and world demand which had been developing over the past decade. In less than twelve months, grain surpluses changed to comforting reserves, then to disturbing shortages.

But the question must be asked: Is the sudden shift in grain supply-demand balance a short-run problem, a mere flash-in-the-pan, or does it represent a fundamental change in world food prospects?

World demand for grains has been growing along with population increases. Rising incomes in Japan and western Europe allow consumers to spend more of their incomes for food. And a major share of the increased spending goes for more meat. It is this shift toward more meat, milk, and eggs in western Europe and Japan which is creating demand pressure of feed grains and soybeans. These pressures are in addition to those created by the two percent more people in the world each year.

Each person born into the poor countries of the world adds a demand of about 400 pounds per year from grain supplies. As incomes increase, the amount of grain utilized rises rapidly. But after per-capita incomes reach $500 a year, *direct* grain consumption declines, and more is consumed indirectly in the form of meat, milk, and eggs. The peak grain consumer is the average North American whose per-capita grain consumption is over 1800 pounds per year, much of it in the form of livestock products.

In the United States, two factors are of crucial importance in assessing future grain supply prospects—land and technology. In the U.S., some 20 million acres of cropland were held out of production in 1973 compared with an average of 53 million acres during the 1960s. For 1975, no such restraints on cropland use existed. But because cropland held out of production usually is the more marginal land, any long-term increase in production will not be proportional to increases in acreage. And there is an annual attrition of cropland to other uses.

Agricultural technology is harder to measure. The U.S. with its public supported land-grant university and USDA agricultural research system has increased greatly the productivity of its farmers. In 1952, the average U.S. farmer produced food and fiber for himself and sixteen others. By 1972, the average U.S. farmer was producing food and fiber for himself and fifty-one others.

An efficient agricultural education and communications network has carried new agricultural technology to U.S. farmers. And where farmers of two generations ago were slow to adopt new agricultural practices, today's farmers grasp much of the new technology as quickly as it is available and clamor for more.

As a result of this efficient system of transmitting agricultural technology to farmers and farmers' ready acceptance, the unused technology pool is very low. For example, extension agronomists at Iowa State University agree that Iowa farmers are using practically all available technology in producing that state's most important crops, corn and soybeans.

There is only so much land available to use in producing food in this country. No such immediate restrictions apply to production technology—the methods and techniques we use in producing and processing agricultural commodities.

The salutary effects of U.S. investment in agricultural research and education are illustrated by several measures. U.S. citizens in recent years have spent less than 16 percent of their disposable incomes for food. This is less than in any other country in the world. With a smaller proportion spent for food, more remains to support a high living standard.

Another measure is the percentage of the work force engaged in direct agricultural production. Only six percent of the U.S. labor force is engaged in farming. That leaves ninety-four percent to provide the services and other goods (including farm inputs) which U.S. citizens use and enjoy. The six percent who do the farming have been producing abundant food for U.S. consumers and also vast amounts for foreign trade.

From half to three-fourths of the U.S. wheat crop is exported, one-fifth of its corn, about one-third of its cotton, and more than half of its soybean crop.

U.S. exports of farm products added to $12.9 billion in the fiscal year ending June 30, 1973. Our agricultural trade surplus was a record $5.6 billion—bringing the U.S. balance of payments much closer to balance. Many foreign countries produce industrial goods more economically than we do. None produce corn and soybeans as efficiently.

So, U.S. investment in agricultural research and education has paid off in abundant low cost food for consumers at home and also in commercial gains in world trade. It has paid off so well that the cooperative land-grant university-USDA research and education system is a marvel of the world. Literally thousands of foreign officials and students have come to work in and study that system.

It is clear, therefore, that one answer to the world food problem is to increase the investment in agricultural research and technology transfer so that more food can be produced here. But that is not the whole answer to the world problem. With the best of will, there is no way that America can feed the world, no matter how much we produce. There are not enough bottoms to carry what would be needed, and the less prosperous countries are mostly adding to their populations with might and main. Therefore, the technology transfer must be from us to them: they must learn to feed themselves.

The effort to bring this about has been underway a quarter of a century. American land-grant colleges have been in the vanguard, in partnership with the Agency for International Development and the Department of Agriculture. New initiatives are afoot in 1975 to renew the international aid impulse and begin new extensions. The response of the American public is not encouraging, but it is an effort that has to be made. It is not easy to look away as parts of the world face famine.

Equal Access to Higher Education

The public university, with its low tuition or none at all, certainly has done more than any other socially established mechanism to ease the financial barrier to access to higher education. The American tradition of a student working his way through college depended on a low-cost institution which made it possible for summer work, perhaps a part-time job during the school year, a little help from the family, and some modest borrowing to see the student through. Although tuitions at public universities have gone up, some to levels that surely are too high, the officers and supporters of these institutions fight to keep them down. The burden of the student has been eased by the burgeoning of the community colleges, but the problem of the last two years must be faced if the student is to get what is accepted as a college education.

The most dramatic aspect of extending access lies, in 1975, in the attempt to get to students who cannot get to the campus with external programs which serve him where he is. Dramatic examples are everywhere. The statewide Empire State College, which is a part of the State University of New York system, and the State University of Nebraska are two examples of ambitious programs. Most promising, perhaps, is the coalition of the State University of Nebraska with five other midwestern public universities to set up an extended-education university called the University of Mid-America. A basic part of all these programs is a dedication to lifelong learning. Today both state and land-grant institutions are assuming increasing responsibilities in adult education.[2]

The growing need to provide lifelong learning experiences is lead-

[2]The following discussion is adapted from *People to People,* a publication of the National Association of State Universities and Land-Grant Colleges.

ing these universities to extend themselves even more than they have in the past. Changing career patterns and new demands for updated knowledge have made it essential that higher education institutions offer an increasing number of opportunities for adults to drop in and out of the university at will.

"Higher education has traditionally focused upon the education of youth, the 18–24 year old group whose potential lay in the future," noted Clifton R. Wharton, Jr., president of Michigan State University. "Today it is no longer adequate to educate the youth of our society and expect that educational experience to suffice a lifetime. For in the 20 to 30 year interim between graduation and their rise to positions of influence, the fundamental values and knowledge of our society may have changed dramatically."

While some form of continuing education has existed almost from the start, the needs of an urban society now demand that this concept pervade all aspects of the institution. State and land-grant universities are attempting to meet the new challenge with the same vigor and directness with which they met the needs of rural America more than a hundred years ago. In some states the continuing education program is already so comprehensive that it is probable that at least one person in every township is participating in one of the activities provided.

Academic courses are taught in formal daytime and evening classes, conferences, seminars, workshops, and institutes. They are conducted by correspondence, television, radio, and cassette. They may be taught in local high schools, factories, elaborate residential centers, or in regular college classrooms.

They are taught by full professors, student teachers, volunteers, and professionals eminent in their fields. They may last a few weeks or a full semester. They may or may not be taken for credit.

They may enroll grandmothers, doctors, grade school dropouts, teachers, laborers, businessmen, housewives—in short, any person who wishes to further his education.

Many adults take such courses to increase their earning potential by the acquisition of higher degrees. Others seek to enrich newly-found leisure time. Still others, perplexed by changing times and mores, are seeking answers in books.

Continuing education is particularly appropriate for professionals such as teachers, lawyers, dentists, doctors, engineers, and business-men who take extension courses in order to update their skills. So rapidly is new knowledge being produced in these fields that profes-sionals who do not return periodically to the classroom quickly lose their effectiveness. In some cases universities actually contract with business, industries, and school systems to provide "in-service" training for personnel.

Continuing education divisions of state and land-grant universities also provide job training for persons who want to learn new skills in a large number of fields as diverse as fire fighting and data processing.

This determination to teach people whatever they need to know, wherever they are, whatever their circumstances, surely is an exten-sion of the egalitarian impulse of Justin Morrill.

Quality and Equality

It must not be forgotten that Justin Morrill's vision was not just that there should be equality of opportunity for higher education, but that this education should be *quality* education. He had in mind four years of truly liberating education.

One of the great developments of our time has been the rapid growth of community and junior colleges all across the land. Close to home, conversant therefore with local problems and job oppor-tunities, they have opened up the classroom to hundreds of thou-sands of people who doubtless would have missed out altogether. Their success has led one member of Congress, a person whose credentials as a friend of education are beyond any question, to suggest that a two-year community college education for every young person is what the government should guarantee. The idea is good as far as it goes, but questions arise. Will this become a "track" for the disadvantaged, who have thereby no guarantee of the last two years and so will aim for the vocational courses, while their more fortunate neighbors lay the groundwork for a profession? What guar-antee is there that all who finish two years can transfer to the third and fourth? A scheme akin to that is the so called "K-14," which simply adds two more years to public school. The idea is appalling

to one who thinks the public school holds young people too long now
and that efforts should be directed at reducing, not lengthening, this
experience.

A problem shared by higher education institutions generally is the
grade inflation which plagues many institutions, causing some to
abandon the dean's list because it is meaningless with half the student
body on it. There are those who argue that there should be no grades,
because grades themselves are meaningless, or that grades put brands
and stigmas on young people which they cannot live down. Some
even oppose any kind of certification. But we do not hesitate to make
other discriminations. Beauty prizes do not go to ugly persons, nor
varsity letters to weaklings. And grades and diplomas certify, not to
the worth of the person, but to that person's academic performance.
To deny grades, or to make them meaningless, is to cheat the good
performer of the validation of his good performance, that he or she
has earned.

The grand goal of equality of opportunity is not met by granting
equally to all a poor education. There can be no true equality without
quality.

Relations with the Federal Government

One source of great strength in higher education throughout our
history has been the capabilities of colleges and universities to maintain their institutional integrity. But the rapid development of federal
programs of assistance to higher education has not allowed time for
an orderly pattern of mutual responsibilities to evolve. Indeed, we
believe that in many cases the devices and regulations introduced by
the government have invaded the autonomy of institutions and have
threatened their integrity, which should be maintained at all costs.

Each program carries its own requirements, spelled out in guidelines or administrative regulations. Sometimes these rules go beyond
legislative intent; sometimes they seem clearly to contradict it. The
prerogatives of colleges and university administration are overridden. Enforcers unfamiliar with academic procedures, and sometimes
even with the law and their own agency's regulations, make judgments on most complicated matters. Regional offices are allowed to

make conflicting interpretations. And the same requirement may be enforced by as many as four agencies plus the courts, permitting the same matter to be litigated again and again.

No particular programs are selected for criticism; the point is that there is no hint of general policy in them. Some centralize, some decentralize. Some support one concept of governance, some another. They seem to be provisions developed by well-meaning officials dealing only with the matter at hand.

On another front, it is important to higher education that public officials who develop and enforce national policies which all support should evolve a flexible array of sanctions. The policies multiply but the sanction stays the same: withdrawal of federal funds. Capital punishment. And the lethal sanction is, of course, in the end, unusable. Would the government of the United States close a medical school when one-third of new physicians each year are graduates of foreign medical schools? Almost certainly not. There are many available sanctions that can be tailored to the offense. Court orders, fines, monetary penalties, reimbursements for discrimination are among them.

It is time for representatives of higher education to sit down with their friends in Congress and the executive branch and discuss these problems. No one should expect blanket solutions. But forthright discussions and better understandings can result. And that will be worth a lot.

Conclusion

Today the historic land-grant institutions and their sister state universities address the large and demanding problems of the nation and all mankind—energy and the environment, inflation and recession, and the need for an adequate and nutritious food supply—and accept responsibility for helping to solve them. At the same time, we should suggest with modesty and candor what they can and cannot do.

What they can do—which is what matters—is to continue to carry out higher education's historic mission of helping to prepare humanpower which can, in its many individual capacities, do the job. We must see that this humanpower is not wasted—through financial barriers which shut off access to poor though competent students and through the continuation of any practices which discriminate on the basis of ethnic origin or sex. We must commit ourselves once again to the democratic goal of equal opportunity for all which, in a very fundamental way, embraces education.

Furthermore, humanpower is wasted if the intellectual power of the nation is over-committed to practical ends. The technology which has added so much to our lives, and which finally must be adequate to solve the problems it has created, is simply all an end-product of what began as basic research. Nuclear fission is not the creation of a technician but, in its origin, of a solitary thinker seeking the answer to a basic question. To place undue emphasis on end-products is to condemn ourselves to a ceaseless rearrangement of what we already know.

Needless to say, the government of the United States must continue to be our partner in what we and they do. The die is cast; there is no changing that. But we ask the friendly giant to tread lightly. Too close a supervision of what colleges and universities do, and over-zealous intervention in the affairs of higher education, cripple the academic partner and limit its productiveness in the grand endeavor. Each partner has its proper role and context for its performance. Mutual respect and forebearance are needed if each is to perform well.

Chapter 3

THE LAND-GRANT UNIVERSITY:
MYTH AND REALITY

DAVID MADSEN

IT is more than a century now since the Congress of the United States voted into law the Morrill Act of 1862, under which the several states were given grants of public lands to be offered for sale, with the proceeds used "to promote the liberal and practical education of the industrial classes in the several pursuits and professions of life." To achieve this aim, colleges or universities were to be established—at least one in each state—in which the major emphasis would be on branches of learning related to agriculture and the mechanic arts.

Within eight years of passage of the land-grant legislation, thirty-seven states had authorized some kind of educational enterprise affording instruction in the prescribed areas. Subsequently, many new institutions were created; several others, already in existence when the Morrill Act was adopted, also benefited substantially. Today the seventy-one land-grant colleges and universities in operation in the fifty states, two territories, and Puerto Rico are an integral part of the American higher learning enterprise. In common with all such institutions, they are increasingly subject to demands from within and without the academic community for a general reappraisal of the educational philosophy they espouse, the services they purport to render, and the methods by which they are governed and financed.

In light of the phenomenal expansion of higher education in the United States in the past quarter century and the turmoil that has descended on the nation's campuses in the decade just past, these demands for reassessment appear to have considerable merit, and even some urgency. So it is appropriate that the land-grant institutions, like their various counterparts in the higher educational enterprise, undertake to study their origins, their relative achievements and failures, and their prospects for the future.

To do so, they must look beyond the self-laudatory evaluations of their centennial committees. Those who would seek to assist land-grant institutions in their scrutiny must ask several questions: What forces gave impetus to the demands for "industrial" education in the United States during the latter half of the nineteenth century? What goals were envisioned by the early educators, the politicians, and the spokesmen for agrarian and industrial interests who worked to establish the land-grant institutions? With what degree of success have these goals been attained in the decades since 1862?

Widespread Scientific Education for the Working Classes

Among the diverse forces that culminated in demands for widened educational opportunity in the mid-nineteenth century, one of the most potent was the widespread belief in the essential dignity and worthiness of the laboring man. One hears frequent references these days to the so-called Puritan work ethic, with the inevitable inference that the virtue of hard work was unique to American Puritanism. On the contrary, work was glorified in the rules that governed the ancient monasteries; the men of the Renaissance understood and appreciated the value of disciplined labor; intellectuals throughout the centuries have regarded work, for all classes of society, as one of the worthiest activities of humankind. The founders of the land-grant colleges, in keeping with historical thought and experience, acknowledged the essential importance of work, as they dedicated their institutions to helping the industrial or working classes better their lot in life.

It was increasingly recognized, however, that the role of the laboring man would be profoundly altered by developments in science and technology. By the middle of the nineteenth century, the industrial and scientific revolutions that have induced in our age the symptoms of "future shock" were already well advanced in Europe and were gathering momentum in the United States. Long before the American Civil War, the Germans had established both agricultural and technical schools, and their universities were the admiration of the Western world. Other European peoples—notably the English, the

French, and the Russians—also had founded technical and agricultural schools in recognition of the revolutionary potential of the forces of industrialization.

Early American Institutionalization of Science

From the earliest days of the Republic, many American statesmen and intellectual leaders were keenly interested in science, invention, and technology. These advocates of science included Benjamin Franklin, Thomas Jefferson, Benjamin Rush, John Quincy Adams, Joseph Henry, Albert Gallatin, Samuel F. B. Morse, Benjamin Silliman, and Asa Gray.[1] A number of institutions in the young country actively pursued practical and scientific ends, and from time to time proposals were advanced to extend the benefits of modern technology to a larger proportion of the working population of the land. Several such institutions, still in existence today, recognized the need for men trained in technological and scientific areas. The United States Military Academy at West Point, early in the nineteenth century, initiated a course of study which embraced civil engineering, chemistry, mathematics, drawing, and French, as well as instruction in matters military.

Rensselaer Polytechnic Institute, founded at Troy, New York, by Stephen Van Rensselaer in 1824, aimed at the "diffusion of a very useful kind of knowledge, with its application to the business of living."[2] Under the skillful leadership of Amos Eaton, and later B. Franklin Greene, Rensselaer Polytechnic emerged as a most important source of highly skilled schoolteachers, engineers, bridge-builders, factory and shop managers, railroad builders, and other workers.

The Smithsonian Institution of Washington, in many ways a

---

[1]Defenders of the classical studies were many. A writer for the *Western Review* in Cincinnati in 1820 insisted: "Should the time ever come when Latin and Greek should be banished from our Universities, and the study of Cicero and Demosthenes, of Homer and Virgil should be considered as unnecessary for the formation of a scholar, we should regard mankind as fast sinking into absolute barbarism, and the gloom of mental darkness as likely to increase until it should become universal." Quoted in Frank Luther Mott, *A History of American Magazines, 1741–1850* (Cambridge: Harvard University Press, 1930), p. 146. The new universities did not banish Latin and Greek so much as they changed the definition of the word "scholar."

[2]Quoted in Frederick Rudolph, *The American College and University: A History* (New York: Alfred A. Knopf, 1962), p. 230.

unique American educational institution, opened its doors to scientific research and discovery in 1846. A bequest of a half million dollars by an English chemist, James Smithson, was used by the United States government to achieve Smithson's desire to promote "the increase and diffusion of knowledge among men." Over the years, the Smithsonian Institution has encouraged the researches of many of America's most eminent scientists, among them Asa Gray, George Bancroft, James Dana, Louis Agassiz, Joseph Henry, and Alexander D. Bache.

The years before the Civil War saw scientific studies gaining some ground at such private institutions as Harvard, Yale, and Dartmouth; several other schools launched engineering programs. Some institutions offered the degrees of Bachelor of Science and Bachelor of Philosophy in addition to the traditional Bachelor of Arts. The first Doctor of Philosophy degree patterned on the German doctorate was awarded at Yale in 1861.

Need for Public Effort to Provide Education for Laboring Classes

Much still remained to be done to make scientific education accessible to the laboring classes who might be presumed to have the greatest stake in the technological revolution. Hence, there was agitation in the public press, in journals such as *Scientific American* and the *American Journal of Science and Arts,* and in publications specializing in engineering and its related fields. As early as 1838, Solon Robinson, writing in the *Albany Cultivator,* affirmed the need "in every county and principal town in the United States [for] a well-founded agricultural school in which young men and girls can acquire such an education as will be USEFUL" instead of a "piano, French, Spanish, or flower daub education."[3] In New York, Simeon De Witt pressed for the establishment of agricultural schools; in

[3]Quoted in Edward Danforth Eddy, Jr., *Colleges for Our Land and Time* (New York: Harper and Brothers, 1956), p. 12. This book, which traces the history of the land-grant college movement, is one of the most important ever written on that topic. Another good book, albeit an older one, is Earle D. Ross, *Democracy's College* (Ames, Iowa: The Iowa State College Press, 1942).

Massachusetts, a college of agriculture was proposed in the late 1820s. Francis Wayland, in his plea for the revitalization of Brown University in mid-century, took pains to point out that with more than 100 colleges, law schools, and theological seminaries throughout the land, there still existed not a single institution "designed to furnish the agriculturalist, the manufacturer, the mechanic, or the merchant with the education that [would] prepare him for the profession to which his life [was] to be devoted."[4] Apparently Wayland overlooked the claims of Rensselaer Polytechnic to instruct "the sons and daughters of farmers and mechanics . . . in the application of experimental chemistry, philosophy, and natural history, to agriculture, domestic economy, the arts, and manufactures."[5]

There were, to be sure, institutions created before the Civil War that ostensibly dedicated their efforts to furthering the education of the industrial or the working classes. The People's College of Havana, New York, waged a continuous struggle to stay alive after its opening in 1858. In Pennsylvania, the Farmer's High School, chartered in 1854, metamorphosed into the Agricultural College of Pennsylvania by 1862.[6] Michigan State University, begun about 1857, was the recipient of the state's beneficence under the Morrill Act; Penn State and Michigan State were to become two of the most prominent of the land-grant institutions. And there were other early stirrings in Georgia, Kentucky, Massachusetts, and Virginia.

Jonathan Baldwin Turner's Efforts

Of all the men whose efforts culminated in the establishment of educational institutions for the industrial classes, none is more notable than Jonathan Baldwin Turner of Illinois. A man of vision, Turner was a graduate of Yale College and a student of the classics. His Massachusetts upbringing had imbued him with the stern virtues of hard work, independence, and a love for the land. He was also "stern, often sarcastic and vituperative in his wars for

---

[4]John S. Brubacher and Willis Rudy, *Higher Education in Transition: A History of American Colleges and Universities, 1636–1968* (New York: Harper and Row, 1968), p. 64.
[5]Quoted in Rudolph, *The American College*, p. 230.
[6]Ibid., p. 249.

reform."[7] Although he believed education should inculcate moral values, Turner had early acquired an antipathy for sectarianism. As a student at Yale, he had been unhappy with the unremitting study of the classics, yet he would have had the public school curriculum include both classical studies and agricultural and mechanical pursuits.

In 1847, after fourteen years as a professor at Illinois College, Turner resigned, and shortly thereafter dedicated himself to the "uplift of the industrial classes." His action was prompted by his conviction that the salvation of the largely agricultural United States was in the hands of the sturdy farmer, and that an enlightened agrarian society stood the best chance for survival. Time and again Turner reiterated his belief that the destiny of the country would be shaped by the hands that had guided the plow—a romantic notion, perhaps, but one voiced by many before and since.[8]

Working through such organizations as the Illinois Horticultural Society, the Illinois Agricultural Society, and the Industrial League, Turner wrote articles for newspapers and periodicals, and spoke at state fairs, educational gatherings, school dedications, and the like, always with the aim of advancing the interests of the working man. It was Turner's conviction that Illinois—indeed, the whole country —needed a common school system, from the elementary level through the university, and a "National Institute of Science"—although he supposed the Smithsonian to be already functioning admirably in this capacity. Moreover, he favored a "University for the Industrial Classes" as well as an "institute, lyceums, and high schools in each of the counties and towns."[9] A university was essential, said Turner in 1851, because "no people ever had . . . any system of common schools and lower seminaries worth anything, until they first founded their higher institutions . . . from which . . . [to] draw supplies of teachers."[10] Moreover, such institutions ought to meet the needs of the communities in which they were located, whatever

---

[7]Judith Ann Hancock, "Jonathan Baldwin Turner (1805–1899): A Study of an Educational Reformer" (unpublished doctoral thesis, College of Education, University of Washington, 1971), p. 12.

[8]Ibid., p. 270.

[9]Richard A. Hatch, ed., *Some Founding Papers of the University of Illinois* (Urbana, Illinois: University of Illinois Press, 1967), p. 37.

[10]Hancock, Jonathan Baldwin Turner, p. 116.

might be the nature of those needs. The industrial classes, on their part, wanted "and they ought to have, the same facilities for understanding the true philosophy, the science and the art of their several pursuits . . . and of efficiently applying existing knowledge thereto, and widening its domain, which the professional classes have long enjoyed in their pursuits."[11]

But it was opportunity for the farmers and mechanics to attend college that seemed preeminent in Turner's thought in later years. In a speech in 1871 at the laying of the cornerstone of University Hall at the Illinois Industrial University, he dismissed as unimportant the fact that only a small percentage of the graduates of agricultural colleges remained in industrial pursuits. "If . . . the sons of our farmers and our friends are educated in our Industrial institutions . . . I care not into what particular professions they may choose to go in after life! This is a free country, and they have a right to go where they please." Indeed, they would carry the "broad, scientific, catholic, American and truly christian [sic] spirit of their *Alma Mater* along with them."[12] This particular comment might well have afforded some little comfort to the several land-grant college presidents whose jobs in later years would be imperiled by the accusations of farmers and newspaper editors that they had done too little to advance the cause of agricultural education.[13]

The campaign to create an industrial university for Illinois was pressed by Turner and his colleagues on many fronts. His "Plan for an Industrial University" was received with gratifying enthusiasm and no more so than by his friend John Kennicott, who proclaimed it the "best thought of the nineteenth century." Turner's words, Kennicott insisted, "should be written in letters of Gold [sic] on the front of every capitol, and on the walls of every college in the land —and should be read, as his bible [sic], by every son of labor in happy Illinois."[14]

[11]Hatch, *Some Founding Papers,* p. 35.
[12]Ibid., p. 138.
[13]The first president of the University of Rhode Island, John H. Washburn, was hounded from office charged with not having been zealous enough on behalf of agricultural education in his state. See Herman Eschenbacher, *The University of Rhode Island: A History of Land-Grant Education in Rhode Island* (New York: Appleton-Century-Crofts, 1967).
[14]Hancock, Jonathan Baldwin Turner, p. 140.

The Morrill Land-Grant Act and Land Ordinances

These demands by reformers in mid-nineteenth-century America
for more scientific and technical training to benefit farmers and
industrial workers eventually were to see fruition as a bill introduced
in Congress under the sponsorship of Justin Morrill of Vermont.
Like Turner a man of sturdy New England stock, Morrill was undoubtedly one of the most single-minded supporters of the land-
grant movement; during his long tenure in Congress, first as a representative, and later as a senator, he introduced measure after
measure relating to higher education. Although the source of his
ideas for the land-grant institutions is unclear, he became so im-
mersed in the cause that he seems to have assumed an almost proprietary interest that led him, at least later in life, to overlook the
contributions of equally dedicated men. Yet whatever debt Morrill
may have to others for the details of his plan, he was the acknowledged parliamentary master who engineered its passage, and for that
achievement he has acquired a kind of immortality.

The timing of Morrill's original bill was inauspicious, however,
and Congressional approval was overridden by President James Buchanan's veto in 1857. Not until 1862 did a second bill become law
as the Morrill Federal Land-Grant Act. By that time the civil strife
of the intervening years had removed from the legislative scene a
number of Southern representatives who might have made objections
on Constitutional grounds; moreover, a new provision for the training of military officers at the proposed institutions added a timely
appeal that helped secure passage of the measure. Signed into law by
President Lincoln in one of the darkest hours of the Civil War, the
Morrill Act prompted the distinguished educator, Andrew D. White,
to exclaim in the grandiloquent prose of his era, "In all the annals
of republics, there is no more significant utterance of confidence in
national destiny out from the midst of national calamity."[15]

There was nothing especially innovative, to be sure, in the setting
aside of public lands to the support of public, or for that matter,
private schools. The practice had been long accepted in Europe,

[15]Quoted in Eddy, *Colleges for Our Land*, p. 45.

where such institutions as Oxford and Cambridge had had land apportioned for their use. On this continent, the precedent was set in Colonial days with the founding of Harvard, Yale, Dartmouth, and William and Mary.

Even before ratification of the Constitution, Congress, acting under the Articles of Confederation, had passed two important pieces of legislation that were to have far-reaching consequences for American education. These ordinances of 1785 and 1787 (the Northwest Ordinance), provided for, among other matters, the division and sale of public lands and laid down the conditions for the entry of new states into the Union. The Northwest Ordinance declared, moreover, that "religion, morality, and knowledge, being necessary to good government and the happiness of mankind, schools and the means of education shall forever be encouraged." To promote this worthy end, the authors of the ordinances reserved section sixteen in every township for the support and maintenance of the public schools. The Northwest Ordinance went on to stipulate that "not more than two complete townships [were] to be given perpetually for the purposes of a university."

Although their significance may not have been fully recognized at the time, the land ordinances, with these provisions for grants in behalf of higher education, carried within them the seeds of the great American state university system. By setting a precedent that could be invoked as new states entered the Union, these first major efforts of the central government in aid of higher learning have had far-reaching and enduring consequences. Over the years, the revenue from some 118 million acres of the public domain—an area approximately four times the size of New York State—has been used to finance all areas of the nation's educational effort.

The Morrill Act directed that public lands be apportioned to each state "in quantity equal to 30,000 acres for each senator and representative in Congress." States which lacked the necessary public lands within their borders were to be issued land scrip in equivalent amount. Given the enormous size of the public domain, it was perhaps inevitable and at the same time singularly appropriate that land should afford the means of financing new institutions of higher learning. For many decades, and particularly after the 1830s, the disposition of the extensive western territories had been a bone of legislative contention. The sale of public lands to finance educational enterprises provided an acceptable means of coping with the problem and at the same time achieved certain useful political ends. With 30,000 acres apportioned for each representative and senator, every state was assured of benefiting in some tangible way and, theoretically at least, on an equitable basis; moreover, there was political hay to be made from the fact that the land-grant institutions were undeniably designed to serve the educational interests of the multitude of hard-working Americans rather than the privileged few. Finally, there was an irresistible appeal in the prospect of the scientific and technological resources of academe arrayed against the problems of the agricultural community; in theory, at least, the effect would be to preserve and, hopefully, to increase the fertility of the very acres that provided the funds to finance the new educational ventures.

Similar political ends were served by the passage of the Homestead Act in the same month as Morrill's legislation. Compared to the 234 million acres made available to homesteaders and settlers and the 181 million acres granted the railroads to extend their rights-of-way across the continent, the 17 million or so acres set aside for the support of land-grant colleges and universities may appear somewhat niggardly. Again, it may not be surprising that the popular press took slight notice of the enactment of legislation that over the years would provide the wherewithal to establish dozens of institutions of higher learning. Nonetheless, the allocation of even this relatively modest amount of public land to "promote the liberal and practical education of the industrial classes in the several pursuits and professions of life" was no small feat.

State Implementation of Land-Grant Provisions

If there were those who thought that the states would not take advantage of the land-grant provisions under the Morrill Act, they would have done well to consider the fact that, by the Civil War, seventeen states had set aside the necessary townships for the support of a state university as called for in the Northwest Ordinance. It has been said that the state universities, especially those in the West, were "reared on national grants and that no restricted or selfish policy is worthy of their origin."[16] On the whole, the land-grant institutions were conscious of the great debt they owed to the public largess. The concept of the public university responsibly discharging its debt to the society that created it was expressed, for example, by Charles Van Hise of the University of Wisconsin, who said he would never rest content "until the beneficient influences of this University . . . shall be made available in every home in the state."[17]

The Morrill Act of 1862 did not require the states to create new institutions to administer its charge; indeed, some states—notably Iowa, Michigan, and Pennsylvania—already were served by agricultural colleges, and in some instances, a state university as well. The state of Iowa, it seems, was the first to avail itself of the benefits of the Land-Grant Act; Oklahoma, Texas, and Washington were among the states that established new colleges of agriculture and the mechanic arts; still others, including Minnesota, Missouri, North Carolina, and Wisconsin, expanded the offerings of existing public institutions to include courses in agriculture and thereby combined the state university and the land-grant enterprise under a single roof. A few states set up new universities which incorporated extensive work in the agricultural and mechanic arts; other states, most of them eastern, took still another path—turning over to existing colleges all or part of the required programs to be financed by the funds raised from land sales under the Morrill Act. Among the institutions affected by arrangements of this sort were Dartmouth, Brown, Vermont, Transylvania College in Kentucky, the Sheffield Scientific School at Yale, Rutgers, and the Massachusetts Institute of Technology. In Indiana and New York, the land-grant funds, bolstered by private monies, were used to found Purdue and Cornell Universities. A century later each state in the Union had this type of institution; in some states, there were two.

Since under the terms of the law only the interest on the proceeds could be used to support the colleges, it was essential that the land

---

[16]Andrew C. McLaughlin, *History of Higher Education in Michigan* (Washington: Government Printing Office, 1891), p. 18.
[17]Eddy, *Colleges for Our Land,* p. 114.

be sold at the highest possible price. Regrettably, the record of the disposal of these 17 million acres of land is clouded by scandal, fraud, and poor management. Many states realized less than one dollar an acre for their land, and some were even swindled out of the proceeds of the sales altogether. A notable exception to a generally dismal picture prevailed in New York, where Ezra Cornell, through judicious selection of lands and exemplary sales methods, secured for Cornell University an endowment of several millions. Cornell's accomplishment is particularly noteworthy in view of the fact that when New York's 980,000 acres were first offered for sale, they were bringing less than one dollar an acre. California and Minnesota also benefited from better than average management; Pennsylvania and Connecticut were less fortunate.[18] The problem of the disposal of land was complicated by the fact that it was so cheap—and was, in fact, free for the claiming by settlers and railroad builders in the western United States. To complicate the situation further, few states other than the western ones had enough land within their borders to offer for sale; some, in fact, had none at all and had to rely entirely on land scrip to secure funds.

Interpretation of the Land-Grant Act:
Defining the Curriculum

In a sense, the aims of the Morrill Act were clear enough. Colleges were to be created "where the leading object shall be . . . to teach such branches of learning as are related to agriculture and the mechanic arts . . . in order to promote the liberal and practical education of the industrial classes in the several pursuits and professions of life." Not to be excluded from the curriculum were "other scientific and classical studies, and military tactics." Clearly, something was to be undertaken to benefit the working classes—but precisely what was needed? Andrew D. White's answer to the puzzle of what to teach was: "Make your student a master-farmer, or a master-mechanic; but make him also a master-man."[19]

[18]Allan Nevins, *The State Universities and Democracy* (Urbana, Illinois: University of Illinois Press, 1962), pp. 30–34.
[19]Quoted by Eddy, *Colleges for Our Land,* p. 55.

One of the first problems was to define the curriculum, including a definition of "practical education." Did this phrase suggest only studies of a purely vocational nature, such as blacksmithing, carpentry, animal husbandry, horticulture, veterinary medicine, bookkeeping, botany, and vegetable physiology? If so, what would be the fate of such traditional disciplines as geometry, rhetoric, astronomy, and logic, the mainstays of the old liberal arts curriculum? Some interested voices insisted that too much should not be expected on the practical side, that students ought to receive the bulk of their training in matters intellectual and social. Others wanted to know how the practical problems of farmers and mechanics were to be solved: "We want no fancy farmers; we want no fancy mechanics."[20]

The answer, in time, was to retain the old and to incorporate the new "practical studies" into the curriculum. This blend of the old and new often achieved an interesting juxtaposition of the practical and the theoretical. In a sense, the courses usually characterized as "elitist" were offered along with those regarded as more "egalitarian." And a most interesting fact was that, in time, students of every social background were enrolled indiscriminantly in both kinds of courses.

At Cornell all the "good" studies were welcome, including those that tended to promote "Christian civilization." In addition, physical training was to be offered, student and faculty relationships were to be enhanced, and students were to be allowed choice in the question of what to study. This latter provision was a result, in part, of the general interest in the elective approach to the curriculum advocated so many years earlier by Thomas Jefferson and others, and more recently championed by the new president of Harvard, Charles Eliot. Cornell's insistence on equality among course offerings undoubtedly prompted the land-grant colleges as well as other institutions to introduce a flexibility into the curriculum that encouraged the rapid expansion of higher education. Cornell's entering student body in 1868 numbered 412, making it perhaps the largest class to that date to enter an American college or university.[21] Undoubtedly, too, the enrollment was augmented by the advertising campaign that

---

[20]Ibid., p. 31.
[21]Nevins, *The State University,* p. 21.

preceded the opening day ceremonies. And, indeed, the entering classes at Cornell and elsewhere might have been larger had there been more academies and high schools affording preparation for college.

Interpretation of the Land-Grant Act: Agriculture

Whatever may have been the intention of Jonathan Baldwin Turner and Justin Morrill, agriculture was the first order of business in the new land-grant colleges. The industrial revolution was not yet in full swing in the United States, and the country was still essentially agricultural in outlook and spirit; the small town and farm, not the city and factory, still dominated the affairs of the nation. At the outset, however, the colleges had difficulty finding students to enter their programs in agriculture. It was not until 1889, for example, that the first students in agriculture came to Minnesota, although the state had adopted provisions of the Morrill Act in 1863.

There were other serious problems resulting from the lack of a firm scientific base for agricultural experimentation and development in the United States. To begin with, the basic pattern of agricultural studies had to be established. In some quarters, agriculture was regarded as an art rather than a science; but even those who considered its scientific nature to be preeminent were hard put to identify the agricultural scientists of the day. There were other questions: Was the land-grant college essentially a teaching or a research institution? What of the college farms? Were they to function primarily as sources of revenue, as training grounds for future farmers, or as demonstration facilities for the introduction of new techniques? And, later, would graduates be willing to return to farms after their taste of the outside world, or would the new colleges have the effect of weaning the future farmers away from the soil?

To guard against this last possibility, the legislatures often chose sites far from any populous areas to prevent students from imbibing the noxious airs of the metropolis. (Unfortunately, when the day came for the land-grant colleges to switch their emphasis from the needs of the farmer to those of the urban dweller, the colleges found themselves miles away from the cities—cities whose burgeoning populations included many former farmers.)

Among early critics of the land-grant colleges were such college presidents of the day as James McCosh of Princeton, Noah Porter of Yale, and Charles Eliot, the young president of Harvard. Some churchmen were quick to characterize the new enterprises as "godless" even before they opened their doors. In many cases, the opposition of the former group was based on condescension; others objected to the very concept of financial aid to agricultural institutions. Charles Eliot, for example, regarded subsidies to agricultural schools as symptomatic of a "deep-seated disease" resulting from governmental interference in the affairs of citizens.[22] (Eliot seems to have forgotten that Harvard College, founded by the Commonwealth of Massachusetts, had been the beneficiary of a not inconsiderable amount of public monies over the years. Furthermore, he had served as president of M.I.T., another recipient of public funds.)

On the other hand, it was often difficult to convince the agrarian interests that their needs were being given a full measure of attention. At Illinois Industrial University in 1870, for example, only about twenty students in 200 were taking Latin; however, when it was later proposed that the name of the institution be changed to the University of Illinois, a rural newspaperman was to sneer that the change represented a switch from "learning and labor" to "lavender and lily white."[23] Over the years, both the National Grange and the Farmer's Alliance were to accuse the colleges of following the old classical curriculum too closely and doing too little for farmers. Populists fomented investigations of the land-grant colleges in both Ohio and California in the 1870s. Predictably, farmers themselves were often among the most vociferous critics of the land-grant institutions when their expectations for massive and immediate assistance with the problems of farming were not realized. The unfortunate truth was that few American agriculturalists were familiar with the principles of scientific farming which even in Europe were just beginning to be

[22]Charles Eliot to Daniel C. Gilman, October 21, 1873. Quoted in Louis D. Corson, "University Problems as Described in the Personal Correspondence among D. C. Gilman, A. D. White, and C. W. Eliot" (unpublished doctoral dissertation, School of Education, Leland Stanford Junior University, 1951), p. 143.
[23]Quoted in Rudolph, *The American College*, p. 257.

practiced in a limited way; even fewer occupants of American university chairs had the requisite knowledge to make substantial contributions to agricultural science. Indeed, the success of the efforts on behalf of farmers would have to await progress in the whole body of science and then encounter further delays as scientific principles were translated into practical solutions to agrarian problems.

It must be understood, however, that things were not hopeless for the friends of scientific agriculture; quite the contrary. A "Convention of Friends of Agricultural Education," held in Chicago in 1871, was attended by some of the chief administrative officers of leading land-grant universities—among them, Andrew D. White of Cornell and Daniel Coit Gilman of California.[24] The proceedings of this body suggest that while the delegates were aware that progress in agricultural research would be slow, they also recognized that new techniques of experimentation such as statistical analysis would be profitably applied to the solution of research problems.

The discontent of the farming community was somewhat allayed by the passage in 1887 of the Hatch Act, which encouraged the creation of experimental stations to perform agricultural research and service. The later success of the colleges was due in part, at least, to the activities engendered by the experiment stations with their well-equipped barns, their carefully nurtured fields, their laboratories and demonstration facilities, and to the services they provided through county agricultural and home economics agents as well as through correspondence with persons seeking answers to questions having to do with agriculture. To be sure, experiment stations were not unknown before 1887; as many as two dozen and possibly more were in operation in the United States, notably at Wesleyan University in Connecticut and at other schools in California and North Carolina; the Hatch Act, however, gave them official sanction and continuous funding. In time, the numbers of faculty and staff at the experiment stations increased rapidly, and with the continuing encouragement of the federal government the interests of the land-grant college became even more inextricably bound up with those of

---

[24]Richard A. Hatch, ed., *An Early View of the Land-Grant College: Convention of Friends of Agricultural Education in 1871* (Urbana, Illinois: University of Illinois, 1967).

the Department of Agriculture. The impressive list of achievements in agricultural experimentation includes improvement in fertilizers, seed corn, pesticides, fruits, hog breeding, disease control, and tests for butterfat. At Minnesota, scientists worked to improve alfalfa yields, while Missouri soy beans, Louisiana sugar cane, and Oregon poultry were improved.[25] The University of California at Davis today has more students enrolled in the liberal arts than in agriculture; nonetheless, research now underway there will continue to have a significant impact on the wine-growing industry of the state. The effect of chemicals on milk has been studied, and an effort has been made to think of agriculture in the broadest sense from the nature of the seed to the effect of that seed on human life.

Extension in the Land-Grant Institution

Too often the land-grant universities are cited for their agricultural and engineering enterprises and for the impressive number of doctorates they award: of the fifteen universities in the United States that grant the most Ph.D. degrees, nine trace their origins to the land-grant movement of the nineteenth century. However, there is a large though less visible aspect of the enterprise that deserves more attention than it has received heretofore—the extension services of the land-grant institutions. From the outset, the extension services have faced the problem of defining their mission and determining the direction their activities would take. In the last century, the farmers' claims were recognized as preeminent, but how to reach the farmers remained a vexing question. The efforts to accomplish the work of liaison with agricultural interests deserves extensive treatment that cannot be undertaken here. In brief, however, the land-grant schools have pursued several lines of activity that include research at the experiment stations, the dissemination of those research discoveries, the preparation of future generations for an agricultural vocation, and the general schooling made available to the sons and daughters of the soil. But there were special difficulties to overcome in efforts to deal directly with the farmers themselves. The concept of the

[25]Eddy, *Colleges for Our Land*, p. 170.

whole state as a campus was espoused at Wisconsin and at Michigan State at one time or another; as proof of this, farmers' institutes brought farmers to the campus for brief periods to learn about the latest developments in materials, techniques, and methods. Other institutions offered short courses for farmers, and still others utilized some of the features of the old Chautauqua movement, combining reading programs with short summer sessions. Still later, the Smith-Lever Act of 1914 authorized extension work to "aid in diffusing among the people of the United States useful and practical information on subjects relating to agriculture and home economics, and to encourage the application of the same." Partners in this venture were the Department of Agriculture and the state agricultural colleges. Incidentally, this act had one ingenious and somewhat regrettable aspect in that it provided for the matching of federal funds by state-generated revenues, the very technique that has been used in recent years to underwrite the ubiquitous and occasionally environmentally disastrous highway construction programs. The authors of the Smith-Lever legislation had hit upon a psychological device—in earlier days some might have termed it an appeal to man's innate sense of greed—that was extremely effective, for within a short time most states were able to raise state and local funds with which to participate in the program. In a few years the Department of Agriculture had reorganized its bureaucracy the better to coordinate work in extension, agricultural experimentation, demonstration, and the like.

Of course the federal government did not initiate university extension programs, nor did the authors of the Smith-Lever Act invent them. For example, 4-H clubs had been organized before the act was passed, and Clemson University, for one, had been cooperating with the Department of Agriculture through the medium of a state agricultural agent. Nor was home economics as a field of study an innovation; "domestic economy" had been offered in some schools long before the Civil War and a number of home economics departments were organized in land-grant colleges before the turn of the century. Nevertheless, the recognition of the value of extension activities and, equally significant, the authorization of the funds for their support, were of crucial importance to development of programs that today reach into all parts of the country. By 1919, seven-

ty-five percent of the nation's counties were served by county agricultural agents, thirty-five percent by home demonstration agents.
These agents, who eventually served almost every county in the
nation, were influential in engendering a spirit of cooperation among
farmers; in time many of these farmers united to form cooperatives
for the purposes of buying and selling produce. In the 1930s, of
course, this tendency proceeded apace until farm cooperatives were
commonplace.

The depression of the 1930s demonstrated that, whatever its earlier aims, farm extension work would have to expand beyond mere
education and demonstration; clearly, the tremendous improvements in farm production methods and other farm-related activities
would not suffice to stave off the crushing effects of economic depression. Furthermore, new and more efficient farming practices were
having the unforeseen effect of forcing farmers off the land. With
economic survival increasingly dependent on large acreage, modern
machinery, and generous capital, the small family farm often became
an uneconomical enterprise that even governmental subsidies could
not save. Many of them passed into the hands of the holders of large
acreage or the agricultural corporation bent on making a profit from
large-scale farm operation. Today, of course, the number of farm
dwellers has dwindled to well under ten percent of the total population and is still declining, whereas when the land-grant act was
passed the bulk of the American populace, perhaps as much as ninety
percent, lived on farms or in nearby towns and villages.

The Agricultural Adjustment Act (1933) was the first of the New
Deal programs to attempt to coordinate activities in aid of the
farmer. As its provisions were implemented through the land-grant
university extension services, the directors of these offices, and, indeed, the institutions themselves, were drawn inexorably into the
federal net, although not without profit to the universities and to the
farmers they served. As time passed, however, the extension offices
became mired in a morass of federal rules and regulations, shifting
policies, and interference from government agencies. Before the
muddle could be satisfactorily resolved, World War II erupted, and
the land-grant enterprise joined itself to the national effort in these
words:

They [the land-grant colleges] offer to the Nation, through the military and civilian channels, all their facilities for such essential scientific, technical, and professional training and research and other educational activities as may be necessary for the success of the country's war effort.[26]

The broadening of extension activities continued after World War II to include such areas as the management of school lunch programs and the operation of infant health clinics, as well as a vigorous 4-H club program that introduced young Americans to the importance of conservation long before the media popularized it under the term ecology. Several land-grant institutions—Iowa State, for one—early recognized the educational possibilities of television and established their own stations. All of these activities were part of an extension program that was becoming far more complex and sophisticated than anyone could have imagined. The earlier efforts to promote soil conservation and improve farming practices, machinery, materials, and livestock, were gradually augmented by a growing body of information on better marketing techniques, and, in a somewhat more controversial area of the program, instruction on governmental policies with a direct bearing on the agricultural enterprise, i.e., problems of crop surpluses, and international agricultural and financial exigencies. As more and more farmers left their lands to move to the cities, investigations were initiated into the problems of adjustment from rural to urban life, into educational and medical needs, and related matters.

In the long run, one consequence of the decline in the number of farmers on the land in recent decades has been this redirection of extension efforts to serve urban as well as rural areas. The demographic change has occurred with much greater rapidity than could have been predicted. Less than twenty years ago, Edward D. Eddy, Jr., whose book, *Colleges for Our Land and Time,* is one of the best general histories of the land-grant college movement, concluded that "it would be a long time, if ever, before urban work matched the rural program."[27]

---

[26]Quoted in Eddy, *Colleges for Our Land,* p. 201.
[27]Ibid., p. 241.

In recent years the land-grant institutions have even gone beyond the borders of the United States to exert an international influence. They have dispatched farm experts, sanitary engineers, and technical experts all over the world in response to local needs; they have welcomed countless students from foreign countries. Many of these students have returned to their own lands to create technical schools, agricultural colleges, and a host of other enterprises inspired by their stay in the United States.

Land-Grant Contribution to Engineering

Among the most impressive undertakings of the land-grant institutions have been their accomplishments in the training of engineers and the furthering of research in all areas of engineering. To the engineering field, once dominated in the United States by the graduates of the West Point Military Academy, the land-grant colleges annually contribute thousands of graduates. (In fact, all American higher institutions turn out about 60,000 engineering graduates each year, of whom about 15,000 earn the master's degree, and another 3,300 the doctorate. Surprisingly, this figure exceeds by only about 10,000 the total for 1948–49, but in that year only 4,798 master's degrees and 417 doctorates were awarded.[28])

The substantial achievements in engineering education and research have come about despite early uncertainties in the interpretations of the terms mechanic arts and engineering. Their ambiguity was perhaps the more marked in contrast to the widespread popular understanding of the word agriculture, especially in matters curricular. The preponderantly agrarian bias on the part of the early sponsors of industrial education also failed to stifle the claims of the mechanic arts, whatever their precise definition.

When the Morrill Act was passed in 1862, the scientific and engineering programs engendered by the industrial revolution were only beginning to gain popularity in the universities; by 1900 they were common at most institutions. The precise nature of programs to be

[28]Alvin Renetzky, ed., *Yearbook of Higher Education* (Orange, N.J.: Academic Media, 1971).

offered by land-grant universities was unclear then and continued to be so for some time. Programs involving manual labor were in vogue on the land-grant college campuses for a number of years, and in the early days many campuses had shops which produced a wide variety of items, especially metalwork. Engineering programs began in civil and mechanical fields; by 1885 they had been extended to include electrical engineering. In some states, particularly in the West, mining engineering had a place in the curriculum. The influential Andrew D. White of Cornell obviously had in mind the preparation of skilled engineering talent when he insisted on the importance of trained minds as well as practical skills. In 1909 the land-grant college association declared that the laws that "constitute the charter of the land-grant colleges, distinctly prescribe work of collegiate grade in agriculture and mechanic arts, including engineering in all its branches and the science related to industries."[29] Still no definition of mechanic arts was offered, and, with the demands of industrialization pressing heavily on the nation, a satisfactory definition was sorely required.

Gradually, with the creation of engineering experiment stations and the advancement of science, research and development in engineering made great strides. Experiment stations were to be found in five land-grant colleges in 1910 and in forty-six by the end of World War II; for the most part, however, they were poor and struggling enterprises. By 1925, the annual sum spent in agricultural research in the land-grant colleges exceeded more than twentyfold that allotted to engineering research.[30] Surely, this imbalance did not reflect the dedication to the mechanic arts implicit in the institutions' early charge.

Military Training in the Land-Grant Institution

Another feature of the land-grant institutions, the subject of so much recent controversy, was the provision for military training. In 1862, when the Union Army was on the verge of military disaster, the prospect of a reliable source of commissioned officers was for

[29]Quoted in Eddy, Colleges for Our Land, p. 41.
[30]Ibid., p. 173.

many people one of the most appealing features of the legislation introduced by Senator Morrill. Yet, as the Civil War faded from memory, the relatively small regular army became increasingly indifferent toward the military programs in the colleges; it was not until much later that the holder of a reserve officer training corps commission could stand a chance on the regular army promotion lists. A flurry of interest in the officer training program occurred within the War Department during the Spanish-American War. But it was the National Defense Act of 1916 that created the modern Reserve Officer Training Program and aroused considerable interest in the colleges' military training endeavors. By the early days of World War II about three-fourths of active military officers were graduates of R.O.T.C. programs. High-ranking army officers have been lavish in their praise of those programs and have looked to the colleges for a large portion of their young officers. When in recent years the R.O.T.C. program came under heavy assault, its critics seemed to ignore the fact that the United States historically has been suspicious of professional military castes—and with good reason. Over the years, many Americans have found reassurance in the presence within the officer grades of a large number of men whose training was essentially civilian in character. Forgotten, too, or largely ignored is the role R.O.T.C. stipends have played in making college attendance possible for many young men and women from lower-income families.

Failures and Current Problems:
Current Criticisms of Land-Grant Institutions

Current critics of the land-grant enterprise point to various inadequacies discernible in its diverse operations nationwide. Land-grant institutions have been accused (with some truth) of having grown complacent, of having been less receptive to criticism than they should have been. The quality of their leadership, it is claimed, has been uneven.[31] Nor have they been as generous in providing as wide a measure of opportunity to various minority groups and to

[31]Louis G. Geiger, *Higher Education in a Maturing Democracy* (Lincoln, Nebraska: University of Nebraska Press, 1963), pp. 73; 82–84.

women as might have been expected in view of their egalitarian origin.

Some critics go beyond even these serious charges to question whether the ultimate effect of the land-grant movement has not, after all, been deleterious to the interests of the small independent farmer. Have the colleges been in a curious way the enemy of the farmer as well as his friend? One critic thinks so: "While mechanization and incorporation of the farm has led to great agribusiness wealth for a few, it has produced enormous poverty for millions. The land-grant colleges have lent their considerable resources to development of that industry instead of a total rural community.[32]

It is not possible here to support or refute so broad a charge, but it must be noted in passing that the land-grant institutions have long been sensitive to the broad spectrum of the farmers' needs beyond the mere increase of product yields; nor have they been unaware of the complex problems engendered by some of the very scientific and managerial successes they have helped to bring about. Perhaps this sensitivity has not been as effectively communicated as it might have been; surely the answer to the farm problem, if there is one, has not been made common knowledge.

To some extent, however, the ultimate success or failure of the land-grant institutions must be judged in terms of their ability to respond to the needs of all the working people of the United States, whether rural or urban. How well have the colleges discharged their responsibilities to the laboring man, the industrial worker, the mechanic? As the population of the country has become increasingly concentrated in urban environments, the land-grant institutions have not always been adequate to the challenge of shifting demographic patterns. Any harsh judgments on the relative success or failure of the land-grant institutions in addressing the urban segment of their mission must yet be tempered by the recognition that they originated, after all, in a day when agriculture was still a dominant mode of life. Often purposely located away from metropolitan centers, the land-grant colleges inevitably have been closer to the nation's agrar-

---

[32]James Hightower, "The Shame of an Agricultural School," *Change Magazine* Vol. 3 (Summer, 1971): 15–16.

ian community, in both a physical and a spiritual sense. As it became apparent that farmers were leaving the farms and moving to towns and cities, the land-grant institutions might well have seen their way clear to pursue them with educational opportunity; they might even have been the prime force in bringing the American community college movement to the larger towns and cities of the nation. The fact that the most rapidly growing enterprise—the community college—would appear to be duplicating some of the purposes originally assigned to the land-grant colleges—and doing so with great public encouragement—raises some questions about the degree to which the land-grant institutions have succeeded in meeting their commitment to make higher education widely available to the industrial classes.

Achievements:
The Varying Image of the Land-Grant Institution

Throughout their first hundred years, the land-grant colleges and universities have presented a varying image. To those who were allowed to matriculate without having earned a formal high school diploma, as was the case at several land-grant schools until the turn of the century, they were truly the "open door" colleges of their day. To many politicians and educators, their role was like that of dedicated public servants affording their facilities and the fruits of their research to all the people of the state, a manner most notably exemplified by the University of Wisconsin in the time of Governor Robert M. LaFollette.

To early twentieth century historians, they symbolized a new and pragmatic spirit in American education. Allan Nevins, for one, sees the land-grant curriculum as palpable evidence of the "rejection of the tyranny of classical and theological studies."[33] In all fairness, however, it must be admitted that those disciplines continued to enjoy a satisfying measure of favor long after their predicted demise. Now a newer generation of critics would refurbish the image of the

[33]Nevins, *The State Universities,* p. 2.

early liberal arts colleges, whose supposed faults and inadequacies were so loudly decried by the nineteenth-century proponents of the emerging American universities, including the land-grant institutions.[34]

What of the future? Will the institutions Eddy referred to as "colleges for our land and time" continue to deserve this accolade? What accomplishments of America's land-grant colleges and universities are still ahead? Predicting trends can be a discouraging and a futile exercise. Certainly, if land-grant institutions can channel the current demands for reassessment into a constructive discussion of new goals and redefinition of their unique role in American education, the future of the land-grant institutions yet holds promise.

[34]For three such articles see the *History of Education Quarterly* (Winter, 1971); James Axtell, "The Death of the Liberal Arts College," pp. 339–52; Hugh Hawkins, "The University-Builders Observe the Colleges," pp. 353–63; David B. Potts, "American Colleges in the Nineteenth-Century: From Localism to Denominationalism," pp. 363–80.

Chapter 4

COLLEGES OF AGRICULTURE REVISITED

HENRY R. FORTMANN, JEROME K. PASTO, THOMAS B. KING
with the assistance of Carol Kersavage

THE traditions, history, and spirit behind the concept of state colleges of agriculture and the staggering obstacles that impeded their establishment are chronicled in detail in *State Agricultural Experiment Stations: A History of Research Policy and Procedures.* The full impact of the frustrations is conveyed most poignantly in a discussion of the efforts of John Pitkin Norton to establish an agricultural college with a viable research arm.

In order to combat conservatism he first had to change the educational system; but to change the system he first had to conquer conservatism. Norton could see no escape from this predicament. He resigned hope of introducing a system of scientific agriculture into New England. He turned instead to New York State, a 'newer country' where farmers perhaps might appreciate the advice of scientists, and in 1851 put his willpower and overtaxed physique into a movement for a State university there. That campaign halted his missionary work; he encountered a frustration more decisive than discouragement and disillusionment: death in 1852 at the age of 30.[1]

The commitment of men like Norton was countered for ten more years by the public's apathy and the policymakers' greed, selfish expectations, myopic conservatism, and blatant ignorance. Finally, on July 2, 1962, President Lincoln signed into law the first Morrill Act (Land-Grant Act).

[1]H. C. Knoblauch, E. M. Law, and W. P. Meyer, *State Agricultural Experiment Stations: A History of Research Policy and Procedure,* Misc. Pub. No. 904, (Washington D.C.: USDA, 1962), p. 13.

Tripartite Organization of Colleges of Agriculture

The colleges of agriculture within the land-grant system encompass the agricultural experiment stations, resident education, and the cooperative extension service. A series of acts provided the enabling legislation for appropriations to carry out the missions of these three components.

The first of these acts (Hatch Act of 1887) established the agricultural experiment stations and provided federal grants to states for agricultural research in cooperation with the colleges established by the Morrill Act of 1862. This research output provided the basic knowledge without which there would have been no resident instruction programs and no initiation of the science of agriculture. Experiment stations and resident instruction were complemented by the addition of the agricultural extension service (Smith-Lever Act of 1914), which aided in dissemination and application of research.

In the relatively short span of time since the passage of the Hatch Act, the colleges of agriculture in the land-grant universities have achieved tripartite integration of curriculum, research, and extension unique in the land-grant university. In addition, these colleges have led the evolution of a complex operation of food and fiber production, and processing and marketing so sophisticated that it reaches into the total life of man and accomplishes what has been called the Green Revolution.

These achievements have been possible because of strong internal control and cooperation among the three components of the agricultural colleges and because of federal support. During the 110 years of cooperation and service with USDA, a unique and workable system has evolved. The scope of this operation can be clearly defined by examining the experiment station, resident education, and extension components of the colleges of agriculture.

The State Agricultural Experiment Station:
Orderly Administration for Planning and Coordination

The state agricultural experiment station system now functions with one station in each of the fifty states; two in New York and

Connecticut; and designated stations in Puerto Rico, Guam, the Virgin Islands, and the District of Columbia. In 1974 total scientific effort involved about 6,250 scientist-years. Expenditures totaled over 330 million dollars. In the 88 years since passage of the Hatch Act, experiment stations have been efficiently operated, due to care in planning and monitoring research and in continuity of funding and appropriate use of research monies.

The backbone of control in each of the state stations derives from systematic procedures to identify priorities, develop projects, and maintain a competent research staff. Several administrative arms coordinate all efforts: the four regional associations of experiment station directors meet three times a year to consider problems of mutual concern, including coordination of research efforts and development of effective research policies and procedures; the Experiment Station Committee on Organization and Policy (ESCOP), proposed and organized in 1905, disseminates general policies and procedures; the Experiment Station section of the National Association of State Universities and Land-Grant Colleges (NASULGC) provides the connecting link between the regional associations and the governing board of NASULGC. As the federal agency charged with carrying out the legislative mandate of the Hatch Act, the Cooperative State Research Service (CSRS-USDA) aids in approving and improving research proposals, planning and coordinating research, and providing a buffer against pressures by various forces to misdirect, if not misuse, federal and state funds appropriated for agricultural research.

The report of the Dabney Committee, adopted in 1887, set a major precedent for NASULGC and the stations by differentiating between the stations' and the colleges' operations and by enunciating the standards to be observed in the expenditure of federal funds:

> All appropriations . . . should be applied in good faith to agricultural research and experiment, and the dissemination of the results thereof among the people and any diversion of funds to the general uses of the college would be a direct violation of the plain spirit and intent of the law.[2] . . . The experiment stations . . . should be so far

[2]Proceedings of the First Annual Convention (1887) of the Association of American Agricultural Colleges and Experiment Stations, 6 pp. (Note: No account of this convention was

separate and distinct from the colleges that it shall be possible at any moment to show . . . that all of the funds . . . have been expended solely for the purposes of agricultural experimentation according to the intent of the law.[3]

These safeguards against misuse or misdirection of research funds have not precluded the development of strong and mutually beneficial ties between research and teaching functions in the colleges of agriculture. In fact, the majority of scientists on experiment station staffs devote assigned portions of their time to teaching duties, with commensurate arrangements for salaries and operating expenses.

The Long-Range Study of Agricultural Research Needs

In 1965, the Senate Committee on Agricultural Appropriations[4] requested a long-range study of agricultural research conducted by the states, USDA, and industry. The joint experiment station-USDA task force document produced by the study defined the goals and scope of agricultural research; devised a classification system of experiment station and USDA research; and introduced an automated information storage and retrieval system of research—public and private. The task force estimated research priorities and projected a needed increase of 76 percent in public research effort over the 1965 level.[5] The study's recommendations were to employ a regional coordinator or regional director for each of the four regional associations of SAES. These regional directors now plan and coordinate individual and collective research programs; participate in federal planning and advise on policy matters; and prepare, support, and project appropriation requests three years in advance.

Another recommendation, creation of regional planning committees, was an attempt to assess priority of research needs within

---

printed originally. However, a manuscript summary by C. E. Thorne, secretary of the convention, filed in the Office of Experiment Stations, was ordered printed by the Executive Committee of the association on May 5, 1941.)

   [3]Knoblauch, *State Agricultural Experiment Stations,* pp. 64; 79.

   [4]Senate Report No. 156, Committee on Appropriations, April 9, 1965, p. 11.

   [5]No increase in research effort had occurred by fiscal year 1971, and in terms of 1965 dollars, there was some decrease.

respective regions and to recommend division of effort among potential researchers.

Establishment of an effective information system was the culmination of efforts of the task force. The Current Research Information System (CRIS), initiated in 1966 and fully operational in 1970, is one of the most useful scientific research information storage and retrieval systems in existence. CRIS was designed to "improve communications among scientists with regard to research which is presently underway and provide more effective management information on the total research programs of the State stations and the U.S. Department of Agriculture."[6]

The system of classification for agricultural research used by the fifty-five stations and the USDA is unquestionably the most extensively and intensively used of any system in the world, mainly because it is usable and useful. It is comprehensive, comprehendable, and manageable, both to the scientist and the administrator. Ninety-eight research problem areas encompass the total research program and include such divergent areas as: Soil, Plant, Water, Nutrient Relationships; Non-Commodity-Oriented Biological Technology and Biometry; Food Products Free of Toxic Contaminants Including Residues from Agriculture and Other Sources; and Improvement of Rural Community Institutions and Services.

Included in the system is information on all current research in about 25,000 state projects and 6,000 USDA work units including: (1) title, project leaders, objectives, procedures, reports of progress, and publications; (2) location and performing station or agency; (3) funds expended for the previous fiscal year by source of funds; (4) scientist-years devoted to each project; and (5) complete classification by research problem areas. Further specification is provided by designating the commodity, resource, or technology not oriented to specific commodity; by activity; by field of science; and by certain special concerns (e.g., pollution, health-related). Useful in planning and determining research needs with task forces and commodity groups, research program groupings are: natural resources; forest

[6]James Turnbull, "Current Research Information System," *Agricultural Science Review* 5 (1967):p. 30–33.

resources; crops (field and horticultural); animals; people; communities and institutions; and competition, trade, adjustment and price, and income policy.

The Will to Be Responsive to Current Needs

Each of the four SAES regions have developed varying procedures for approaching the problems of programming-planning-budgeting. By 1967, four northeast stations in New Jersey, New York, and Pennsylvania joined forces to effect better agricultural research coordination within the subregion. Corn and forage breeding programs were terminated at Rutgers and expanded at Penn State and Cornell. Rutgers in turn expanded efforts in waste disposal and pollution control. The corn-breeding programs of Cornell and Penn State were modified to expand effort on the short-season hybrids by Cornell and the long-season hybrids by Penn State. Agreement was reached on shifts within facets of many programs whereby each of the stations took portions of the problem in order to concentrate efforts.

The New England States Agricultural Research Coordination project, activated in July 1971, has taken a broader viewpoint, encompassing research, education, and extension. Its activities involve consideration of the value and impact of resources, commodities and programs on the people of each state; research, teaching and extension resources, responsibilities, and opportunities; and an analysis of current staff resources in order to shift programs within the constraints of existing personnel.

State experiment stations seek to solve problems of people they serve by participating and cooperating in needed planning and coordination with scientists, administrators, industry groups, consumers, and the public. Members are in close contact with the extension network functioning in every state and are therefore in touch with producers, processors, consumers, and "user" groups. However, administrators of research must strike a reasonable balance between maintaining adequate continuity of research projects and running the risk of obsolescence. Balance is achieved by having feasible procedures for project development, project review and approval, and continuing procedures for program planning and coordination.

The stations' responsiveness to changing needs is reflected in changes in both the absolute and relative allocations to various research programs. For example, environmental quality research totaled $2.8 million in 1966; in 1970, $7.7 million was expended. Included in a $15 million increase in Hatch payments to states requested for 1974 were increased funds for rural development; environmental quality and resource conservation; and consumer needs, including nutrition, adequacy of food and fiber supply, and food safety. The urgency of these problems is widely recognized; what is important is that they have been included in budget requests during the past five or six years. Unfortunately, appropriations of recent years have not made provisions for financing new research required. Both in terms of dollars and percentages, agricultural research has declined since the Senate committee study of 1965.

However, colleges of agriculture are equipped to solve present-day problems. James G. Horsfall, director emeritus of the Connecticut Agricultural Experiment Station, feels that solutions to problems in the plant and animal sciences can be applied to man's problems today. He says:

> Crowding of men together is certainly one of the great environmental issues of the day. We in agriculture have been dealing with the crowding of organisms since we got into the science 100 years ago. We called it competition, of course. Competition in a species—that is sociology. But agronomists call it spacing research. . . . The chicken men call it pecking order . . . a plant pathologist calls it host-parasite relationships; the foresters call it succession. . . . This is the result of our environmentology research over all these years. Let us adapt it to man.[7]

Experiment stations are unique among research organizations because they are not only problem solving but people oriented. Economists, in looking at research and researchers' abilities and capacities to solve social problems, have used a systems approach in their scrutiny of experiment stations' work. They have examined the sta-

[7]James G. Horsfall, "Agricultural Strategy in the Tragedy of the Commons," *Agricultural Science Review* 10 (1972):20.

failed to understand the purposes of the land-grant college, and for twenty-two years the college's aim was not only to educate scientific agriculturists but also to fully explain this mission to the people.[13]

Educators varied in their zeal to establish a relevant or practical yet liberal education. The Board of Trustees at Ohio Agricultural and Mechanical College in 1887 insisted that liberal courses be added to the practical subjects in education, while other educators vocally endorsed classical studies. Both farmers and proponents of a scientific education questioned the worth of a classical education at universities in the 1870s. Many faculties and students in liberal arts felt their area of education superior to agriculture; possessing the strength of tradition, the early course offerings in agriculture at many land-grant colleges leaned towards classicism. Moral philosophy, German, French, logic, and literature were listed along with botany, chemistry, vegetable economy, animal physiology, and other scientifically related courses. Despite this, rural students gradually enrolled in the colleges to learn how to improve their farming. Urban youth were attracted to the agriculture curriculum because tuition was low or nonexistent.[14]

In 1890, the Negro land-grant colleges were established by law as part of the dual system of education in southern states, to enable Negro youth to obtain the only higher education in a public institution available to them. Unfortunately, federal and state support was inequitably divided between the main land-grant college, with its tripartite segments, and the black college. The programs of both colleges often weakened in the conflict.

During the early part of the twentieth century, colleges were graduating men who were taking up farming or seeking ag-related careers that were becoming available as the science of agriculture flourished. Students, who in the early days were destined to become hired hands on their families' farms, could now begin farming on their own or

[13]H. W. Hannah, "Curricular Genesis in Agriculture" *Proceedings-RICOP*, 1971 Summer Work Conference (Branson, Mo., 1971), p. 40.

[14]As a case in point, 40 percent of the students in Cornell's college of agriculture in 1914 were from urban areas; therefore, farm practice requirements, though criticized, continued to be used as a test for eliminating potential arts and science students who had enrolled in agriculture to escape tuition.

elect any one of the new occupations in agriculture. Enrollments in specialized courses increased; student labor in the fields was replaced by laboratory sessions. Teaching expertise grew. Eventually, some colleges reduced the mathematics, basic sciences, and humanities courses because "now we have more to teach about agriculture." This approach was contrary to the Morrill Act, which stressed the inclusion of scientific and classical studies in the agricultural and mechanical arts programs.[15]

Liberty Hyde Bailey Promotes Agriculture

Progress in agricultural education was greatest during Liberty Hyde Bailey's tenure at Cornell. His single-handed dedication and enthusiasm for agricultural education, specifically in New York State, fostered awareness in other states.

Where Roberts was the father, Bailey created the science of agriculture. He viewed the college as an important center of research; each faculty member had to prepare at least one bulletin representing original work each year. Bailey himself was the most prolific contributor. He also expounded the worth of graduate study; Cornell was the first institution to award a Ph.D. for study in agricultural subjects. During Bailey's long association with Cornell's college of agriculture, he repeatedly said it was not the main purpose of the college to train farmers, but to provide a broad education through ag-related subjects. He sought to direct agricultural education into areas which met the needs of the time. He initiated programs designed to prepare students to assume significant roles in organizations related to agriculture. "Needs of the individual student," said Bailey, "must be met by relying on electives." This approach remains today as the basis for resident education.[16]

Liberty Hyde Bailey came at the right moment in history. The country in the second half of the nineteenth century had shifted from an agricultural to an industrial base. Industrialization brought ugli-

[15]Charles E. Kellogg and David C. Knapp, *The College of Agriculture: Science in the Public Service* (New York: McGraw-Hill Book Company, 1966), p. 11.

[16]Goold P. Colman, *Education and Agriculture* (Ithaca: Cornell University Press, 1963) p. 508.

ness, creating a nostalgia for country life. The mood was reflected in the resurgence and growth of agricultural colleges. Theodore Roosevelt's Country Life Commission, with Bailey as chairman, helped to keep alive the dream of the pastoral life. Subsequently, the Extension Service was founded; and, in 1917, the Smith-Hughes Act established teaching of vocational agriculture in the public schools.

Resident Education Expands

More rural young people were now attending high school who had no intention of leaving the family farm. Consequently, many universities initiated a curriculum in agricultural education to train teachers to teach agriculture in high schools. Farming became more rewarding; winter short courses were added and in some cases were expanded into technical two-year programs.

The period from 1925 to 1940 has been characterized as one of questioning amidst a changing agriculture and economy:

> There was an addition of new courses and new curricula but in a cautious vein. Resources were sometimes limited—there was a depression—and before much that was really innovative could be done, World War II came along. But as early as 1924, in the University catalogue, the College of Agriculture (Illinois) announced that one of its objectives was to train '. . . for technical positions in industries closely related to agriculture' and for public service in research and extension and for teaching. There was a recognition of change, but the response was sporadic and . . . varied markedly between institutions. 'Agriculture' was again up for definition.[17]

During this period, growth of instructional programs survived the depression, natural disasters, and resultant low farm prices. In the late 1930s, federal agencies sought to control production, conserve soil, and help marginal farmers, recruiting specialists from universities to carry out the work. The New Deal undertook drastic measures to restore order to farm marketing and finance; agricultural colleges emphasized interdisciplinary research. Stimulated by enormous de-

[17]H. W. Hannah, "Curricular Genesis in Agriculture," p. 42.

mands of World War II, American agriculture changed to encompass not only the dwindling number of farmers, but also non-farm workers, processors, and those in the booming agribusinesses. The number of farmers and family farms declined rapidly while farm production and efficiency soared.

The tripartite segments of the colleges—experiment station, resident education, and extension—had to adapt their programs to societal changes and needs. How successful the adaption has been is reflected in the individual college's adjustment to the changing focus in agriculture from a production to a process orientation with resident education curricula aiming for a proper balance between basic and applied courses.

Nondegree Programs Important

Short courses, winter courses, or twilight school at the land-grant colleges began in the early 1900s offering specialized programs for farm youth. Like the "shorthorns" of Cornell or the "chilblains" of Michigan State, students were given intensive training for existing jobs. Their immediate success on the job showed people that college training helped.

Educators today recognize the continuing and growing need for less-than-degree-level programs, e.g., short courses, two-year technical programs, correspondence courses, and adult education offerings. One of Kellogg's and Knapp's recommendations in their three-year study of the 50 principal land-grant colleges of agriculture and some 250 other institutions offering higher education in the field was the expansion of terminal, technical programs in agriculture, supplemented with study in English, mathematics, and science. Many nondegree programs are designed to provide educational opportunities for farm youth, particularly in areas of farm services and food industries. Currently, in Pennsylvania, 215 public schools offer programs in vocational agriculture to nearly 13,000 students and 4,000 adults.

Since the establishment of correspondence courses in agriculture and home economics in 1892 at Penn State, nearly a half-million people have studied materials at home. Currently, 105 noncredit correspondence courses are available in agriculture, family living, home economics, public affairs, and ecology.

The land-grant institutions have a responsibility, under the Morrill Act, to provide education beyond high school for rural and working-class youth. Kellogg and Knapp point out in *The College of Agriculture: Science in the Public Service*: "Success cannot be measured alone by the improvements in farm practices for crop and livestock production. Increased efficiency in agricultural production ought not to overshadow the progress in the education of farm people."[18] Therefore, the major responsibilities of resident education administrators in agriculture are to (1) project future professional manpower needs; (2) direct programs and resources to meet these needs; and not the least of these, to (3) improve educational opportunities in rural areas.

Resident Education Programs Today

No one body has been more aware of issues in undergraduate education in the agricultural sciences than the Commission on Education in Agriculture and Natural Resources (CEANAR). Formerly the Committee on Educational Policy in Agriculture, CEANAR was created to reevaluate and improve education in agriculture and natural resources and functioned until 1969. The commission initiated regional conferences for faculty in agriculture, natural resources, and biology; cosponsored conferences with scientific and professional societies; assessed teaching materials; offered guidelines and suggested mechanisms for development of purposeful teaching materials; and sponsored a visiting specialists program to assist colleges with evaluating courses and curricula.

The increased emphasis on large agricultural production agencies has caused shifts in many resident education programs to process orientation courses, which focus on how to maximize profit, optimize delivery of products to markets, and enhance product marketing. Consequently, more courses and majors in areas such as economics, marketing, and the pure sciences have evolved. Kellogg and Knapp concluded that the majority of many colleges have increased their

[18]Kellogg, *The College of Agriculture*, p. 130.

general-education requirements; reduced the number of technical, how-to-do-it courses; reduced the number of specialized curricula; and are stressing flexibility in individual student's programs. New majors and new curricula have been developed over the years, but it would be impossible for any college to meet all the new and changing demands.

Each college has a core of departments that are responsible for teaching, research, and backstopping the extension staff. Traditionally, they include agricultural economics, agricultural education, agricultural engineering, agricultural mechanization, agronomy, animal industry, animal science, food technology, forestry, horticulture, and general agriculture. Quality of environment today means conservation of our natural and physical resources. As agriculture's involvement in the quality of our environment becomes more complex, an increasing need for qualified people to administer the business of agriculture must be met. Recently, on many campuses, curricula or institutes in environmental science have been established or proposed. Penn State's environmental resource management major, begun in 1971, is designed to educate managers to deal with environmental problems and to integrate course work from several disciplines into a coherent picture of the correct use and management of natural resources. At other institutions, new interdisciplinary majors in plant protection and pesticide management have been added. As more regulations regarding pesticides, herbicides, and insecticides are implemented, more knowledgeable men will be needed.

Many schools recognize the need to incorporate a ladder and lattice structure into curricula, enabling graduates to move vertically as well as horizontally. Dr. R. E. Larson, provost of The Pennsylvania State University and former dean of the College of Agriculture, has pointed out that today's graduates are choosing careers in food science, plant and animal genetics, nutrition, wood product science, sociology, environmental resource management, or in any one of more than 500 distinct occupations found in eight major fields of agriculture.

In our present society colleges tend to teach what students wish to study. This necessitates strong career counseling in order that some fields of work are not overburdened with graduates. But colleges of agriculture realize that while they have the responsibility to provide students with job-entry skills, they also have a mission to provide an education in the broadest sense to those students who want a college education, through the avenue of agriculture.

Within the very last few years there has been a new awakening in public interest in agriculture and agricultural education. Food surpluses have vanished, severe hunger again haunts parts of the world, international trade in basic food commodities has increased, and there is concern for environmental protection of our land and water resources. These factors, along with modernized instructional programs, have encouraged young people to look to agricultural training in larger numbers than ever before. For the 70 institutions of the National Association of State Universities and Land Grant Colleges, baccalaureate enrollment in agriculture increased by 34 percent from 1970 to 1974, to a total of almost 82,000 students. In the last decade, enrollment has just about doubled.

The Cooperative Extension Service: Education for All People

Extending knowledge to the public has passed through several developmental stages since Benjamin Franklin organized the Philadelphia Society in 1785 to acquaint members with improved methods in agriculture. One of the prime factors in the advancement of agricultural technology in this country has been the opportunity for farmers to gain new knowledge, much of which was taught outside the formal classroom—at institutes, fairs, demonstrations, short courses, and workshops. The "university without walls" concept has been in operation for the farmer and his family since the early part of the nineteenth century.

Societies for Promoting Agriculture, similar to the Philadelphia Society, were prevalent in many eastern states prior to the Morrill Act of 1862, and they laid the groundwork for extension education as it was to evolve in the colleges of agriculture many years later. By 1852 there were about 300 active societies spread over 31 states and five territories. By 1860, there were well over 900.[19] Societies which functioned as state or regional organizations encouraged formation

[19]Alfred C. True, *A History of Agricultural Extension Work in the United States* (Washington D.C.: Misc. Pub. No. 15, USDA), p. 4.

of similar groups in counties; members held fairs—not only to sell animals or farm products but also for educational purposes. Frequently the societies requested the universities to provide speakers on agricultural subjects. The Massachusetts Agricultural Survey of 1840 reported a series of public meetings, held in 1839 in the hall of the Massachusetts House of Representatives, at which prominent agriculturists and scientists lectured. In 1840 the first meeting of the series was addressed by Henry Colman, Commissioner for the Agricultural Survey of Massachusetts, the Honorable Daniel Webster, and Professor Benjamin Silliman, soil scientist and chemist of Yale University.

The Farmers' Institutes

About the middle of the nineteenth century, both Massachusetts and Connecticut organized a series of public lectures for farmers patterned after successful teachers' institutes. Within a few years, farmers' institutes were being organized and conducted by agricultural societies, state boards of agriculture, and educational institutions across the country. The institutes were usually held at the state agricultural colleges and dealt with many agricultural related subjects. However, programs often dealt with improvement of rural schools and roads, how to keep young people on the farm, recreation in the rural community, and other educational as well as recreational programs.[20] In the beginning, the institutes were sponsored and financed by agricultural societies or local communities. Between 1890 and 1900, many state boards of agriculture were influenced to provide financial support to the farmers' institutes, which were often managed by the land-grant colleges.

The national significance of the farmers' institute movement was recognized by the federal Office of Experiment Stations in 1889 "as one of the most encouraging features of the agricultural and intellectual progress of our times." In 1901 the association was brought closer to USDA through the Office of Experiment Stations, expanding programs and broadening influence, partly because of increasing state and federal aid and because of growing popularity among rural

[20]True, *A History of Agricultural Extension*, p. 41.

people. Following the passage of the Smith-Lever Act in 1914, federal financial support was withdrawn from the institutes, and the maintenance of a separate national organization to represent the farmers' institutes became increasingly difficult. Its demise came in 1919.

Extension Work of the Colleges of Agriculture

Many early American universities and colleges considered extension work one of their major missions. Originally, universities used the term "extension" to denote their practice of "extending" their services beyond the campus, mainly for continuing general education. Kellogg and Knapp suggest: " 'Extension' may not have been the happiest term to have chosen for what in agriculture became primarily an advisory service to help people with up-to-date knowledge . . . agricultural extension is clearly directed toward helping people solve specific problems and improve the quality of decisions they make."[21] By 1890, enough educational institutions were engaged in extension endeavors to warrant the organization of the American Society for the Extension of University Teaching. In 1897, the University of California established a department of university extension in agriculture. In 1902, the University of Wisconsin began organized extension work and in 1906 established a department of university extension. Between 1906 and 1913, 28 institutions formally organized university extension work.

Farmers' reading courses or correspondence courses were often developed. Free publications dealing with many aspects of agriculture and home economics were prepared and distributed. Subsequently, a faculty emerged whose major responsibility was to the people who could not attend college as resident students, relieving the experiment station worker to devote more time and effort to research.

In 1905, the Association of American Agricultural Colleges and Experiment Stations appointed a committee on extension to complement committees on teaching and experimentation. Extension teach-

---

[21]Kellogg, *The College of Agriculture,* pp. 186–87.

ing in agriculture was to encompass instruction in improved methods of agricultural production and the general welfare of the rural population for people not enrolled as resident pupils in educational institutions.[22]

Seaman Asahel Knapp (1833–1911) was responsible for the growth and widespread use of farm demonstrations, an important tool in extension teaching. Acknowledged nationally as "father of extension work," a New York native, Phi Beta Kappa, teacher in New York and Vermont, and professor of agriculture at Iowa State Agricultural College, Knapp also served a short term as Iowa State president. He co-authored an experiment-station bill which laid the foundation for the passage of the Hatch Act in 1887. In 1886 he moved to Louisiana, where he managed a land development company for seventeen years. It was in the Gulf states that he established a number of demonstration farms, believing that farmers would more readily change their practices by observing demonstrations carried out on their own farms rather than on farms operated at public expense.

In the fall of 1903, the Bureau of Plant Industry assigned $40,000 to Knapp for farm demonstration work, specifically earmarked for cotton growers plagued by the boll weevil. In 1904, agents were employed to hold meetings and conduct demonstrations in Texas, Louisiana, and Arkansas. By the close of 1904, more than 7,000 farmers had conducted five to twenty acre cotton growing demonstrations. By 1908, the number had grown to 32,000. Considerable private financial and local tax support of extension work was generated in the South during 1906–14. The General Educational Board, established by John D. Rockefeller, was a major supporter of Dr. Knapp, supplying funds for improving agriculture throughout the South using the county agent approach and allocating monies to employ both white and black agents.

[22]Proceedings of the Association of American Agricultural Colleges and Experiment Stations, 2–39, 1889–1925.

Boys' and Girls' Club Work

Early farmers' institutes incorporated youth programs into their sessions such as corn-growing contests for New York State boys in 1856. Between 1900 and the passage of the Smith-Lever Act, boys' and girls' clubs became well established throughout many parts of the country. Observing the success of this movement in northern states, Professor Knapp organized boys' clubs in the South in 1909, not only to teach better agricultural practices but also:

> To prove to the boy, his father, and the community that there is more in the soil than the farmer has ever gotten out of it; to inspire the boy with the love of the land by showing him how he can get wealth out of it by tilling it in a better way and keeping an expense account of his undertaking.[23]

The 4-H national emblem evolved in 1913; the symbol (head, hand, heart, and health) is used worldwide.

Extension Becomes a Federal and County Funded Organization

The involvement by agricultural colleges, their experiment stations, and USDA in extension work during the first decade of the twentieth century became so great that steps were initiated by the Association of American Agricultural Colleges and Experiment Stations to secure federal appropriations to supplement state and local appropriations. Almost from their inception, agricultural colleges had relayed information to farmers, informally and formally, on and off campuses. At both the 1908 and 1909 meetings of the association, Congress was asked to appropriate money for extension work in the land-grant colleges, but it was not until 1914 that President Wilson signed the Smith-Lever Cooperative Extension Act. It provided:

> that in order to aid in diffusing among the people of the United States useful and practical information on subjects relating to agriculture and home economics, and to encourage the application of the same,

---

[23]True, *A History of Agricultural Extension Work*, p. 65.

there may be inaugurated in connection with the college or colleges in each state now receiving, or which may hereafter receive the benefits of the Land-Grant Act of 1862 and the Morrill College Endowment Act of 1890, agricultural extension work which shall be carried on in cooperation with the United States Department of Agriculture. . . .[24]

Passage of the act clarified the relationship between extension and the federal-state-county governments. The act provided a $10,000 annual grant to each state; additional funds, based on rural population, were to be matched by the states. In addition to a memorandum of understanding with USDA, land-grant institutions also entered into a series of agreements with county boards of commissioners. The counties accepted responsibility for maintaining the program and managing funds, permitting the county agricultural extension associations to determine each county's program in cooperation with the college.

Most agricultural colleges integrated the vast force of extension agents scattered around the country into their programs, and a unified system of cooperative extension work in agriculture and home economics was established in all the states.

The Smith-Lever Act provided the impetus for the colleges to employ subject-matter specialists to backstop the county-based staff with technical information. Specialists prepared publications and exhibits; participated in various meetings, extension schools, and conferences; and visited communities, farms, and homes where special problems had arisen. Today's subject-matter specialist continues to be a viable force in the total cooperative extension program. Usually, he or she is a member of an academic department of the university, fully integrated with its research and teaching activities, and housed either on the university's main campus or a district extension office or branch campus.

[24]Ibid., p. 114.

Extension Since World War I

During World War I, state extension employees worked closely with U.S. Food Administration personnel and county and state defense councils. Congress directed extension personnel to help farmers produce and distribute maximum farm and food products; to assist the Department of Labor relieve the acute farm labor shortage; to carry out an emergency seed program; and to work in Liberty Loan, war savings, and Red Cross campaigns.

In the decade of the 1920s, agents stressed more productive farming, crop rotation, greater diversification of production and economic aspects of agriculture, and helped develop state forestry extension programs. The 1930s brought the depression. Markets dried up and agriculture was in trouble until passage of the Agricultural Adjustment Act of 1933, which sought to sharply reduce production of corn, wheat, cotton, hogs, and other commodities. Extension workers helped implement this program and also helped organize local committees and boards, training them in other New Deal program objectives and procedures, informing farmers of program regulations, and conducting educational programs to help farm families plan in terms of total, long-range needs. World War II ushered in an era of greatly increased agricultural production. Extension workers with the War Food Administration helped farmers and city gardeners set unprecedented records in food production.

In 1945, representatives from USDA and the Association of Land-Grant Colleges and Universities summarized the effects of technological progress affecting extension's future role—the widening gap between efficient and inefficient farmers; displacement of farm labor; increased production requiring soil conservation programs and marketing and distribution assistance. Extension's role in public service was recognized and called for expansion of farm and home planning, recognizing the decreasing number of farm families and the increasing number of rural non-farm families; improvement in rural health and rural educational services; and conservation of natural resources.

The 1950s brought new and growing consumer demands, new agricultural technology, and a growing economy. Efforts that had previously been directed towards increasing production were now centered on managing production that exceeded demands. Increased federal and local funds in 1954 provided about 1,000 new county and home agents to furnish intensive counseling to families in the nation-wide Farm and Home Development Program launched by extension. In 1955, USDA, federal and state agencies, and extension coordinated a comprehensive rural development program attacking low-income problems on a community basis—a program which continues today.

Extension Expands and Broadens Focus

Extension's thrust in the 1960s emphasized marketing and consumer education programs. Youth work penetrated deeper into the urban areas; educational programs sought to reach the part-time farmer and urban dweller; and community resource development programs assisted in solving problems of pollution, health systems, land use, taxation, waste disposal, schools, job opportunities, and housing. Computerized farm record analysis programs, for a fee, were made available to farmers in most states. Performance evaluation programs in all areas of animal agriculture benefited not only the producer but also the consumer. Better marketing programs dealt with improved efficiencies in the marketing system, development of new products, maintenance of quality during marketing, and a tailoring of production and processing methods to consumer wants.

Extension's responsibility to the consumer was not restricted to rural areas. Programs reached into the cities, serving both low and middle income clientele. The Expanded Food and Nutrition Extension Program, funded by Congress in the late 1960s, provided money for a nutrition program for the low-income and disadvantaged segment of society. Many paraprofessionals were hired as nutrition aides to reach families in their own neighborhoods with information designed to improve their diets and their lives. The 4-H Club program was expanded for youths from cities, small towns, suburban communities, and farms, for boys and girls from every economic level and ethnic group.

A People and a Spirit

In 1968, a joint USDA and Land-Grant University Extension Study Committee completed *A People and a Spirit,* a comprehensive analysis of the challenges and opportunities confronting the Cooperative Extension Service.

Extension, said the report, should be the "educational arm" of the USDA and educational support arm for other governmental agencies. Extension should help strengthen the local Cooperative Extension Service office in its role as a primary source of information and focal referral point for the many programs involving direct relationships between units of government and the people, especially in rural areas. This office should be the public's point of contact for the entire land-grant university. The administration of various extension functions funded from different sources within the federal government should be at the university level. The university, in turn, should provide access to and support from all colleges and departments which have competencies relevant to the extension function.

The committee's program recommendations were: (1) to seek maximum effectiveness from manpower resources; (2) to maintain an effective program in agriculture and its related industries; (3) to assist in alleviating problems related to the American community and unequal opportunity; and (4) to further develop extension programs related to quality of living. Detailed suggestions for carrying out these recommendations were made, although the committee recommended the appropriation of sufficient additional funds by the proper federal, state, local, and private agencies to substantially strengthen their overall capability.

The committee also recommended a long-range program strategy for the U.S. overseas agricultural development programs. Efforts should be made to adapt existing U.S. institutions, including extension, to long-range overseas programs of agricultural development, including the establishment of International Extension Training Centers at one or more land-grant universities.

A People and a Spirit will be used to guide future extension programming. How far and how fast programs change will depend on how much emphasis and resources are placed in the various program elements. Advice and recommendations of local advisory groups representing the people in each state will also be considered. Using these guidelines, extension can continue to assist a contemporary society in solving contemporary problems. Nowhere else in society is there an organization better equipped to handle these problems, because of extension's closeness to the people, its teaching techniques, and its informal methods of transferring knowledge.

Colleges of Agriculture: Their Image

Colleges of agriculture are not what people often perceive them to be. Kellogg and Knapp have said:

> One of the greatest fallacies in thinking about land-grant colleges of agriculture stems from simple comparisons between numbers of farm families and the size of the colleges. Questioners have asked: If the number of farmers is declining, why shouldn't the college budgets? The question itself implies that only farmers . . . benefit from agricultural research and education. Such a fallacy can seem reasonable to people who have lacked opportunities to become acquainted with modern specialized farming, with the other great sectors of agriculture, or with the growing problems of resource use and human welfare in rural and urban-fringe areas throughout the country. At the high level of technology that commercial farmers work today, their individual needs for knowledge in depth are far greater than ever. So the total cost is higher, not lower. And the principles learned to service them have direct applicability to resource use for other purposes.[25]

But what of the other farmers? The science of agriculture that solves problems also creates them. Farmers with limited resources cannot compete today in specialized agriculture, and too often rural communities offer little or no employment alternatives. Edward Higbee, in his book, *Farms and Farmers in an Urban Age,* says:

> The small farmer can no longer establish contact with the small consumer on a scale required to feed the population. Food must be assembled by the trainload rather than by the wagonload, and trans-

[25]Kellogg, *The College of Agriculture,* p. 33.

ported across the continent rather than across a township. This calls
for a new gigantism in production and in distribution. A few little
farmers may survive by lying between the rails as the freights thunder
by, but they are becoming as rare as old-fashioned butchershops in an
age of supermarkets.[26]

What are the colleges doing for the displaced or impoverished
farmer, whether he is on or off the farm? Many administrators feel
the answer is to provide more educational opportunities for rural
youth, and are meeting the challenge through less-than-degree-level
programs that train youth for non-farm jobs. Extension programs in
many states are also geared to the low-income family in both rural
and urban centers.

The problem of providing blanket help to the displaced rural
population, says Higbee, rests with who will bear the financial responsibility:

> . . . The federal budget to relieve the problem of farm surpluses has
> been more generous than the federal budget to relieve the urban
> problem of surplus people. This, in part, is due to the influence of rural
> spokesmen who contend that the problem of human surpluses is one
> for local governments to resolve with local tax funds while the prob-
> lem of farm surpluses is one for the national treasury.[27]

In 1963, at a seminar on Agricultural Administration in the Land-
Grant System, educators voiced their concern that colleges have
not fully met the research and education needs of the displaced
rural population. The change in structure of agriculture as productivity grew and labor was displaced affected the demand for goods
and services provided by non-farm persons and institutions in communities. Colleges, the administrators felt, have concentrated disproportionately on particular services to a small section of the
community, and have not solved the problems which they helped
to create.

Programs in the 1970s reflect this concern; some colleges are using

[26]Edward Higbee, *Farms and Farmers in an Urban Age* (New York: The Twentieth Century
Fund, 1963), p. 4.
[27]Higbee, *Farms and Farmers,* p. 5.

a multi-discipline approach to solve problems of resource use, recreational development and management, urban and rural poverty, and educational and cultural opportunities for rural people. Regional rural development centers have recently been established by Cornell, Iowa State, Oregon State, and Tuskegee Institute. Kansas State already has such an action-oriented center that focuses on solving community problems, such as attracting new businesses or using existing resources productively.

Colleges' Programs, Policies Attacked

Criticisms of the land-grant colleges of agriculture—with their tripartite organizations of extension, experiment station, and resident education; their diversity of emphasis of the three segments according to individual state's agricultural economy and climate; and their vast differences in program scope, direction, and administrative structure—are necessarily very general. A recent, well-publicized critique by James Hightower, *Hard Tomatoes, Hard Times,* accuses all colleges of agriculture of diverting millions of tax dollars annually to the service of large agricultural corporations while ignoring the pressing concerns of consumers, environmentalists, American farmers, farm workers, small-town businessmen, and other rural residents.

The report was the product of a six-month investigation by the Task Force on the Land-Grant College Complex, a self-described public interest organization, which conducted research in Washington, D.C., and on nine land-grant campuses. Hightower's indictments triggered a hearing by Senator Adlai Stevenson III (D., Ill.), chairman of the Senate Subcommittee on Migrant Labor. The National Association of State Universities and Land-Grant Colleges responded to the charges through a panel headed by Chancellor John T. Caldwell, North Carolina State University; President Alvin I. Thomas, Prairie View A & M College; Dean Orville Bentley, College of Agriculture, University of Illinois; and Assistant Dean George McIntyre, Director of Extension, Michigan State University. In brief, the allegations were refuted; though it was agreed that "the nation has not done enough to assist displaced farm workers or others adversely affected by changing farm economy, either in rural or urban areas. . . . We (land-grant colleges) have, however, never been given the funds to pursue an individual counseling-guidance-retraining program for the rural dweller, either displaced or on the way to being displaced from farming."[28]

Charges that research benefits private firms were labeled inaccurate; every new development is made available to the small farmer as well as to the absentee-owned corporate enterprise. Hightower's insistence that the land-grant complex tolerated discrimination which deprived Negro land-grant colleges from research funds was justifiable, according to President Thomas of Prairie View A & M, an "1890 institution," in that "black colleges have been less than full partners in the land-grant experience. . . . These conditions are not only true of the land-grant system, but they have been true in general for the nation as a whole. . . . In recent years, the National Association of State Universities and Land-Grant Colleges has taken positive and affirmative steps to insure the full partnership of the 1890 colleges in the land-grant college system. . . . Through USDA, $12.8 million for research and extension became available to the 1890 colleges in FY '72. The major thrust of practically all of the funds provided 1890 colleges went into people's problems."[29]

A law suit was filed (and subsequently dropped) by various self-described consumer interest groups against federal officials charging they (officials) head land-grant aid programs which cater to big business and special interest groups. Administrators of colleges of agriculture are currently preparing briefs for the Justice Department to respond to the allegations.

Penn State's College of Agriculture administrators felt that every college should continuously scrutinize its programs as part of its ongoing function; this is true not only of colleges of agriculture but also in other areas of the universities. The absence of accountability, a theme throughout Hightower's thesis, was dismissed by Penn State officials, who pointed to the voluminous progress reports required by USDA and to Penn State's Agricultural Advisory Council, composed of representatives from farm organizations, farmers, and farm-

[28]NASULGC Circulating Letter, No. 12 (July 7, 1972), p. 7.
[29]NASULGC Newsletter, pp. 9–10.

related associations who meet with college officials to discuss and oversee the college's future and present programs.

Penn State experiment station directors feel their segment is an agent for both the consumer and the farmer; any short-range research monopoly gains to industry are not captive but are transferred to the consumer sector. In many instances, research in agriculture, especially in farm mechanization, was stressed in order to compete with low labor costs available in foreign countries. All research, they emphasized, benefits farmers both large and small, whether they be innovative or subsisting.

Research on people problems has not been voluminous because often there were no researchable hypotheses to pursue with tools now available. Who should or could pursue these research hypotheses? Administrators stressed that colleges of agriculture are not "action" agencies. Their role is education and research, to point out alternative courses of action but not to make public policy. Colleges cannot distribute funds. Legislators must implement services and control welfare programs.

It is significant that legislators are becoming aware of research needs. This year, Congress gave USDA four times as much money as it requested for sociological research. Jerry Carlson, managing editor of *Farm Journal,* reporting on the Hightower-NASULGC Congressional Hearing, said:

> Back in the 1930's, Congress killed the Farm Security Administration, a vital USDA drive to help small farmers out of the Depression. The axe fell again from Capitol Hill in the 1940's, gutting the Bureau of Agricultural Economics for 'socialist schemes.' BAE had dared to push for both social research and action, including federally financed training to help farmers diversify.
>
> Today, one of the strongest advocates of social-economic research is USDA's ag economics head, Don Paarlberg. He says, 'in the past, we had an implicit policy that drove rural people to the cities. What we now propose is an explicit policy that gives them a choice.'
>
> However, if people prod Congress into giving our land-grant leaders a chance, we can work another series of new wonders in the countryside which will far surpass our technical achievements.[30]

---

[30]Jerry Carlson, "More Research and Extension for Small Farmers," *Farm Journal* (August 1972):27.

Educators and administrators within the colleges and universities feel the tripartite organization offers an institutional model useful in solving urban and rural problems. What is needed are reevaluated and redefined purposes and objectives. The rich experience and successful research contributions of the colleges of agriculture; their unique closeness to the people through the extension segment; their existing network of communications between governments—federal, state, and local—and between universities and their publics, offer an existing model usable and applicable for years of service to the people.

One final observation seems warranted. While this observation cannot be made by "revisiting" colleges of agriculture and their multiple facets in isolation, it does emerge after reviewing colleges in the context of the total university. The observation is that the colleges of agriculture alone deal with a total social system. They encompass agricultural production plus processing and marketing; they are concerned with the human aspects of production and labor as well as the farm family in its totality; they utilize the science disciplines to create a science of agriculture; they expand the use of the social sciences and the humanities to create new perspectives on both rural and urban life. Perhaps the challenge to the land-grant university of the future is answerable in terms of this totality.

Chapter 5

HOME ECONOMICS AND THE DEVELOPMENT OF NEW FORMS OF HUMAN SERVICE EDUCATION

THEODORE R. VALLANCE

THIS examination concentrates on the forces and administrative processes of change and their outcomes as of this writing.[1] Hopefully, it will illustrate how some programs of home economics have participated in the process of evolution within land-grant universities in the responsiveness of those universities to the continuing trends of change in society at large. Three examples of this adaptive process will be presented—the developments at Cornell, West Virginia University, and Penn State—with the principal attention directed to the experience at Penn State.

In order to set the stage, it will be helpful to provide a review of some of the forces which gave rise to colleges and departments of home economics.

The Evolution of Home Economics

A conference, held at Lake Placid in 1902, was the fourth of a series of meetings of people concerned with the welfare and importance of the family in our society. Among the actions of this meeting was the adoption of this definition of the nature of the field which they named home economics:

> Home economics, in its most comprehensive sense, is the study of the laws, conditions, principles, and ideals which are concerned on the one hand with man's immediate physical environment and on the other with his nature as a social being and is the study especially of the relation between these two factors.[2]

---

[1]November 1972.

[2]Hazel Craig, *History of Home Economics* (New York: Practical Home Economics, 1945), p. 15.

The report of that meeting goes on to identify home economics as "a philosophical subject, something to connect and bind together into a consistent whole many pieces of knowledge"[3] at that time unrelated.

The intervening years have seen the evolution of home economics along considerably more specialized and, at times, fragmented lines. As frequently happens, the legislative and financing programs from the federal government played a major hand in shaping the evolution of home economics in its various services and institutional forms; Henderson[4] summarizes the results and the trends away from the broad objective cited above into a series of programs which became tied closely to the production, distribution, and use of agricultural products.

Home economics was written into the Smith-Lever Act of 1914 as the means of helping farmers' wives through the association with the Agricultural Extension Service which that law brought into being. While this act initiated a trend that brought funds to home economics, it contributed, according to Henderson, to years of confusion about the purposes of home economics by uniting it with agricultural programs and purposes that many of its early adherents neither understood nor especially cared to support at the expense of foregoing their broader aims.

The Smith-Hughes Act of 1917 provided a strong, federally supported thrust to vocational education in many fields, particularly in agriculture, home economics, and the trades. The emphasis in home economics was on using evening, day, and part-time schools in the preparation of homemakers and jobs related to homemaking. Calvin described the influence of the Smith-Hughes Act by noting that prior to its passage:

Home economics education provided in the land-grant institution was theoretically directed toward the preparation of women for their

[3]Grace M. Henderson, *Development of Home Economics in the United States* (University Park, Pennsylvania: The Pennsylvania State University, College of Home Economics, 1954), p. 6.
[4]Ibid., pp. 16–17.

home activities. The training designed to prepare for teaching home economics was but incidental to the major objective, training for home administration.

The Smith-Hughes Act directly affected home economics teacher training in land-grant colleges. In most states the Federal money provided for teacher training and vocational home economics was allocated to the land-grant college. This made possible larger salaries for home economics faculty and also provided for increased personnel. Whereas previously teacher training had been incidental to other objectives of home economics instruction it now became the major objective in many land-grant institutions for the stimulus of Federal aid.[5]

McGrath and Johnson[6] thereafter recorded in 1967 that the number of home economics departments in the land-grant colleges grew from four in 1890 to eighteen in 1905 and, after the Smith-Hughes Act, to forty in 1920. They also observed that the structure of the 1960 home economics college was established in higher education essentially through the impact of the Smith-Hughes Act.

In 1925, the Purnell Act provided research funds for home economics. These funds, administered by the U.S. Department of Agriculture through its experiment stations in the land-grant universities, again helped to shape the programs of home economics departments and colleges.

The expansion in home economics fostered by the federal programs of agricultural development, research, and education, made serious demands on the energies and talents of those who identified themselves with home economics and diverted these energies away from the original objectives as stated in 1902.[7] Because of accelerating migration and the impact of modern technology in the post-World War II period, home economists found a renewed and growing interest in problems of family, community, and environment. Along with the increasing interest was a relatively de-

[5]Henrietta W. Calvin, "Survey of Home Economics Education in Land-Grant Colleges," *Bureau of Education Bulletin,* No. 20, Department of the Interior (Washington: Government Printing Office, 1925), pp. 1–3.

[6]Earl J. McGrath and Jack T. Johnson, *The Changing Mission of Home Economics* (New York: Teachers College, Columbia University, 1968).

[7]Grace M. Henderson, *Development of Home Economics.*

clining interest in problems connected with the production, processing, and distribution of agricultural products.

Therefore, by the late 1950s and the early 1960s, conditions bode
well for more rapid changes in the field of home economics. By the
1960s the field of home economics could be summarized in approximately these terms: It had become female-dominated because of
emphasis on the home and processes within the home and the way
in which this emphasis had been affected by a half-century of ties
with agriculture. In 1966, 90 percent of resident instruction faculty
members in home economics were women.

Factioned into diverse and frequently competing and poorly
related programs and subfields, home economics had also become
inbred through the development of strong programs in a small number of institutions: ten universities accounted for 75 percent of the
doctorates earned by home economics faculty members from 1945
to 1965.

Home economics units remained highly dependent on agriculture
for research funding. Funds appropriated under the Hatch Act and
experiment station funds supported 43 percent of research projects
with which home economists were associated. Other contributors
financed a very small proportion of the total of home economics
research: National Institutes of Health, 5 percent; other components
of the U.S. Department of Health, Education, and Welfare, 7 percent. Home economics had not evolved a research program responding clearly to interests outside the field of agriculture: 43 percent of
home economics research projects were concentrated in seven land-
grant universities which enjoyed substantial subsidies of federal
funds through agriculture channels.[8]

Its administrative placement within parent universities was diverse. Forty-nine percent of home economics units within land-grant
and state universities existed as separate colleges reporting to top
administration, 30 percent reporting to the top by way of an agricultural channel, and the balance through liberal arts, education, or
other professional schools.[9]

[8]McGrath and Johnson, *Changing Mission,* p. 73.
[9]Ibid.

Home economics in the land-grant universities was ripe for change. By the 1960s several of the larger schools in the field were the scenes of reviews of purpose and program structure, initiated from within or in response to other administrative forces. According to McGrath and Jackson:

Was it merely a collection of disparate specialties or did it have a distinctive and unifying core? What research should it include and how should such research be organized? . . . What should happen to home economics extension? How should home economics respond to the major changes occurring in society, increasing urbanization, the shift of values and attitudes about family life and even new international efforts to assist the developing nations?[10]

Of special concern to administrators in a number of universities was how the universities might provide leadership in coping with the increasingly evident problems of modern society. Unavoidably, colleges of home economics within these universities were being caught up in the sweep of institutional change.

The Transition at Cornell:
Committee Study of the College of Home Economics

At Cornell, the evolution of the College of Home Economics into the College of Human Ecology began officially in 1965 when President Perkins appointed a committee to study the college and make recommendations about:

One, the objectives and functions of colleges of home economics in the United States during the remainder of this century and two, the specific objectives, functions, and approaches of a state supported institution for home economics education and research located on the campus at Cornell University.[11]

---

[10]Ibid., p. 20.
[11]*Final Report of the President's Committee to Study the College of Home Economics,* Cornell University, December 1966.

The committee had nine members: four from the college and one each from chemistry, psychology, agricultural economics, sociology, and cooperative extension. A panel of technical consultants from outside the university was appointed to advise the committee. Provisions were also made for participation by the provost and other officers of the State University of New York because of the statutory nature of Cornell's college which links it with public education. (Cornell University has the unusual characteristic of having a private endowment and a board of trustees that controls the use of that endowment through a set of internal colleges, while at the same time administering some publicly financed colleges—including Agriculture and Human Ecology—that are the responsibility of the administrators and regents of the SUNY system.)

Internal forces which generated and influenced this committee included:

1. A series of internally initiated studies extending as far back as 1960 when the dean appointed a long-range planning committee which, in several incarnations, successfully advocated several changes in the college.

2. Desire on the part of President Perkins to move a number of elements of the university from what was seen as limited applied specializations to broader views.

3. The opportunities for taking a new look at missions, programs, and structure with the foreseeable retirement of the incumbent dean.

4. A growing belief on the part of many faculty members within home economics that some changes were desirable—in fact, overdue. The largest and strongest department, Child Development and Family Relations, had both the largest proportion and the largest number of men. Many of them had gained a degree of eminence in fields related to home economics, though not commonly seen as a part of it. Several were uncomfortable in their identification with what they regarded as a high degree of specialization within home economics and with what many of their colleagues in other universities saw as a low-status profession.

5. Faculty concern about focusing home economics interests and skills on problems of the broader society—to attend to the ever more evident needs of cities and so to loosen the tie with agriculture which

had come to dominate the home economics field as a whole.

6. The feeling of several faculty members that the college should also take steps to attract more men students. (This action would focus on more urgent contemporary problem settings.) Very few men applied for admission to the college, and women students heavily predominated. This was brought about in part by an admissions screening practice that sought to admit students with a commitment to home economics and by a curriculum requirement that every student take the introductory course in each department of the college.

7. A tuition pattern at Cornell that tended to reinforce isolation and specialization within home economics. Being state supported, the home economics college was able to charge lower tuition rates. However, it also posed a problem when students took extensive courses in the endowed colleges of the university—which required a transfer of tuition payments.

Thus, conditions had developed over a number of years which generated a considerable readiness for change. The readiness was neither equally distributed across the college faculty, nor was there unanimity on the directions which changes should take.

In this context, then, the president's committee set about its work. More than forty meetings were held between September of 1965 and the end of October of 1966. Its report was submitted in December of that year. A general idea of the report is as follows:

1. The college's program should focus on the study of human development and the quality of the human environment, and its name should be the College of Human Development and Environment.

2. Student preparation should emphasize societal problem areas but should be built upon enough exploration of adjacent academic areas to permit movement across professional lines. Within this process the requirement of taking the introductory course in each department should be abolished.

3. A strengthened graduate faculty should be assured of freedom to select their research areas and projects.

4. Research should be more clearly related to teaching and to public service obligations of the college, and joint research-teaching,

and research-extension appointments should be encouraged.

5. Public service functions should be developed more aggressively for consumer groups.

6. Continuing education programs for professional people and community leaders should be given priority over established programs for nonprofessionals.

7. The organizational structure of the college should be reviewed to incorporate these criteria:

    a. Each department should focus on an area of study derived from one or two basic disciplines and have a majority of its graduate faculty belonging to the same field.
    b. Each department should be large enough to provide for a rich interchange of ideas and for subgroups to work together on selected areas of interest.
    c. Interaction of faculty across departments should be encouraged.

The committee suggested department names which would reflect the use of the guiding criteria and imply the reasonable incorporation of existing faculty and programs. These were:

    a. Department of Child Development and Family Relations
       Department of Consumer Economics
       Department of Environmental Design
       Department of Food and Nutrition
       Department of Housing and Community Development
    b. Department of Community and Social Welfare
       Department of Consumer Resources
       Department of Design and Allied Arts
       Department of Human Behavior
       Department of Nutrition and Food Science

8. New faculty members should be recruited for their demonstrated competence and promise for continued growth in at least two program functions (continuing education, research, teaching) more than on the basis of their fitting into detailed position specifications.

9. Recruitment and selection should be a responsibility shared by many faculty members.

Faculty Action

Given these recommendations, each of which was supported by a clearly stated rationale, the faculty began an extensive self-study aimed at bringing about a significant change in the focus, organization, and program of the college. One principal instrument of this study was the organizational committee called for in the earlier report of the president's committee. It, too, was intercollege in nature, having representatives from the Departments of Engineering, Physics, Industrial and Labor Relations, and Sociology, in addition to five members of the Home Economics faculty. Between July 1967 and June 1968, the committee held about thirty meetings mostly involving various faculty groups. They explored a very wide range of concerns: mission and educational philosophy, basic and applied research, program articulation within the college, relations with other segments of the university, and humane issues unavoidably to be involved in changes of emphasis.

Following submission of the committee's report[12] to the faculty, a small *ad hoc* group, including the new dean, formed a plan for the college. This plan, as presented to the faculty in February 1969, provided for college governance, a system for administration and management, and department organization.[13]

The changes that came about as a result of this work are summarized in the table on the following page.

The aims of the undergraduate program in the college now were to provide "a liberal education in the social and natural sciences, the humanities, and the arts; and to provide specialized instruction, based on these disciplines, as preparation for professional careers in which the interests and well-being of the individual, the consumer, and the family are paramount."[14] The interdisciplinary approach to these aims was provided through programs in five departments: Community Service Education, Consumer Economics and Public

[12]*Report to President James O. Perkins from the Organization Committee,* Committee Report, Cornell University, College of Home Economics, June 1968.

[13]David C. Knapp, *Memorandum to the Faculty on College Organization,* Cornell University, College of Home Economics, February 1969.

[14]*Cornell University Announcements,* New York State College of Human Ecology, 1972–73.

	College of Home Economics 1965	College of Human Ecology 1972
Department Structure	7 Academic Departments	5 Academic Departments
Number of Faculty		
Men	19	53
Women	89	86
	108	139
Number of Students		
Undergraduate		
Men	0	63
Women	738	1099
	738	1162
Graduate		
Men	17	45
Women	128	174
	145	219
Administrative Structure	1 Dean	1 Dean
	3 Coordinators	3 Associate Deans

Policy, Design and Environmental Analysis, Human Development and Family Studies, and Human Nutrition and Food.

As a result of these undergraduate modifications, graduate study was offered in four fields corresponding generally to the last four named departments but with opportunities for interdepartmental study.

The Transition at West Virginia University

At West Virginia home economics was different in two major respects from either Penn State or Cornell. The tie with agriculture was especially strong, and home economics did not have autonomy or the strength normally associated with college or school status. In 1962, home economics was a department of about twelve members within the College of Agriculture, Forest Resources, and Home Economics.

The transition which affected home economics began essentially with the appointment of Paul Miller as president of the university in 1962. Miller had for some years been associated with the efforts of many home economics leaders to revitalize and redirect their field. Therefore, he brought with him hopes to reshape home economics at West Virginia, while developing plans to promote reorganization of the university as a whole from numerous small units to fewer large units. This restructuring was to promote better use of faculty and other resources. One of these larger units was to be related to the development of human resources. One of the early planning papers stated:

> The rationale for a human resources unit rests on the assumption that programs which share a broadly designed common concern, which share common roots in a social and humanistic discipline, which share similar research methods, which share an obvious theoretical and professional interdependence, which share a common concern for graduate education, and which share a common need and desire for rapid development can best achieve their mutual and separate objectives in concert.[15]

A planning committee was appointed by President Miller in October 1964 to study the university's human resource-related programs. Accordingly, a rather intensive analysis of the programs in education, psychology, sociology, social work, rehabilitation counseling, and home economics was undertaken. Curriculum emphases, faculty composition, faculty rank and salary structure, research productivity, and sources of financial support were analyzed in considerable detail.[16]

The faculty members of the Departments of Psychology and Sociology on reflection decided that their best interests lay in the further development of their basic disciplines, rather than applying them to contemporary problems. They believed that application could as well be made by continuing from their base within the College of Arts and Science.

[15]*Notes on Human Resources,* West Virginia University, October 1964.
[16]Human Resources Planning Group, *An Overview,* West Virginia University, January 1965.

Home Economics, on the other hand, saw an opportunity to grow in a new setting. Faculty members saw the new enterprise as moving into a current concern for the quality of family life and away from what some considered an exclusive concern for the production and distribution of agricultural products. Action toward such an opportunity was made easier by the fact that the new dean of the College of Agriculture, Forestry, and Home Economics was an appointee of the incumbent president and shared his views on the general reorganization of the university.

Thus, the president's planning committee concluded after its year-long study that:

> the transfer of the division of home economics from the College of Agriculture, Forestry, and Home Economics is not simply an administrative realignment. Nationally the profession of home economics is seeking what it calls 'new directions.' Among other things, these new directions involve a return to a fundamental concern with the family and the home and a new emphasis on the basic social sciences. Inclusion in the program in the new College of Education and Human Resources as the Division of Home and Family Studies would be a step in this direction.[17]
> The basic recommendations of the study committee were:
> a. that current university programs in education, social work, rehabilitation counseling, speech correction and audiology, and home economics be brought together in a single college to be named the College of Education and Human Resources;
> b. that the new College of Education and Human Resources be organized, in effect, on a divisional basis, including a Division of Education, a Division of Clinical Study, a Division of Home and Family Study, a Graduate School of Social Work, and a Human Resources Research Institute. . . .[18]

The committee recommended that the new college go into effect as of July 1, 1965.

Within the new college, priorities of public need and opportunities for change led to the decision that developmental emphases should

[17]*Recommendation and Rationale for a College of Education and Human Resources*, Committee report, West Virginia University, 1965.
[18]Ibid., p. 1.

go in the beginning to the modernization of the Division of Education. The feeling was that greater societal advantages would come from emphasizing education in the first few years rather than quickly trying to raise the status of a small division whose faculty held mixed views about the change. The program appears today, at least as reflected in a comparison of old and current course offerings, much as it was in 1965. Administrators of the new unit nonetheless have stated that a number of benefits have accrued from this combination in better communication between home economics faculty and other divisions of the new college. The belief is also held that, through the Division of Family Resources, home economics has made definite progress in several of its programs as a result of an increased degree of autonomy. Plans for the next few years called for further attention to be given to the rejuvenation of home economics by further capitalizing on the opportunities of sharing an administrative framework with several closely related fields.

The Changeover at Penn State

The experience at Penn State in its original focus and its outcome is highly dissimilar from those at Cornell and West Virginia.

Home economics at Penn State is now diffused throughout the university with much of it in programs that have major thrusts not readily identifiable as home economics. Nonetheless, a close look behind program names and into several colleges of the university could show that there is as much home economics at Penn State now as before the College of Home Economics ceased its existence as an organizational entity.

The 1980 Committee Study

Penn State's president from 1956 to 1970, Eric Walker, was a far-seeing president as well as a strong leader, skilled at capitalizing on the boom conditions in higher education that characterized most of his time in office. In 1960 he appointed a committee to make recommendations about what The Pennsylvania State University should be like in 1980. Dr. Walker believed that the rapid rate of

change in society's ways and means would continue or even accelerate for the foreseeable future, largely driven by the opportunities
provided by a rapidly expanding technology and its scientific base.
He also thought that changes for both ill and good could be expected
and, given sufficient skill and wisdom, forestalled or used well.

This committee was told to consider new educational and research
needs. President Walker reminded the committee that by 1980 all of
the present administrators would be gone, and so admonished the
committee to be imaginative about proposing changes in the organizational structure of the university according to their judgment.
Interestingly, this 1980 committee, as it came to be known, contained
no representative from home economics. Its members came from
mechanical engineering, biochemistry, Slavic languages, political science, psychology, meteorology, the president's staff, biophysics, and
accounting. Their concern stemmed from the virtue of their own
work or of their being serious avocational students of the current
scene, competent in many of the areas that were foremost in providing the new ideas that were promoting technological and social
change. They did not represent any kind of politically balanced
ticket.

In June 1963 the report was given to the president and the university faculty.[19] Two early paragraphs set the tone of the report. They
note that a university is:

> both a product of and a creator of the society in which it exists.
> Therefore, it must think of itself not only as *responding* to conditions
> in its changing world but also as one of the basic energies *responsible*
> for creating those varied changes. Similarly, individuals strive not
> only to maintain their physical existence through control over their
> own environment and their body, but also to give some meaning to
> their lives. Man is not satisfied just to exist to relieve his biological and
> animal urges. He also innately seeks the excitement of new experience
> and new accomplishments.
>
> In this context, we seem to be creating a great dilemma for our-
> selves. Through our science and technology, we are, and will be,
> fantastically successful in gaining control over our physical environ-

---

[19] *Penn State in 1980,* The Pennsylvania State University, June 1963.

ment and in maintaining our good health. This gives us new freedom from fear, pain, and the requirement that most of our life be spent primarily in maintaining our existence in physical comfort. But what will we use this new freedom for? Is it really a menace—something to be feared as has sometimes been suggested? If the University shares the basic responsibility for creating these new conditions, should it also assume some responsibility for discovering how man can use his new powers to enhance his own life rather than being the victim of his knowledge? Can the University help create conditions in which people learn to live meaningfully and harmoniously as well as to exist efficiently and comfortably for a long life time?[20]

The report goes on to refer to the vocational thrust that had developed from the land-grant character of the university and the scientific thrust that grew out of the practical needs of modern man. Then, following a preview of likely political conditions affecting man's relationship to the state, and a set of assumptions about man's control of the environment, the committee identified a new thrust likely to be critical in guiding the development of a major university —the Human Development Thrust.

The University should focus a major effort on the objective of how to make human life significant in the context of a society in which people will live in good health much longer, will spend a much smaller portion of their lifetime at economically productive jobs, will live in closer proximity to one another, will have much greater control over their environment and will be subject to much greater centralized control themselves. . . . For example, increasing control over our physical environment will pose the critical questions of how new control should be exercised by whom and for what purposes. Who should decide about the human genetic control, or control of weather, both of which will undoubtedly be possible in the near future? Our continuing industrial revolution will lead us to increasing amounts of free time and energy for people to use in ways other than on economically productive jobs. Must we evolve a society in which a few people (for want of a better term we will call them government) provide for the comfortable physical existence of everyone else and invent things to keep them busy? We think not.

For what purposes shall man live if not simply for physical exis-

[20]Ibid., pp. 6–7.

tence or economic productivity? We do not consider ourselves wise enough to answer this question for all people for all times. However, we are convinced that recreation as loosely defined today will not be sufficient even though remaining an important healthy part of life. We think the phrase "the energetic use of abilities" coined in one of our meetings may provide a valuable lead. Certainly man's capacity to transcend his immediate physical environment through his abilities to think, imagine, create, and communicate opens up all of the phenomena of the universe for his investigation and enjoyment. We are convinced that if the University devotes an important portion of its energies and resources to this thrust, consequences of great importance to all our lives could result. We do believe it will take new resources and energies. It is true that the University has active and flourishing departments studying within the framework of the scientific ethic. They are studying man as an object and organism like any other. This is quite proper and productive, and will undoubtedly lead to fundamental and important new knowledge. However, they demonstrate relatively little interest in how human life can be given personal significance within the context of a world rapidly changing because we are changing it. These are not just questions of what can be but what should be: not only questions of fact, but questions of values.[21]

The report goes on to present thirty major and minor proposals relating to university organization and policy. It also discusses how instruction and instructional policy, research and research policy, would be articulated with one another and with the proposals on university organization and policy.

One of the more far-reaching recommendations was that a new College of Human Development, Health, and Welfare be established. This college would serve as a vehicle for translating man's advancing knowledge of man into constructive and remedial social applications. The report recommended that portions of the (then) Colleges of Physical Education and of Home Economics should be brought into such a college, along with programs for training people in medical, psychological, and sociological professions. Clearly, its faculty would have to be broadly interdisciplinary.

The committee's report went on to address a number of issues, including expansion of continuing education and activity in interna-

[21]Ibid., pp. 16–18.

tional affairs, the development of the health and biological sciences, the development of libraries and research centers, and the changing role of the faculty.

College of Home Economics Self-Study

During the period when the 1980 committee was at work, the leadership and a significant part of the faculty of the College of Home Economics was struggling with the general disciplinary ferment that had begun in home economics. The college's annual report for the 1959–60 academic year summarizes the outcome of a two-year self-study directed toward modernizing the curriculum in order to bring it more into tune "with the needs of the third quarter of the twentieth century."[22]

That study led to the adoption of a new curriculum that deemphasized instruction in the specifics of how-to-do particular homemaking tasks and increased the emphasis on the social significance of the several aspects of family life and on the professions that would serve families. More requirements were laid down for general liberal arts and science subjects, in sociology, psychology, economics, bacteriology, literature, chemistry, and other fields that related to home economics programs. Emphasis continued to be placed on the family, although with a revised and strengthened program in the management of hotels and other residential institutions and their food services.

At this time, too, consideration was being given a name change that would reflect the change in emphasis; several were recommended to the president's office including College of the Family and Community, and College of Family and Community Services.[23] Thus, the family, while clearly continuing its domination as a center of interest, was coming to be seen in a community context.

Comparison of that new curriculum with the rhetoric of the objectives and philosophy of home economics as represented in the annual report for 1959–60 suggests that the changes were somewhat less

---

[22]Grace M. Henderson, *1959–1960 Annual Report of the College of Home Economics,* The Pennsylvania State University, July 1960.
[23]Ibid.

dramatic than the college leadership might have sought. The curriculum adopted by the university senate still closely tied its course structure to a fairly traditional departmental organization which emphasized child development and family relationships, foods and nutrition, clothing and textiles, home management and family economics, commercial consumer services, home art, home community relationships, home economics education, and hotel and institution administration. However, plans were being made for further evolution—primarily a new departmental organization which would reduce the number of administrative personnel and provide for an increasing emphasis on community relationships of the family.

University-wide Discussion

With the release of the 1980 committee report in 1963 a series of university-wide discussions began to define and implement the human development thrust which that report advocated. Several meetings of top administrative officers were held where the deans of the several colleges that might participate in such a program made formal presentations, commenting on the general merits of expanding a human development emphasis within the university, how their colleges might participate, and how a new college to incorporate it might be set up.

The leadership of the College of Home Economics was quick to see in this prospect the potential for realizing many of their own ambitions for increasing social relevance. Within the college a number of additional studies of possible reorganization were conducted, along with renewed thinking about name changes, including Human Development.[24] As discussion proceeded throughout the university over the next few years, plans were developed within the College of Home Economics to make it feasible for home economics to be centrally involved in a new college when and if such a college were to emerge. The home economics section of a general university-wide

---

[24]Committee Reports: *Proposal for a New College at The Pennsylvania State University,* College of Home Economics, November 1965; *Increased Emphases Needed in the College of Home Economics by 1970,* The Pennsylvania State University, September 1965; *The Expanded Proposal for the College of Human Development,* College of Home Economics, The Pennsylvania State University, September 1966.

self-study, prepared for the Middle-States Association of Colleges and Secondary Schools in 1966, says:

> Recognizing this University's responsibility (in the human welfare area) is President Walker's recent proposal for a college devoted to human welfare. Although this proposal is still in the early discussion stages, it is hoped that the present College of Home Economics may become in name, as it has been in substance, the College of Human Welfare, and that its departments and faculty may be augmented by essentially related parts from other colleges.[25]

In July 1966, after several petitionings of the university's administration by the home economics faculty, the name of the college was changed officially to the College of Human Development.

The rounds of discussion prompted by President Walker and his staff led to a decision in 1967 to establish a new college that would embody the main intent of the 1980 committee report. These discussions reviewed a number of options for implementing human development. Among them was the creation of an intercollege institute which would combine the resources of a variety of related departments throughout the university into a research and service mission in human development. This was finally rejected, however, because previous experience indicated the relative transitoriness of faculty commitment to such intercollege programs. There was general consensus that the human development thrust as advocated in the 1980 report was of such significance that a collegiate organization should be devised to implement it, and thus provide continuity of management, coordination of faculty efforts, and care for the development and welfare of the associated faculty members over time.

It was evident that significant portions of the College of Home Economics were ready to participate actively in the evolution of a successor college—broader even in concept than had been considered by the home economics faculty in their deliberations during the period in which the 1980 report was under discussion. The retirement in late 1965 of the dean of home economics was followed by the appointment of an interim dean who continued to prepare the home economics faculty for change.

---

[25] *Report for the Middle States Evaluation*, p. 67.

Formation of the College of Human Development

In January 1967, Donald H. Ford was assigned the task of developing a new College of Human Development, building upon major components of the home economics college and utilizing its facilities. In order to signal the fact that Human Development was indeed to be a new and different college rather than a new name for the College of Home Economics, several significant actions were taken. The first of these took place prior to the designation of Ford as dean: in late 1966 the Department of Home Economics Education was transferred to the College of Education, there to continue its principal task of preparing secondary school teachers. Second, the recently established Department of Nursing within the College of Health and Physical Education was transferred into the College of Human Development to emphasize the general concern within the new college for health services. Third, the Center for Law Enforcement and Corrections which had been established by contractual agreement with the Pennsylvania Department of Justice within the Institute for Public Administration (in the College of Liberal Arts) was transferred to the College of Human Development.

Another factor contributing to the evolution of the new college was the sizeable number of senior faculty members from the former College of Home Economics who were soon due for retirement. These retirements, plus a commitment of additional funds by the top administration of the university, made it feasible to develop a new organizational structure and set of programs.

For the first part of 1967, the new dean interviewed extensively the remaining faculty members of home economics who were to become a part of the new college. The resulting conceptual and operational scheme was presented to the university's board of trustees June 15, 1967 and is most simply represented in the diagram presented as Figure 1.[26] The new dean was thereupon charged to proceed in developing a new college on the lines of his presentation, was given funds with which to acquire new faculty, and was

[26]Donald H. Ford, *Rationale for the College of Human Development,* The Pennsylvania State University, May 1967.

assured of support from the central administration.

During the academic year 1967–68 faculty members—inherited from home economics and a growing body of new faculty members, both newly recruited and transferred from elsewhere in the university—worked toward implementing the administrative design. They also strived for the evolution of new curricula combining the old with new programs in community services, man-environment relations, and health planning and administration.

By the end of 1967–68, seven departments remaining from Home Economics had been dissolved and the faculty reorganized into four broadly based problem-oriented divisions. Four new division directors were appointed, and about forty additional new faculty members were recruited to begin implementing the several new majors in the following year.

The academic year that began in the fall of 1968 was marked by continued adaptation within the new college of old and new faculty, old and new programs, and increasing recognition from outside the college of the implications of a new degree-granting, student-attracting, and resource-using element within the University. Withall, however, the emergence of the College of Human Development and its growth from about 1,200 undergraduate students in the fall of 1967 to over 3,900 in the fall of 1972 (including about 1,150 at the outlying Commonwealth Campuses) was accomplished with goodwill and cooperation in most quarters of the university. Some of the more obvious comparisons are summarized in the table on page 101.

Rationale for the College

As of late 1972 the college was professional in orientation, designed to educate people to work in a variety of roles of human service professions. Each of the four academic divisions—Biological Health, Community Development, Individual and Family Studies, Man-Environment Relations—was therefore composed of faculty and students with diverse backgrounds but with interests converging on a more limited set of problems. These public problems involve a variety of disciplines. Thus, for example, the Division of Biological Health had a faculty numbering fifty-five whose highest degrees

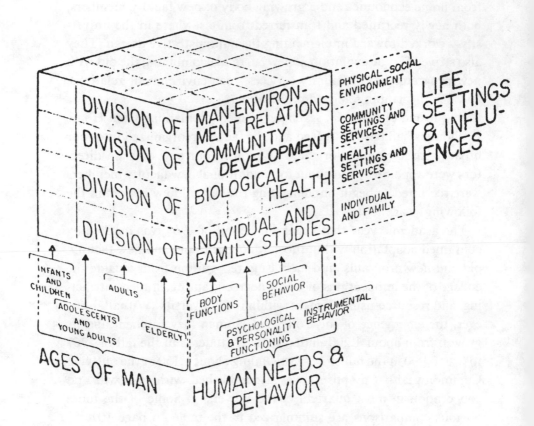

FIGURE I
Conceptual Model for the College of Human Development of The Pennsylvania
State University

	College of Home Economics 1965	College of Human Development 1972
Department Structure	8 Academic Departments	4 Academic Divisions 1 Research Institute
Number of Faculty		
Men	17	84
Women	61	85
	78	169
Number of Students		
Undergraduate		
Men	208	1712
Women	674	2363
	882	4075
Graduate		
Men	11	58
Women	124	95
	135	153
Administrative Structure	1 Dean 3 Assistant Deans	1 Dean 3 Associate Deans 1 Assistant Dean

(most of them doctorates) were in psychology, cultural anthropology, nursing, medicine, political science, public health, human development, education, physical anthropology, public administration, economics, biochemistry, nutrition, and physiology.

The number of undergraduate programs offering majors in each division is kept to a minimum in order to discourage faculty compartmentalization and encourage cooperation across programs. For example, the faculty in the Division of Individual and Family Studies, numbering forty and representing academic backgrounds mainly in psychology, sociology, human development, family economics, and their specializations, offers but one major and one degree, Individual and Family Studies. There are several optional areas of concentration, however, ranging chronologically from early infancy through adolescence, adulthood, and old age, and emphasizing the family as the principal socializing instrument.

In graduate programming the conceptual organization of the college is seen most clearly. A program of Community Systems Planning and Development, for example, emphasizes research, analysis, and planning methodologies that are applicable to a considerable range of human service systems including health services and health planning, welfare services, community and economic development, and the administration of justice. It draws on faculty members from all four of the college's divisions.

This openness of curriculum, easy to conceptualize but difficult to maintain in a traditionally specialized professoriate, makes combinations of expertise on particular problem areas possible. Interest in several human development and social problem areas may be pursued across a number of degree-granting programs. For example, if one is interested in problems of the aged and the process of aging, he can study the psychological and sociological problems in the Individual and Family Studies Division, the dietary, nutritional, and nursing care needs of old people in Biological Health, the special environments needed by old people and the criteria for designing such environments in Man-Environment Relations, and the economic and political positions of aged people and an aging population in Community Development. His degree may be in either Human Development and Family Studies or Community Systems Planning and Development, depending on whether his interests focus more on the individual or on the broader social and policy issues surrounding old people.

In the College of Human Development, the functions of research, resident education, and continuing education, traditional in land-grant universities, are administered by a team of associate deans whose jobs are to insure quality and suitable volume of activity in their respective areas. These deans also strive for steady feedback such that innovations and new ideas coming from research and scholarship are put early into continuing education and community services as well as into regularly scheduled courses.

Research in the college is conducted both within the divisions and in the Institute for the Study of Human Development. This institute brings together a variety of interests and competencies. One program model being pursued is somewhat analogous to the agricultural experiment station because it maintains a close and continuing partnership of an academic institution with a governmental agency responsible for a significant segment of public interest. The major example is in the Center for Human Services Development, which is a continuing working relationship with the Pennsylvania Department of Public Welfare. The center administers a variety of projects in policy research (e.g., in the analysis of day care programs and of public assistance standards) and continuing education (e.g., devising a pattern of career development and special skill training programs).

How is Penn State's College of Human Development different from an updating and renaming of Home Economics? There are two answers. Some traditions of home economics, such as child development, the family and the home, nutrition, food service, and dietetics, have been carried forward and expanded. But these have been integrated with or supported by several new developments: nursing, health services planning and administration, man environment relations, community development, and the administration of justice. All have been brought together in an administrative scheme that emphasizes cross-program coordination. Relations with the agricultural experiment station continue in research areas, as is the case with other colleges of the university. Home Economics Extension, however, is now an integral part of the College of Agriculture, and the College of Human Development has evolved a new extension program of its own, emphasizing continuing education and community service which is financed partly by appropriations and partly by user fees.

Another way of answering the question is to describe the college as incorporating several aspects of human service oriented professional schools: (1) those concerned with public health and the allied health professions, (2) those providing education in social welfare and social work, (3) those concentrating on community development and urban planning, and (4) schools of home economics. In relation to the concerns of each of these kinds of schools, human development attempts to address both the development of the individual person and the nexus of environing physical and social conditions.

Chapter 6

THE FUTURE OF ENGINEERING EDUCATION IN LAND-GRANT UNIVERSITIES

OTIS E. LANCASTER

THE education of engineers has probably been studied more extensively than that of any other professional group. The first comprehensive study was made in 1849; the latest in 1968. The former was done by Greene[1] of Rensselaer Polytechnic Institute. The latter, "The Goals of Engineering Education," was prepared by a committee chaired by Walker, Hawkins, and Petitt,[2] and had inputs from over 250 engineering colleges and most of the leading industrial companies and consulting firms which employ engineers. Preparation took five years, at a cost of $332,000, discounting the hours contributed by individuals.

I—Engineering

It is important to clarify what engineering really is, for the term is used frequently to encompass a wide range of activities which are not part of the profession. The Engineers' Council for Professional Development defines engineering as "the profession in which a knowledge of the mathematical and natural sciences gained by study, experience, and practice is applied with judgment to develop ways to utilize, economically, the materials and forces of nature for the benefit of mankind."[3]

This definition encompasses all the essential facets of the engineering profession; but, to put the field into perspective, it is well to

---

[1]B. F. Greene, *The True Idea of a Polytechnic Institute* (Rensselaer Polytechnic Institute, 1849) pp. 1–80.

[2]Goals of Engineering Education, Final Report of the Goals Committee, American Society for Engineering Education, 1968.

[3]Engineers' Council for Professional Development, *40th Annual Report,* Year Ending September 30, 1972.

examine its relationship to other fields with which it is often confused —science and engineering technology.

a—Engineering Differs from Science

The differences between engineering and science arise from differences in purpose. An engineer is a *user* of knowledge; a scientist is a *pursuer* of knowledge. The scientist is concerned with the discovery and organization of facts and the development of theory to explain phenomena. The engineer couples knowledge in a way not previously done to create a new machine, device, or structure, or to develop a process which can perform a desired task or serve a suitable purpose. Ideally, he is an innovator—a synthesizer.

The spectrum of engineering activity is very large, with many bands. First, and foremost, is the conception or *idea* band. When the conception process is coupled with specifications of sufficient detail so that the conceived item can be constructed or composed by someone else, it forms the *design* band. The design process may include preparation of sketches, drawings, layouts, models, breadboard models, or mock ups necessary to clearly delineate the combination of components, elements, and concepts. The construction of prototypes and the measurement of their performance, with resulting modifications and improvements, constitutes the *development* band. A significant part of this development is rigorous, systematic testing to insure desirable performance and life with suitable safety tolerances under the desired operating environment—the *testing* band. Following the development, there must be production in sufficient numbers and at a price which will generate a profit to producers or minimum costs to taxpayers. In the *production* band, the question, "How else can we make it?" must be answered so as to reduce the cost without jeopardizing the quality of performance. These considerations include the possible use of different materials, processes, and plant layouts, along with working conditions, schedules, pay scales, training, and maximum utilization of employee skills. Thus, the *production* band blends into the *management* engineering band. Within the spectrum is a *sales* band in which the engineer plays an important role in explaining how, when, where, when not, and where not to use a new idea, device, or construction. Once the products are produced and sold, then come the bands of *service, maintenance, repair,* and *replacement,* all of which require judgment, knowledge, and experience.

In all of the above activities, unexpected performances and other deviations which cannot be answered or explained by present knowledge may arise. Slight improvements in the physical properties of materials (strength, elasticity, weight, conductivity, etc.), or in the fabrication or production environment, might make the difference between success or failure of the design process. It is this critical "cutting edge of engineering" which leads to another band of the spectrum, *research.* In research, the engineer is a seeker of new knowledge and information similar to a scientist. However, his pursuits are directed to solving specific problems. This is an important band; it bridges the information gaps that are often disclosed when the results of scientific research are reduced to practice. According to Theodore Von Karman: "The scientist explores what is, the engineer creates what has not been." Robert W. MacVicar: "The scientist makes it known, the engineer makes it work." Frederick C. Lindvall: "In science lies the foundations upon which the engineer builds toward a goal of the utility, comfort and advancement of men."

b—Engineering Differs from Engineering Technology

A growing confusion has evolved between the terms engineering and engineering technology, even among practitioners in the field. While the objectives of both engineering and engineering technology are similar, their levels of involvement and responsibility differ. A recent American Society for Engineering Education study of engineering technology states in broad outline that the engineering technologist helps achieve what the engineer conceives. The technologist is usually a producer; the engineer is more often a planner. The technologist is valued as an expediter; the engineer is sought as an expert. The technologist should be a master of detail; the engineer the total system. The engineer is responsible for developing methods or new applications. The technologist effectively uses established methods. The engineer's interest and attention must carry through to the final product. His most important work is usually concentrated in a project's early stages; the engineering technologist may perform some similar activities but at a different and usually later stage in the progression from concept to product.

The essential differences between engineering and engineering technology arise from important differences in mathematics, science, and engineering science in their educational backgrounds. While both involve four-year baccalaureate programs, engineering programs emphasize design, while engineering technology programs stress production and implementation. The graduates of both disciplines perform engineering functions; thus, in a way, engineering technology is a part of the engineering spectrum.

Another key set of persons involved in the engineering process are the engineering technicians. Their work preparation consists of training in specific skills, such as developing a high level of proficiency in drafting, instrumentation, and testing. Some are educated in two-year associate degree programs in engineering technology at the college level. Thus, the responsibility of the land-grant colleges and universities for offering both two- and four-year engineering technology education should be included.

II—Elements in Engineering Education

1. An engineer must have a sufficient foundation in physics, chemistry, mathematics, and often other fields such as biology and geology, so that he can comprehend ideas in these disciplines which are appropriate for his use.
2. If an engineer is to use knowledge, he should have practical experience—in the laboratory and in analyzing and synthesizing elements during his education.
3. Since engineers develop products for mankind, or more precisely for the benefit of man in current times, engineers must be aware of society's needs, demands, cultures, and constraints.
4. When an engineer develops a new design, he must be able to convey his ideas to those who will produce it, to those who will sell it, and to those who will use it. He must have communication skills.

5. Last, but foremost in importance, the engineer must have specific technical knowledge in his chosen engineering discipline. *It is this knowledge which makes him a professional.*

Although problems have shifted with time, the general objective of engineering—the use of knowledge to produce industrial and civil products—has remained constant. In the light of this objective, a discussion of the development of engineering colleges and the studies will have a context.

III—First Engineering Education in the United States

After the Non-Importation Agreement between Britain and the colonies, an immediate need arose for skilled workers to produce clothing, tools, and equipment. This need stimulated the beginning of industry and, consequently, the beginning of engineering in this country. The first successful water-powered textile mill was constructed in 1790; Eli Whitney invented the cotton gin in 1793; Oliver Evans made the first machinery for flour mills in 1787; the first high-pressure steam engine was built in 1801; and Fulton created the marine steam engine in 1807. These inventions were made by men without formal engineering training. The Erie Canal was constructed (1817–1825) by self-trained engineers.

The first engineering school was established in Norwich, Vermont, in 1819—almost 200 years after Harvard's founding—as a private military school with a program in civil engineering. Harvard and all of the early subsequent colleges in this country were created in the image of Oxford and Cambridge and were concerned with classical learning. Practical education was considered beneath their dignity. Shortly after the opening of Norwich, civil engineering was also offered at the United States Military Academy (West Point). Rensselaer School, another private institution, was established in Troy, New York, in 1824. Like the classical colleges, these two private technical institutes were modeled after their forerunners in Europe.

For twenty-three years all civil engineers were educated at Norwich, the Military Academy, or Rensselaer. Early programs were of one year's duration but soon developed into two, three, and four years. In spite of the widespread recognized need, only three other engineering schools opened prior to the Civil War.

Greene Report—In 1849, twenty-five years after Rensselaer's beginnings, Greene, the new director, made the first major review of engineering education. After studying instructional methods and curricula of selected European technical schools, he described in a subsequent paper, "The True Idea of a Polytechnic Institute," the subjects, faculty, facilities, and students' living conditions requisite for an ideal technology school. Following these guidelines, Greene reorganized the historic Rensselaer School into the Rensselaer Polytechnic Institute which has since served as a prototype of engineering schools. Greene felt that the truest interest and the highest duty for man was not the vexing problems of what was, or can be, but man's adaption of himself to the demands and circumstances of his time. Hence, the best education for developing and cultivating man's whole process of perception, of thought, of feeling, of expression, and of action, should be based upon the age in which he lives. The subject matter at Rensselaer embraced this philosophy and consisted of fundamental sciences (chemistry, physics, mathematics and mechanics), application of science to practical problems, and liberal studies such as literature and philosophy.

Fundamental sciences and their application formed the core of the engineer's education. The liberal studies, although limited in development, were included to compensate and balance scientific elements. Thus, from the beginning, there was an effort to develop a technical person, liberally educated, who could make a contribution in industrial production.

Influence of Morrill Act—Educational programs for engineers were in existence before the Morrill Act; however, the establishment of land-grant schools had an important impact. The land-grant colleges were established primarily for practical education "related to agriculture and the mechanic arts." Consequently, the number of nonmilitary engineering schools increased rapidly from four in 1860, to seventeen (twelve land-grant) in 1870, to forty-one in 1871, to seventy in 1872. The first schools offered only civil engineering; but when MIT opened in 1865, it also included mechanical and mining engineering.

The number of engineering colleges and students grew during the last half of the nineteenth century despite financial and enrollment problems. Curricula expanded to include mechanical, mining, chemical, and electrical engineering. Professional societies were formed in order to discuss pertinent subjects in particular fields and to promote professional standards.

IV—Comprehensive Studies for Improvement of Engineering Education

In 1893, the Society for Promotion of Engineering Education (SPEE)—the first society with the sole mission of improving education in a professional field—was founded. Under its leadership a series of detailed studies and reports have been made.

Mann Report—In 1907, SPEE, with the cooperation of other professional engineering societies, initiated an examination of the teaching methods and curricula of all branches of engineering education, at both the graduate and undergraduate levels, as well as the proper relationship between engineering schools and secondary industrial schools or foremen's schools. The resultant report was completed in 1918. It revealed that:

> there was almost unanimous agreement among schools, parents and practicing engineers that the present engineering curriculum whatever its organization, is congested beyond endurance. It is obviously absurd to require from the student more hours of intense mental labor than would be permitted him by law for the simplest manual labor. Yet on all sides the pressure of topics and subjects that have become important because of the extraordinary growth of science and industry is constantly increasing. In 1870 a student might choose his specialty at the end of his second year; now he must decide in many cases in the middle of the first year. Formerly the choice lay among civil, mechanical and mining engineering; now (1917) the selection must be made from aeronautical, agricultural, architectural, automobile, bridge, cement, ceramics, chemical, civil, construction, electrical, heating, highway, hydraulic, industrial, lighting, marine, mechanical, metallurgical, mill, mining, railway, sanitary, steam, textile, telephone, topographical engineering and engineering administration.[4]

[4]C. R. Mann, "A Study of Engineering Education," Carnegie Foundation for the Advancement of Teaching, *Bulletin No. 11.*

No one school offered all options, but they were all offered somewhere. Schools also varied in program length and in the time allotted to languages and humanities, science and mathematics, and drawing and engineering, with averages of 19, 29, and 52 percent respectively.

The Mann Report recommended reducing required class hours per week to less than eighteen so that students could do their work thoroughly and also participate in real industrial work (coop programs), utilizing the practical experience as a source of theoretical analysis in the classroom—theory and practice thus being taught simultaneously. It stressed that practical engineering work is essential for a freshman, not only because it appeals to his professional ambition, arouses his enthusiasm, and gives training in practice, but also because it helps him to master the theoretical work more fully and quickly.

Other recommendations were a broader and sounder training in engineering science, four-years of required laboratory work, increased attention and integration of the humanities into the curricula, emphasis on human values, consideration of costs, and the development of a common core of study.

Wickenden Report—Engineers notably demonstrated their capabilities in technical and administrative service during World War I; but, after the war, the validity of the old order and the educational system in general were questioned as to their objectives, methods, and results.

Only four and one-half years after the publication of the Mann Report, the Society for the Promotion of Engineering Education again posed the question, "What can the Society do in a comprehensive way to develop, broaden, and enrich engineering education?" It was felt that the engineer of the future "will be called upon to take a more important part in great enterprises . . . in organization and leadership, as well as technical service in the solution of new problems (industrial, economical, governmental and social) which the engineering applications of science produce."[5]

Therefore, another extensive study by SPEE was conducted, culminating in a final report published in 1933, "The Investigation of

[5]Board of Investigation and Coordination, American Society for Engineering Education, "The Investigation of Engineering Education, 1923–1929," Vol. I, Vol. II, 1934.

Engineering Education, 1923–1929," usually known as the Wickenden Report. The report observed:

> Society has suddenly become engineering conscious . . . As yet, there are no signs on any horizon that science will be dethroned or that society will lose its faith in technology as a means of social progress . . . the social philosophy which had dominated our politics, our education, and our industry, based on the premises that men are scarce while space and materials are abundant . . . that industry must adopt every expedient to save labor but could afford to be prodigal with ore, coal, oil, timber, water, soil and the other bounties of nature, may undergo radical revision.[6]

The Wickenden Report emphasized: (1) that the development, broadening, and enriching of engineering education should proceed from within, rather than by the addition of unrelated elements from without; (2) that the preservation of a unified program better lends itself to this end; (3) that it is desirable to give a more generous place to distinctly humanistic studies and to give these studies form and content which will enrich the students' conception of engineering and its place in social economy; (4) that it is desirable to give the student a more connected and better grounding in engineering principles; (5) that a greater effort be made to develop the students' capacity for self-directed work; and (6) that these ends be gained, wherever need be, at the expense of unrelated studies on the one hand and of detailed technical training on the other.

Changes in instruction had to be made. The majority of students were being trained to accept, to memorize, and to take for granted, rather than to question, to analyze. They rarely distinguished between observation, definitions, conventions, principles, and hypotheses. They solved certain problems without having the scientific background of fundamental principles to appreciate the approximations and limitations of their solutions.

The committee stated that better engineering colleges are wisely avoiding any slavish insistence on faculty with Ph.D. degrees. Specialized scholarship and minute research was, the committee felt, not

[6]Ibid.

the best training for engineering teachers; practical experience was better. Yet they did not recognize the potential of education for design at the graduate level. The report expressed a need for practical aids to assist high school students, and even college freshmen, obtain an understanding of the nature of engineering. It deplored the tendency of technical institutes to drift into the college field, often to the neglect of the group they serve.

In summary, the Wickenden Report recommended a basic acquaintance with science, familiarity with engineering methods, appreciation of social culture, concrete engineering projects with specific economic considerations, some emphasis on continuing education, and a program for the development of the teaching profession.

Hammond Reports—SPEE's subsequent "Aims and Scope of Engineering Curricula,"[7] was initiated in 1937, completed in 1940, and identified as the Hammond Report. The first Hammond Report was prompted by discussion of the need for extending the undergraduate curricula to five or six years. New knowledge and techniques and widening fields of application pressed for adequate attention in the curricula. Consequently, proponents felt that unless the period of study was increased, previously required content must be reduced. This would mean minimizing descriptive material and repetitive tasks and abandoning efforts to develop specialized skills. Such a pruning would not necessarily weaken the curricula but could strengthen it as a preparation for further specialized study, provided it concentrated on the mastery of fundamental concepts and the cultivation of the intellectual powers required in the more advanced use of the engineering method.

The committee recognized that engineering colleges prepare students for a wide range of technical responsibilities and recommended that technological education be made available to serve a variety of purposes. The Hammond Report recommended: a four-year undergraduate program, followed by post-graduate work; broader and more fundamental undergraduate curricula; increased emphasis on

[7]"Report of Committee on Aims and Scope of Engineering Curricula," Journal of Engineering Education, 30, No. 7, (March 1940) pp. 555–566.

basic sciences, humanities, and social studies; transferring advanced undergraduate courses to the postgraduate period; including advanced training for the higher technical levels of engineering in the general program for engineering education; no restriction in freedom for experimentation and change.

During World War II, special training programs evolved with objectives specifically geared to military requirements. In its postwar planning, the society asked another committee, chaired by Hammond, to consider "Engineering Education after the War." This second report, published in 1944, reaffirmed the first Hammond Report's recommendations but, as a result of wartime experiences, two additional undergraduate programs were suggested: one for preparation of careers in the operation and management of industry and the other to prepare individuals for increased scientific and creative accomplishments. The report stressed that principles, assumptions, empiricisms, standards, and practices are the working tools of the engineer, yet knowledge of these "does not constitute ability to practice engineering. There remains the necessity for the young engineer to integrate the applications of these laws, assumptions, data, and codes so as to accomplish a desired result safely and economically. This requires a combination of resourcefulness, skill, experience, and judgment amounting at times almost to intuition— which we call the art of engineering. Judgment matures only through experience, but introduction to the art of engineering and the development of judgment can and should be started in college."[8]

Research in engineering colleges was considered important as a means of fostering a creative environment. However, research should be genuine and should not constitute routine testing. The need for technology education was evidenced: "War conditions have furnished a striking demonstration of the need for technological training of intensive nature, at a level between that of the vocational and secondary schools and that of the engineering colleges."[9] This report was also the first to recommend the establishment of

[8]"Report of the Committee on Engineering Education after the War," *Journal of Engineering Education* 35, (September 1944):
[9]Ibid.

objectives with measurable standards of achievement not based upon memory.

Grinter Report—The American Society for Engineering Education (ASEE), formerly SPEE, published the "Evaluation of Engineering Education" in 1956. Authors were charged with determining the patterns of engineering education necessary to educate leaders in the engineering profession for the next twenty-five years.

The report's philosophy is that the obligations of an engineer are the continual maintenance and improvement of man's material environment, within economic bounds, and the substitution of labor-saving devices for human effort. Within the current limitations of the state of the art, an engineer must decide which of several possibilities provides the best solution. His education should prepare him for the functions of creative design, construction, production, and operation, and give him an understanding of society and the impact of technology upon it. The report spelled out in detail nine engineering sciences: statics, dynamics, strength of materials, fluid mechanics, thermodynamics, electrical circuits, fields and electronics, heat transfer, engineering materials, and metallurgy. It recognized the importance of science for some curricula, but not for all. Hence, the preliminary report suggested bifurcation.[10] The colleges rejected the concept of two types of engineering education and adopted one with more theory.

In summary, the Grinter Report advocated a strong social-humanistic stem, a strong core of basic and engineering sciences, a program for recruitment and development of faculty, the extension of some of the work downward to high school, the provision of opportunities for gifted students, and bifurcation of programs.[11]

Walker, Hawkins, Pettit Report—The last of the series of comprehensive studies sponsored by ASEE was "The Goals Study,"[12] an attempt to indicate the direction engineering education should take

[10]*Report on Evaluation of Engineering Education,* American Society for Engineering Education, June 15, 1954.

[11]*Report on Evaluation of Engineering Education, 1952–1955,* American Society for Engineering Education.

[12]*Goals of Engineering Education,* Final Report of the Goals Committee, American Society for Engineering Education, 1968.

to meet the needs of the future. In process from 1963–68, the report called for more flexibility, expanded opportunities for interdisciplinary study, reduction in credit hour requirements, and a minimum number of prerequisites in undergraduate programs. It recognized the importance of cooperative education and the need for a means for transferring into engineering from other areas of study.

In graduate programs, the report stressed additional experimental and design projects at the master's level and the expansion of doctoral programs. The master's should be the first professional degree.

An urgent need for continuing education was emphasized, to enhance the competence of an individual as a practicing engineer rather than to attain an additional academic degree. In summary, the report urged the preparation of students for the solution of broader societal problems as the goal of engineering education. Such a goal requires lifelong study preceded by a basic five-year formal education.

V—The Common Thread

A common thread runs through this 116-year reporting period. All reports stressed the importance of (1) social-humanistic studies, (2) physical science and mathematics, (3) engineering sciences, (4) preparation for practice (design), and (5) communications. Historical changes occurred: the percentage of time devoted to theory increased; the amount of shop work and engineering art decreased; new subject matter was added and some was deleted. Yet, the thrust and objectives of engineering education have remained the preparation of professionals for industry and public service. The shift in emphasis from the reduction of manpower to the conservation of resources which was predicted in the Wickenden Report has occurred. Also, the importance of societal needs began to be stressed more than the needs of industry per se, and there was a growth of emphasis on large systems and away from the concentration on components. In each of the successive reports, the need for engineering technology programs to supplement engineering programs became stronger. This trend was a consequence of ever-increasing demands for technological products.

Although there has never been and there should never have been satisfaction with the curriculum, for it must change continuously, one part which has continuously been judged inadequate is the *social science stem,* as much with regard to purpose as to content. A second unsolved problem throughout the years has been insufficient time for study of all the desired topics.

VI—Views of Engineering

There have always been those who resist change. The bicycle, the automobile, the airplane, electrical home wiring, nuclear power plants, etc., have all encountered obstacles—automobiles scared the horses, and God did not intend for man to fly. The resistance and reservations—some well founded—have delayed developments. However, the delays were beneficial if they forced the engineers to perfect the items. People wanted more products. Faith in technology as a means of social progress was mentioned in Wickenden's Report. This faith in engineering persisted and gained strength for thirty more years.

R. G. Jahn has pinpointed three eras of engineering as classical, transitional, and future. He suggests the first era began in the eighteenth or early nineteenth century and extended until recently. In this era, activities (e.g., prime movers, telephones, power generators, computers, airplanes, nuclear reactors, automobiles, and radios) rose in popularity, reached a peak of attention from society, and then relaxed into a less dramatic, routinely accepted part of modern life. During this era there was "general satisfaction with and respect for engineering accomplishments, extending to virtual reverence and awe for the most felicitous enterprises, with no more than resigned tolerance for the more objectionable ones."[13]

In the transitional period of the present decade, technology has begun to tarnish as a result of some of its by-products such as pollution, congestion, resource depletion, and depersonalization. There have always been undesirable side effects, calculated risks balanced against the gains. Jahn believes today's comments are different:

[13]R. G. Jahn, "Three Eras of Engineering Education," *University: A Princeton Quarterly* 55 (Winter 1973) 1–7.

Those (mighty) power stations—are polluting our rivers and the air
we breathe.
This (modern, rapid) transit system—makes cattle of us all.
Our (unparalleled) industrial production—is exhausting all of our
natural resources.
The (new, ultra-safe, high-speed) highway system—is paving over the
entire state.
Those (fantastic) computers—reduce man to a punched card.
That (superb) space program—is a colossal waste of money and effort.
Our (powerful, sophisticated) armaments—slaughter innocent peo-
ple. Those (highly trained, dedicated) engineers—must be brought to
heel.[14]

Are the current criticisms just serious attempts to evaluate? Or are
they similar to those which have been encountered at the introduction of any new device? There is some credence to the comments.
There are problems. Society is not willing to give up electrical lights,
radios, televisions, large and small appliances, automobiles, auto-
matic heat control, indoor plumbing, telephones, year-round fresh
fruits and vegetables, elevators, air travel, superhighways, electric
office machines, or air conditioning. Yet the problems evolving from
use of these products cannot be ignored. The challenge of engineering has been to find ways of making things that people want or need.
As the numbers of people have mushroomed, so have their needs and
wants. Remarkably, engineers have kept pace with demands; but
most of what they design or produce inevitably consumes space,
energy, and irreplaceable raw materials—and creates, just as inevitably, waste that will not self-destruct. The more engineers have made,
the more they—and the people for whom they have made it—have
been able to learn about the limits of the earth, its resources and its
ecology. Solutions to the problems concerning resources and ecology
will be achieved not by abandoning technology, but rather by utilizing it to meet the changing priorities of society. Technology offers
the alternative from which engineers select the ways to improve our
well-being.

[14]Jahn, "Three Eras."

VII—Responsibility of the Public

The choices on the use to which various alternatives are put rests with the people, both in day-to-day selections and in the constraints placed on selections by legal process. The considerations involved are not purely technological but are influenced by governmental bodies and the impact of sociologists, environmentalists, and others on the attitudes of people.

The significant engineering accomplishments, such as the moon landing, interstate highways, and nuclear power plants, resulted from the combined efforts of engineers, politicians, attorneys, financiers, and salesmen. Users, through their demands, have also had a tremendous impact on what and how much is built, sold, and used. Developments require that all of society cooperate.

VIII—Responsibilities of Engineering Education in the Future

Because of this need for cooperation, there is a need for mutual understanding of the factors involved. Thus, engineering educators in the future have the responsibility to educate both the engineer and the non-engineer, the liberal arts student and other college students, as well as persons who do not attend college.

This is not the end of the technological age. The use of technological products will continue to increase. Engineers and technicians will be in even greater demand to produce and service the products of the future as well as to modify, maintain, and service existing products.

Engineering colleges should continue to educate men who can assume the design and associated duties detailed earlier by perfecting the present education rather than discarding it for something new. Although there is cause for concern, there is no need for radical departures. Every change that is needed has been recognized in one of the ASEE reports. Some weaknesses may never be overcome, and the nature of the problems will change with time.

IX—Educational Requirements for Engineers

There appear to be eight essentials for the education of engineers.

Technological Capability—Every student should have a sound grounding in his field of specialty. The current trends for broad education with considerable flexibility will have to be kept under close surveillance. Engineering education's response to the growing feeling of a need to prepare the students explicitly to deal with the social and political components of their activities introduced new dimensions to the curricula. These include more study of sociology, politics, governmemt, and economics in formal courses as well as interdisciplinary programs structured along topic lines and an abundance of contemplative "society and technology" seminars and workshops. Unavoidably, the introduction of more of this subject matter into the curricula places certain constraints. If these yield a relaxation in the technical content, there will be shallowness and naivete in the treatment of the problems. Shallowness cannot be tolerated. As systems become further complicated, more, not less, depth will be required. A firmer mathematics and science base, with increased emphasis on design and synthesis as well as laboratory work to obtain perspectives as a basis for concepts, will be needed.

Design—Design is the essence of engineering. It means the creation of devices, structures, and processes deemed useful. It is a process rather than a thing. The term includes all of the thought and action from the identification of a need to the construction of something which eliminates the need without untenable side effects. It is design and synthesis that distinguish engineering education from science education. Scientists synthesize apparatus and equipment for their explorations, while engineers synthesize and produce things for others.

Team Effort—While earlier an engineer could work alone on a specific project (and there will still be a need for this) there will be a greater need for persons who can help design a system which depends on many engineering disciplines. To prepare for this, undergraduate projects should require a team approach. To give measures of achievement, projects should be competitive between schools such as in athletics. The National Urban Vehicle Design Competition

1971–72 is a good example of the nature of such competition. It should be a regular part of design education programs.

Design Dissertation—Multidisiciplinary studies should be extended into graduate programs. Engineering graduate programs have become mainly science-oriented. This should be changed. Synthesis and design education is as important at the graduate level as at the undergraduate.

J. Herbert Holloman, formerly Assistant Secretary of Commerce for Science and Technology, feels engineering schools are oriented to theoretical rather than to real problems. Thus, graduate engineering students are more prepared for research than for "analysis, synthesis, conception, and design . . . the practical approach, the hard solution of problems or the awareness of cost-benefit ratios. These elements are all too often ignored or looked down upon." This is incredible when engineering is basically composed of these ingredients. The graduate student has a strong mathematics and science background. He also has design capability. A large percentage of doctoral candidates should replace the usual research dissertation by a design dissertation. The project should be on a *current problem:* one for which *something will be (done) designed and built:* one that is large enough to require team effort. Such a team of engineers, economists, political scientists, and sociologists, for example, would each be responsible for the compatibility of the result with his discipline. One design and one detailed report for the entire team would be possible, but all members would receive their doctoral degrees based upon their contributions to the total effort. (These ideas on design at the graduate level are one of the rare exceptions to the recommendations in the Wickenden Report.)

Laboratory Measurements—It is generally agreed that laboratory work is an essential part of the engineer's education, but few have emphasized the objectives. In the engineering profession the justification for experimental laboratory work is to provide design information. Measurements are made to confirm calculations, verify approximations, or obtain basic information where there is none available. Curricula should contain more laboratory exercises in measurements beginning in the freshman year and extending throughout the entire education period.

The use of governmental and industrial laboratories for educational purposes should be expanded. Equipment in these laboratories is superior and some of it is not in use continually.

Social Awareness—The expectation that the social-humanistic stem can provide culture for the individual and at the same time develop a background in politics, society, and economics for the engineer's professional needs is far greater than can be realized in the small percentage of time allotted to it, and no more time can be spared. Thus, these courses should be dropped, thereby retaining the goal of developing an understanding of the political, social, and economic atmosphere in which new products or services are to operate. Students might well take special courses in such fields as public policy, labor relations, government, political science, sociology, and economics. Perhaps students should have laboratory experience in the social-humanistic area, such as a summer of field work in a municipality or agency under the direction of a sociologist. These courses might well be given for the sole purpose of making students better engineers, men who would devise things for the benefit of society. Some educators will worry about dropping the cultural objective. Such concern was generated years ago before society became as sophisticated as it is today. The only known research on the effectiveness of the social-humanistic program in engineering education was conducted by Lancaster.[15] The study showed that senior liberal arts majors were only slightly better informed than senior engineers on art, music, politics, sports, and other current affairs.

Communication—Effective communication is an essential requirement of engineering, yet employers say this is the weakest link in the present programs. Engineering students should be able to write clearly, speak effectively, and sketch or draw with some expertness. The present curricula which tries to develop these talents needs to be broadened and expanded. Efforts to increase the effectiveness of the communicatee instead of placing all the stress on the communicator, might alleviate some of the difficulties.

Engineering Faculty—A majority of faculty in the future should

---

[15]O.E. Lancaster, "Engineering Students' Knowledge of Current Affairs," *IEEE Transactions on Education,* E-16 (February 1973): 57–58.

have design and application capability. Research capability and ability to secure research grants would not be a requirement, but ability to attract support and cooperation on design would be. Doctoral degrees would not be sufficient. The minimum acceptable practical experience would be a five-year cooperative program akin to the students' program, alternating six months at an engineering college and six months with industry or an engineering firm. Regardless of his capabilities at the time of appointment, each professor should spend each seventh year in engineering practice. This experience would not be at the expense of formal education. Every professor should have at least seven years of academic learning in the basic and applied sciences. Last and equally important, every professor should participate in in-service programs on effective teaching and learning.

X—Education for Engineering Technology

Although mentioned in many of the ASEE reports, the impact of the four-year bachelor of engineering technology was almost missed in the Goals Study. Graduates of these programs will continue to occupy a significant niche in engineering. In a way, the bachelor of technology programs may be thought of as the other arm of the bifurcation mentioned in the preliminary Grinter Report. These curricula should be directed more to the do-type problems, with modifications and adaptions of known components and verified procedures, rather than the conception of solutions to major current problems. Programs should be directed to usefulness rather than satisfying degree requirements, i.e., education for a purpose.

XI—Education for Nonengineers

The greatest challenge for engineering education for the future is helping nonengineers appreciate the modes of thought of engineers and engineering technologists so that the general public can make rational decisions on community and national projects. The challenge would be to promulgate an atmosphere of cooperation and understanding among all members of society on the use of technology.

Since the inception of engineering education, leaders have realized that engineers should know about the culture of the society in which they live and an effort has been made to accomplish this objective. However, faculty and students in the liberal disciplines have not acquainted themselves with the rudiments of technology. Some progress has been made. Under the auspices of the Commission for Engineering Education, a high school course, "The Man Made World," was conceived. The National Science Foundation sponsors summer institutes to prepare teachers to teach it. Some progress has also been made at the college level. The authors of "Man Made World" have adapted the materials for college-level courses and published them in two companion paperback books. When Florida Technological University was established, a course in technological concepts was required for graduation. New Mexico University has had similar optional courses, with growing success. Penn State requires students to complete a course in technological concepts, but the criteria established for implementation of this requirement emphasizes the interaction of technology and society rather than technological concepts per se.

Engineers are not the only ones responsible for technological advances. Politicians, lawyers, bankers, and citizens help to promote, guide, or *restrict* development. It is in these areas outside engineering where much of the technological impact is often wrought. Engineers, as resource people, are also citizens and should be accountable for their proportional part of any undesirable technological results. Risks and gains from any new undertaking should be explained using technical concepts. Thus, in this sense, engineers have more responsibility. However, the success of technological advances in the future will depend more on the success of the education of the nonengineers than of the engineers.

If the interface between social needs and technological realities continue to be attacked only in the asymmetric, narrowly-based manner of the reaction era, the effort will inevitably stall from lack of broad comprehension of the available techniques, their basic limitations and future potentialities. A stagnant plateau of mutual tolerance will be reached, wherein further technological progress will be inhibited by social and political constraints. This will be an 'if in doubt, do nothing' era of minimum accomplishment under maximum control, where new enterprises will be rejected out of hand because of secondary effects, without fair assessment of their primary benefits.[16]

If there is a full and broad acceptance of technology as an essential operational component in the life of the modern human being and, therefore, as valid an element in education as history or philosophy, farsighted technological development of this world can continue.

There is no question that engineering logic and technique are essential components of liberal education in a technological age. The educational value of:

extended awareness of technological influences, whether for the labor relations mediator dealing with the impact of automation on the manual labor patterns; for the urban planner attempting to assess what can and cannot be constructed in a given area, at a given cost, in a given time; for the legislator or jurist who must allocate resources, and design or interpret legitimate social constraints on technological development; for the housewife who must cope with the steady increase in the number and sophistication of appliances that free her for other pursuits, who must oversee the primary education of her children for life in an ever more technologically developed society, and who must cast her vote intelligently on environmental control legislation cannot be overlooked.[17]

Attempts to teach courses in technology to those with only a knowledge of arithmetic and rudimentary ideas on science will take unusual skills, infinite patience, and many innovations on the part of the instructors. Cleverly designed courses built around current topics should stimulate student involvement. Students representing politicians, air pollution control officers, planners, industrialists, and engineers could use the team approach. Whatever the mode of instruction, the ultimate purpose would be an extention of the responsibility of the populace based upon understanding of technology. This is the challenge of the hour and will be for the immediate future. It can— it must—be met by engineering educators.

[16]Jahn, "Three Eras."
[17]Ibid.

XII—Land-Grant Colleges and Universities

The land-grant movement was initiated with the idea of educating the whole nation. It was to counterbalance classic education—to educate men and women to think about things which they do, see, and handle daily. To make them thinking laborers.

Service Responsibility—Today people in the United States work with electrical and mechanical apparatus created by man. New products appear on the market every day; all affect daily living. These products are such an integral part of the present culture that this should be called the technological age. Yet, too few people understand how or why they function. Most of the items are considered to be of value to society; others are diagnosed as dangerous and harmful. Many people are concerned only with the immediate use without a care for the future; others cling to the past. Surely, in line with the land-grant movement and its objectives, all students should have a cultural grounding in engineering and engineering technology.

The elevation of a whole nation should not be left to a few. It cannot be left to any single group of specialists. Nor should it be left to those people who react on an emotional basis. Or those who react on the basis of a past culture. Logic, utilizing the best available knowledge, gives the answer. All members of society, college graduates in particular, should be thinking workers. They should be educated to realize that in every venture there are potential gains, potential risks. These risks should always be balanced against the gains. That is why an engineer devises several approaches to achieve a goal; then he evaluates and compares them. An engineer considers various "trade-off" (the lessening of desirable characteristics in one area for improvements in another) until he achieves the optimum for the current state of the art (knowledge).

It cannot be hoped that all students comprehend a complicated system. However, they should, from a few simple examples, comprehend the thought processes. They should also appreciate the limitation of achievements resulting from physical laws. For example, it is not possible to produce an automobile engine which does not increase the carbon dioxide content of the air with present hydrocarbon fuel. Thus, in the strictest sense, a pollutionless internal combustion engine cannot be built. There can, at best, be tolerance limits of control. Moreover, people should realize that these tolerances change with changing conditions. There was little or no concern for the emission of the first automobiles, for there were so few that the evidence of their effects on the atmosphere was not noticeable.

The newer responsibilities of land-grant colleges and universities, and, in particular, of the engineering faculties, is to teach engineering concepts, principles, and modes of thought to nonengineering students and to the noncollege student through continuing education. This cannot be accomplished in a three-credit course. Study should be sufficient to give students confidence and background in order for them to comprehend the issue in an engineering endeavor which affects the environment or their employment. This goal is only beginning to be accepted and implemented. Its pursuit should be one of the most vital for years to come.

Engineering Responsibility—In a technological age, engineers and engineering technicians are necessities. Therefore, land-grant colleges and universities have the responsibility to not only give the appropriate curriculum but also to see that there is an ample supply of educated manpower.

Thus, in addition to the general responsibility of educating all students about technology, the land-grant colleges and universities should supply engineers with appropriate education and in sufficient numbers to design and produce the products for the future national needs.

The optimum education for engineers should include a curricula that satisfies the general requirements previously described. Topics and subject matter would be divided into electrical, mechanical, civil, or chemical majors, or center on topics, such as energy, material, or pollution control. This would be done to form a subset of the totality of all engineering knowledge so that it could be pursued in some depth in a four-year program. Regardless of the organization, the type of problems used to illustrate the concepts will change as they have changed in the past from wagons to carriages to automobiles; radios to television; supplying fuels to conserving fuels; faster speed to safer journeys; airplanes to spacecraft; crystals to vacuum tubes to transistors to solid state devices; reciprocating engines to gas turbines; and heating homes to cooling them.

No bold attempt should be made to specify what new developments should serve as illustrations. Erickson, in 1966, pointed out:

> In 1937, just 29 years ago, a number of this country's most distinguished scientists met to form the first scientific advisory council for an American president. They deliberated, they discussed and they brought forth a learned report on the future. All that this optimistic forecast missed was radar, nuclear energy, the Salk vaccine, missiles, antibiotics, transistors, lasers, integrated circuits, inertial guidance systems, the electronic computer and the whole concept of the exploration of space, among other things.
>
> To give them their due, these experts did predict television—by 1960! And jet transports—by 1970!

Although all schools should participate in the education of engineers, it is the land-grant colleges' responsibility to take the lead in developing programs in new areas. For example, currently, land-grant colleges should educate persons to design for the reduction of noise and the establishment of acceptable limits. Other needs relate to energy generation, urban housing, and transportation.

Number of Students—Of the engineering students and the degrees granted, about 60 percent have been at state colleges and universities, with about two-thirds of these, or 40 percent of the total, in land-grant schools. Consequently, the land-grant colleges do, and in the future must, play a most significant role in engineering education.

The projected annual demand of engineers is 48,000 per year, as estimated by the Manpower Report to the President in 1972. Figures show that there is not a surplus of engineers; in 1975 only 30,000+ were graduated. There may, however, be an imbalance in the distribution by engineering fields. Still, actual enrollments and predicted enrollments clearly point to a critical shortage of engineers in the near future.

Land-grant colleges and universities should give stability to the education process. At present, the number of engineering students goes up and down with the employment market and image, as generated by published articles about projects and their effect on the environment and the economy. Consequently, the needs and supply have a lag built into the system because of the years required for education. Land-grant colleges should control their admission so as to give an ample supply of engineers. Based on projected needs, engineering enrollments should be increased to about 18 to 20 percent of the total of the land-grant college enrollments. This could be accomplished by reducing liberal arts enrollments. Originally liberal arts studies were introduced in land-grant colleges to supplement professional training, instead of being goals in themselves.

Responsibility for Engineering Technology—Land-grant universities should assume the responsibility for educating engineering associates, engineering technicians and bachelors of technology. The nature of the curriculum and numbers should be derived from the engineering program, so that graduates of the three programs will supplement each other.

Continuing Education—Because of the rapid changes in the sciences and engineering, the amount of useful knowledge increases daily. Unless an engineer continues to study what he learned in his four, five, or seven years of formal education, it will soon be insufficient for him to perform effectively. Land-grant colleges and universities have a responsibility to help engineers continue to learn. The colleges of engineering should perform a function for the engineers analogous to the one the agriculture colleges and experiment stations have for the farm and non-farm populations. Although the working and employment conditions are sometimes different, the responsibilities of land-grant colleges and universities for similar services are the same.

A model continuing education program consists of: publications written for users, rather than for journal publications; correspondence subjects, where communications employ audio and video tapes as well as printed matter; regular courses by television or radio broadcasts geared to engineers; short seminars at universities or in industrial plants; an answering service for specific questions; and supervised experience on the job and in governmental and industrial laboratories.

In brief, continuing education services should do all the things that are being done now plus other innovative options, and should do them at a higher level and in a more intense manner, including an evaluation by written or performance examinations. The concentration should be on learning for use rather than on degrees and (associated) prestige.

XIV—Summary

The engineering colleges of land-grant colleges and universities have the responsibility in the future:

(1) To explain engineering concepts to nonengineers in a comprehensible way, so those less inclined to precise, analytical thinking can accept them, with the objective of preparing members of society to make public decisions on technological projects on a logical basis.

(2) To give engineering students at the graduate and undergraduate levels curricula which are design oriented and based on a solid foundation of science and mathematics, with special social-humanistic courses to help make engineering activities more relevant to the current culture and with laboratory exercises in measurement to develop skill in obtaining design data as well as contact with the nonideal world. The design emphasis should be continued throughout the graduate program by teamwork on significant current large projects.

(3) To control the enrollment in order to keep the production of engineers consistent with society's needs.

(4) To extend the education of engineers by supplying new information to the practicing engineers.

Only Item (1) is an entirely new venture; the other three are, in a fashion, pursued at present. The main difference is that there should be more emphasis on the art and practice of engineering, especially at the graduate level.

REFERENCES

Board of Investigation and Coordination, American Society for Engineering Education, "The Investigation of Engineering Education, 1923–1929," Vol. I–II, 1934.

Engineering and Technology Enrollments, Fall 1972. Manpower Commission of Engineers' Joint Council.

Engineering and Technology Graduates, 1971 and 1972 issues. Manpower Commission of Engineers' Joint Council.

Fortieth Annual Report, Engineers' Council for Professional Development, Year Ending September 30, 1972.

General Education in Engineering: A Report of the Humanistic—Social Research Project. American Society for Engineering Education, 1956.

Goals of Engineering Education. Final Report of the Goals Committee, American Society for Engineering Education, 1968.

Greene, B.F. "The True Idea of a Polytechnic Institute." Rensselaer Polytechnic Institute, 1849.

Jahn, R.G. "Three Eras of Engineering Education." *University: A Princeton Quarterly* (Winter 1973): 1–7.

Lancaster, O.E. "Dissertation—Engineering Design." American Society for Engineering Education paper, presented at ASEE Annual Meeting, 1966.

Lancaster, O.E. "Engineering Students' Knowledge of Current Affairs." *IEEE Transactions on Education* E-16 (February 1973): 57–58.

Mann, C.R. "A Study of Engineering Education." Carnegie Foundation for the Advancement of Teaching, *Bulletin No. 11.*

"Report of Committee on Aims and Scope of Engineering Curricula." *Journal of Engineering Education* 30 (March 1940): 555–66.

"Report of the Committee on Engineering Education After the War." *Journal of Engineering Education* 35 (September 1944).

Report on Evaluation of Engineering Education, 1952–1955. American Society for Engineering Education.

Wickenden, W.E. "Engineering Education in the Light of Changed Social and Industrial Conditions." *Journal of Engineering Education* 24 (1933).

Wiesner, J.B. "Technology Is for Mankind." *Technology Review* (May 1973): 10–13.

Chapter 7

LIBERAL LEARNING AND THE LAND-GRANT SYSTEM:
FUTURES AND OPTATIVES

MAXWELL H. GOLDBERG

A TRIBUTE to the strength of the land-grant idea is the historic record which shows that, without losing its fundamental integrity and creative vigor, it has kept adapting to changing times and circumstances and to emergent needs—area, national, international, and now global. So far as this last is concerned, it has become a truism that the land-grant idea and forms have proved one of our most exportable items.

This seminal and adaptive potency of the land-grant idea may be appreciated through fresh attention to the career of the liberal arts within the land-grant movement. One of the first impressions is that the history of the liberal arts within the land-grant matrix is a history of confrontations—of polarities more or less successfully maintained in processes of fruitful tension. We might call this the great ongoing dialectic between the liberal arts and other educative components within the land-grant movement and, in recent decades, within the comprehensive land-grant system.

In view of the kaleidoscopic oscillations of society and education, it would be folly to try to predict what forms and functions this creative tension will shape for liberal learning in the land-grant system even of the near future. The most that may be meaningfully done here is briefly to identify the major optatives to be encouraged on behalf of the advancement both of liberal learning and of the land-grant transformative intent.

This is not a pessimist outlook concerning humanistic and other liberal studies. It does not share the Doomsday mood suggested by the *Life* article in which a humanities professor from a prestigious ivy-league university described "the fading pulse-beats of the humanities." On the other hand, it is not the view of a sentimental optimist. Reports such as that by Professor George Devine,[1] chairman of the religious studies department at Seton Hall University, that course requirements for students have been reduced, "largely in liberal arts and sciences, over the past five years . . . primarily to allow students more latitude in selecting courses and to make the curriculum more attractive and 'relevant,' " are taken into consideration, as is the fact that "the effect of the curriculum changes has been felt in virtually all the liberal arts departments." Yet, the hope remains that the liberal arts have a fighting chance to emerge with credit in the endless dialectic between liberal learning and other land-grant pursuits, both thereby making their due contributions to that great educative counterpoint—the land-grant system.

In "General and Liberal Education Today: Problems of Person and Purpose," Edward Joseph Shoben, Jr., climaxes his diagnosis by suggesting that hope itself, "conceived as a sense of positive possibilities, personal in experience and unifyingly social when shared . . . may, in our time, be one of the liberal arts."[2] It is in this spirit that the future of the liberal arts in the land-grant system is discussed.

Democratization of the Traditional Liberal Arts

Essentially, the endeavor to democratize the liberal arts was adopted in Victorian England by Matthew Arnold. As a man of letters, government inspector of schools, and editor of literary textbooks, he became deeply involved in the contemporary moves in this direction. He sought to creatively adapt the classical humanist education designed for an aristocracy to education of the people.[3]

---

[1]"Proselytize or Perish," Education Section, *New York Sunday Times,* July 9, 1972.
[2]*Perspectives: A Journal of General and Liberal Studies* 4 (Spring 1972): 16.
[3]In his *Colleges for Our Land and Time* (New York: Harper & Brothers, 1956), pp. 3–4, Edward Danforth Eddy, Jr., writes that the liberal arts curriculum in the first 200 years of American education was "narrow, restricted, and adhered so to the concepts of the Middle Ages that it refused to entertain any subject which its tradition had refused previously to honor." It "consisted of philosophy, theology, the dead languages, and mathematics; . . . even literature was not approached as a living representation of man's thoughts, but as rote training for a disciplined mind." Actually, men like Erasmus had injected the counter-medievalist "New Humanism" into this so-called "medieval" English curriculum. This movement developed a strongly ethical Christian humanism which stressed the study of philosophy, history, literature, and theology precisely as "living representation of man's thoughts." This "New

Those presently in favor of this move argue that striving for excellence, integrity, magnanamity (liberality of spirit), and largeness of imagination are not the monopoly of any one class or other social group. Nor, they argue, are the pursuit of perfection, love of beauty, devotion to justice and mercy, or personal and social responsibility. These, they insist, are universally valid aspirations. They further insist that, with appropriate interpretations, the same disciplines that have befitted the education of an elite of blood, wealth, or professional status might likewise be appropriate to the average American college student.

Their opponents hold that liberal arts—Old World, aristocratic— have long stressed excellence, the pursuit of perfection, and quality. Therefore, excellence, perfection, and quality education are for an artistocracy; average people should get an average education.

In contrast, Dr. Cornelius W. de Kiewiet, then president of the private University of Rochester, once described the "true greatness of American higher education" as residing in its being "held aloft on the two pillars of quantity and quality." "The ordinary American graduate," he stated, "the run-of-the-mine student who would have little chance of being accepted in a British or French university acquires a literateness in science, an awareness in political and economic issues, a receptiveness in technological affairs, that in the sum total are an incalculable national asset." For America the credit was political and social stability; for elitist Europe the debit was instability.[4]

In our century and country, the proponents of democratization of the liberal arts have had the support of such spokesmen for the blue-collar worker as Emory Bacon and Brendon Sexton. At a Michigan State conference on industry and the liberal arts, as UAW Education Director, Sexton posed the question, *The Liberal Arts and Labor: The Countess Mara Tie?* In effect, he challenged the main

---

Humanist" emphasis was one strain in the European liberal arts education imported and naturalized in the American liberal arts college. Its neglect in twentieth-century American liberal education has resulted in serious loss to the conceptualization and practice of liberal education.

[4]Russell I. Thackrey, *The Future of the State University* (Chicago: University of Illinois Press, 1971), p. 21.

conference sponsor (the Humanities Center for Liberal Education in an Industrial Society) to provide for the blue-collar worker what, with wide acclaim, it had been successfully providing for a management elite.

The Sextonites, and those who agree with them, have insisted that the desire for quality is not the monopoly of a single class—and that, among the common people, too, there is plenty of capacity and desire for quality education. They have maintained that they want to free the term "quality" from the illogical charge that to seek quality education is to be an aristocrat, an elitist. Conversely, they have emphasized that, whatever the sociopolitical form, quality leadership is necessary; that a democracy cannot escape this fundamental political necessity; and that, as Jefferson insisted, it must guarantee, in lieu of an inherited leadership, its own elitist leadership new-grown from within its own ranks. It has been pointed out that, even among anarchistic youth communes, some sort of leadership has to be elicited, and that the success or failure of the group often depends on the quality of this leadership and its acceptance by the group. This has been suggested in Mason Gross's insistence that, while he is against mass education, he is all for education of the masses. With Matthew Arnold, he wants to level up, not down.

The answer to Brendon Sexton's challenge, published in *The CEA Critic* of the College English Association and then widely distributed as a reprint, was an emphatic *yes*. The *yes* was translated into action in 1957 with a program on Politics, Poetry, and Human Values, which became, thereafter, an integral part of the United Steelworkers' programs at The Pennsylvania State University and other land-grant institutions (approximately twenty-four) where, under the direction of Emory Bacon, such programs were held.

Another way of attempting to achieve this same result—the democratization of the earlier aristocratic liberal arts—has its historic antecedent in the doctrines of Matthew Arnold's personal friend and public opponent, "Darwin's Bull Dog," Thomas Henry Huxley. Huxley agreed with Arnold that a quality liberal education was desirable; but he insisted that, if he had to choose between an exclusively literary-philosophical-historical education and an exclusively scientific one, he would prefer the latter. He argued that the study of the sciences themselves—among which he included the newly emerging "social" sciences would be enough to do the job.

This notion of the scientific, technical, vocational, and professional subjects as themselves yielding liberal education increments has been advanced with increasing frequency: in 1953, by Virgil Hancher; in the late fifties by the New England Region of the ASEE; and, not long thereafter, by Eric Ashby, who put his concept into the term "technological humanism."[5]

All in all, the ongoing dialectic between the liberal arts and other forces within the land-grant milieu has been to the good of both liberal learning and of the land-grant movement. It has had its risks; but then, whatever is alive and developing is continually exposed to risk. In spite of the contestations and polarizations, creative tension has been maintained and should continue to be maintained.

Assumptions of Values and Responsibilities
by Disciplines other than Liberal Arts

Liberalizing filaments of growth and development are rapidly developing at the interfaces between the liberal arts as conventionally delimited and other sectors of higher education in the land-grant institution, sectors conventionally (and often stereotypically) regarded as beyond the pale of liberal learning. Similar hopeful observations may be made with regard to the boundaries between the conventionally delimited liberal arts and areas conventionally designated off limits for the liberal arts. These are communal and societal growing fronts—potentially destructive, potentially constructive. These interrelational ties may be discerned as constituting the early phases of a process which ultimately may mean vital interpenetration and synergy between academia and the community-at-large.

Several factors help account for these developing interterritorial

---

[5]See Virgil M. Hancher, "Liberal Education in Professional Curricula," presented at a meeting of the Association of Land-Grant Colleges and Universities, Columbus, Ohio, November, 1953 (mimeographed version); and Eric Ashby, "Technological Humanism," *Journal of the Institute of Metals,* 1957, Part II; and *Technology and the Academics: An Essay on the Universities and the Scientific Revolution* (New York: St. Martin's Press, 1963), especially pp. 81–89. For further commentaries, see my *Design in Liberal Learning,* p. 70.

ties. Among these is a change of attitude with regard to responsibility for the human values concerns of higher education. On the one hand, practitioners of the liberal arts have come more and more to relinquish their at times self-righteously asserted traditional claim to a monopoly on such concerns—as a badge of distinction or a burden to be proudly borne. On the other hand, academic colleagues outside the officially designated liberal arts have been relinquishing their customary practice of passing the 'values buck,' with a sigh of relief or a gesture of indifference, to those professing the liberal arts. More and more these other colleagues have been insisting that they have a right and duty, as well as a capability, to assume a proper share of responsibility for the values components in higher education and in the community-at-large. This reciprocal change of attitude has ushered in a new era of joint responsibility for the human values component in higher education, and, often, of systematic collaboration in meeting this responsibility. To be sure, this collaboration has sometimes meant competition among conflicting value systems which, when free of personal rancor, has yielded positive educative results. Such joint responsibility and effort, therefore, should be included among the optatives for the liberal arts in the land-grant system.

At San José State College, the head of the Department of Material Sciences in the Division of Engineering, with the strong support of his likeminded dean, developed a course in Cybernation and Man which became an institution-wide general education elective. Described in a book-length report, this course has also served as a model for such essentially liberal learning programs at other institutions of higher education both in this country and abroad. At The Pennsylvania State University, the director of the Center for Materials Sciences Research became the catalyzing agent for a newly developed junior-senior and graduate program in Science, Technology, and Society.

Another illustration comes from the same land-grant university. Two professors of engineering designed an experimental course dealing with technology and human values. When they failed to get budgetary and logistic support from their own college, the College of the Liberal Arts invited them to give their new course under interdisciplinary liberal arts auspices. The course persisted beyond the trial-run stage. Then the wheel came full cycle; the course came under sponsorship of the College of Engineering. This is an apt illustration of the interplay between participants in the ongoing dialectic involving the liberal arts and other forces in the land-grant system. Through this counterpoint, a new fabric for liberal learning is being woven.

The beauty of this development is that it is working both ways. As the Penn State STS program moved toward implementation, it turned out that most of the courses being adopted were within the domain of the College of the Liberal Arts—involving literary, historical, and philosophic humanists, as well as economists, sociologists, anthropologists, political scientists, and other "human sciences" people.[6]

Other illustrations have become increasingly available. Thus, *The Program Description and Course List: 1970–1971* for the Cornell Program in Science, Technology, and Society provided for an interdisciplinary program and drew its students, faculty, and research workers from all areas of the university. It included the physical and biological sciences, the social sciences, and the humanities, as well as engineering, business, and public administration. A joint fellowship between the program and the Study for the Humanities was arranged to bring a visiting scholar to Cornell to work on some aspect of the relation between science and technology and humanistic concerns.[7]

The same tendency to interterritorial ties or even coalescence is seen among the several disciplines that comprise the liberal arts. There is a fast-increasing number of conventionally designated scien-

[6]All in all, the new interdisciplinary humanities movement has made far more headway in the schools and the junior and community colleges than in the four-year colleges and the universities. See, for example, Richard R. Alder, ed., *Humanities Programs Today* (New York: Citation Press, 1970); *National Association of Secondary School Principals Bulletin* issue of February, 1972, which is completely given over to *On Humanizing the Schools;* Thomas F. Powell, ed., *Humanities and the Social Studies,* Bulletin No. 44 (Washington, D.C.: National Council for the Social Studies, 1969); Harold E. Taylor, ed., *The Humanities in the Schools* (New York: Scholastic Magazines, 1968); James L. Jarrett, *The Humanities and Humanistic Education* (Reading, Massachusetts: Menlo Park, California: Addison-Welsey, 1973).

[7]See "The Academic Career," *Education in the Age of Science, Daedalus,* 88 (Winter, 1959): 163–64; and my "The Impact of Technological Change on the Humanities," *The Educational Record* 46 (Fall 1965): 388–99.

tists—both natural and behavioral-social—who have been asserting their close kinship with the humanities. Some have even gone so far as to claim that, as they teach their subjects or do other professional work in their disciplines, they, too, are humanists. This notion is seen in the term human sciences, advanced to replace behavioral-social sciences, as well as in the increasing tendency to call social amelioration programs humanistic instead of humanitarian. More: we have had distinguished scientists (both social and natural) insisting that, from their point of view, the sciences themselves are humanities, as their progenitors were regarded in the Renaissance. Examples are: René Dubos and Julian Huxley, biologists; Jacob Bronowski, late director of the Council for Biology in Human Affairs of the Salk Institute, and author of *Ascent of Man,* as well as central figure in the widely presented TV series bearing the same title; Stanley Garn, who has been chairman of the department of growth and genetics, Fels Research Institute; and Harold K. Schilling, former head of the physics department and dean of the graduate school at The Pennsylvania State University. Among Professor Schilling's books are: *Science and Religion: An Interpretation of Two Communities, Physics as a Humanity,* and *The New Consciousness in Science and Religion.* We have had, also, Abraham Maslow and the Association for Humanistic Psychology, as well as Peter Berger and his *Invitation to Sociology: A Humanistic Perspective.* David Riesman has declared: "Social science at its best means to me one of the humanities, one of the most humane and liberating ways of approaching the human condition."

Interterritorial Collaboration to Solve Societal Problems

Granted: from the point of view of the liberal studies seen as academic domains, there is risk in collaboration with other academic provinces. There is the risk that the several liberal arts may suffer depletion, both in their intrinsic and traditional integrity and in such practical matters as personnel, programs, budgets, voice in policy making, and the like.

For the sake of the benefits to be gained and the contributions to be made, the liberal arts leadership within the land-grant system apparently has been willing to assume the risks involved in such collaboration. This is seen in the set of recommendations developed, in 1971, by the Commission on Arts and Sciences of the National Association of State Universities and Land-Grant Colleges, particularly in those recommendations which take cognizance of the "Rapidity of Technological and Social Changes."

These recommendations recognize that, because "of the rapidity of technological and social change, it is no longer possible to wait for a new generation to bring about needed change"; that, certainly, "institutions of higher education will be increasingly involved in preparing students for a life in the future that will be markedly different from life in the present; and that each of the professional areas needs to project the kinds of abilities, knowledge, and skills required by its practitioners a decade down the road and to attempt to prepare present undergraduates to function successfully in this radically changed context." Hence, "if students are to possess the adaptive skills necessary to live meaningfully in a society marked by an accelerating rate of change," the "entire curriculum needs continual revision."

This all-inclusive statement means revision for the liberal arts, too. Thus, to solve the problems of world-wide relations, the liberal arts will need to make their contributions toward developing "programs to provide understanding of cultural and political differences," and "the tools needed to eliminate the tensions between people of different countries." Similarly, the liberal arts program will be called to new emphases and expansions as they contribute toward the solution of the world-wide problems of population and food supply. These programs, the recommendations indicate, will help make a "necessary shift away from materialism" and toward increased stress on "humanitarian attitudes in students." More specifically, the liberal arts programs must help safeguard against brainwashing or thought control and other inhumane coercive techniques for defusing the population bomb. They must do this by conducting the research necessary to provide an understanding of the "freedom," "human," and "value" segments of the population question. In so doing, they must address themselves to that "task of public higher education" which makes it "a point of focus for solutions to issues where these questions of freedom and values are concerned."

In connection with the problem of pollution, the recommendations stress a collaborative role for the liberal arts. While they recognize that the findings of technical research will have to be brought to bear upon this problem, they nevertheless point out that the "technological personnel with engineering, conservation, and ecology backgrounds" will need "a thorough understanding of sociological, psychological, and political implications of the solutions of environmental problems." Students will need to develop "a deeper concern and a clearer understanding . . . of the relationship between pollution and their own value systems." All in all, the recommendations maintain that the "essential attitudinal-value support for this costly investment in survival will be a prime responsibility of the liberal arts."

Later, the recommendations comprehensively generalize this stress on a significant future role for the liberal arts in relation to the other functions of the institution of higher education—specifically, in relation to research. In this endeavor, declare the recommendations, colleges and universities must tackle interdisciplinary problems, systems problems, applied problems, and assessment problems. This means, too, that they must "expand the parameters investigated to include sociological and humanistic factors." Further, they must revise their training of research persons to provide for "instilling sociological and humanistic values"; this training "is primarily the task of the college of arts and sciences."

All these are useful indications of the readiness of the liberal arts leadership in the land-grant system to transcend conventional liberal arts boundaries and to collaborate with those in other academic areas in the solution of societal problems—from the local to the global. Yet, these recommendations likewise raise some disquieting questions. Do they imply too much and claim too little? Does their call for the liberal arts to help achieve a "shift away from materialism" imply that the liberal arts themselves have been free from the implied taint of such "materialism"? If so, are the recommendations not historically and substantially inaccurate? Again, in light of our earlier discussions, does the claim that the liberal arts have a "primary responsibility" for the value components of social problems and issues place too heavy a responsibility upon the liberal arts? Are the liberal arts now—are they likely to remain or become—the prime bearers of responsibility for human values and humanitarian ideals?

On the other hand, do not the liberal arts have contributions to make that are unrelated to their instrumental and applicative utility as so strongly stressed in the recommendations? Should their spokesmen not add the defense that Ralph Waldo Emerson urged for the Rhodora: "Tell them, dear—if eyes were made for seeing, beauty is its own excuse for being." Should these spokesmen not take their cue from John Henry Newman's insistence in the face of the utilitarian challenge that, like good health, the intellectual illumination and enlargement aimed at through liberal education, before it is "good for something," is a "good in itself"?[8]

However one answers these questions, it is quite clear that, with proper safeguards, strengthening the liberal arts within the land-grant system is to a great extent a matter of strategic alliances through interdisciplinary pooling and team operations. This applies in each of the three main functions of land-grant institutions—teaching, research, and direct services to individuals and groups.

This propensity toward interdisciplinary strategic alliances is now being given comprehensive recognition—and on at least three different levels: direct application and operation; policy and program decision making; and principle, theory, and speculation. To this should be added interdisciplinary strategic alliances for the sheer satisfaction of cooperative intellectual endeavor.

Illustrative is Simon Ramo's *Cure for Chaos*—his treatise for the layman on the practical applications of systems science and technology. Ramo urges that values-knowledgeable humanists be included among the interdisciplinary systems teams mobilized for the solution of a given communal or societal problem—such as reform of an entire school district.[9] Another illustration is to be found in an internationally recognized research consultation project carried out by the Center for the Study of Liberal Education at The Pennsyl-

[8]For an elaboration of this line of justification for the liberal arts, see *Design in Liberal Learning*, pp. 18–19.
[9]Simon Ramo, *Cure for Chaos* (New York: David McKay, 1969).

vania State University, with sponsorship of regional and national agencies that deal with problems of blindness. This project culminated in the publication of a volume entitled *Blindness Research: The Expanding Frontiers: A Liberal Studies Perspective.*[10] Not only were the literary liberal arts represented by contributors, but the director of the project and the editor of the volume, who wrote the introduction and the chapter on "Models, Values, and Systems," was a philological humanist.[11]

The recent revolt against the preponderance of positivistic and objectivistic research—with its accompanying emphasis on minutely segmented specialist methodologies—has done a great deal toward opening up fresh channels of exchange between scientific research and humanistic scholarly inquiry traditionally associated with the liberal arts. Researchers in sociology, for example, have discovered, in such writers as Plutarch, a largeness, an urbanity, a generically ethical point of view, a "human touch" which they have found enjoyable, intellectually profitable, and, most surprisingly to some of them, highly relevant.

The optative of strategic alliances for the liberal studies has been encouraged by a number of related developments in land-grant institutions. One of these has been the fast-mounting impetus of interdisciplinary patternings within subdivisions of these liberal arts —notably, on the national scene, in the New Humanities Movement. These patternings show themselves in: (1) the studious humanities (i.e., philological, literary-linguistic, philosophical, religious, and historical); (2) the practicing humanities (i.e., music, the dance, drama, the visual arts—especially multimedia); and (3) the studious and the practicing humanities (e.g., composite programs

[10]Maxwell H. Goldberg, ed. (University Park: Pennsylvania State University Press, 1969).
[11]For a detailed treatment of a number of ventures in strategic alliances and collaboration involving the humanistic and other liberal studies through the Center for Continuing Liberal Education at The Pennsylvania State University, see my "Higher Education: Equalization of Opportunity," in *The American University and the World of Scholars,* a selection of papers at the 1966 Conference for Foreign Fulbright Scholars, at Claremount College, Michigan State University, and Rutgers, published, in celebration of the Twentieth Anniversary of the Fulbright Program and of the Rutgers Bicentennial, by the Committee on International Programs, Ardath W. Burk, chairman; Rutgers, the State University, New Brunswick, New Jersey. See also *Automation, Education, and Human Values,* eds., William W. Brickman and Stanley Lehrer (New York: School and Society Books, 1967; reissued in 1969, by Crowell).

of poetry readings, music, and light shows, as well as dance).

Often, strong social consciousness is exhibited in the New Humanities Movement, and its interdisciplinary programs become directly related to social action. Often, too, such programs become affiliated with the "human sciences," and thus mark processes in which the conventionally designated humanities eventually reach out to the natural sciences and various vocational-professional sectors of higher education, particularly with education.

In achieving alliances, the liberal studies expose themselves, as already mentioned, to a serious risk. Affiliation might turn into absorption by other disciplines. Such risk is endemic to various "inter" tendencies toward which the liberal arts are drawn or are being called. Instances of such at least partial absorption are seen particularly vis-à-vis the liberal arts and education, and between the liberal arts and direct action programs. The latter are seen especially in the burgeoning ecology programs and those having to do with the problems of the slums, the ghettos, racial and ethnic discrimination, world tensions, the new globalistic humanitarianism (c.f. the global village and Space Ship Earth); and the vast and vaguely outlined territory suggested by such terms as "future studies," "futuristics," and "futurology." For his proposed new discipline of "techumology" —purportedly an amalgam of "technical and humanistic wisdom"— Glenn T. Seaborg mentions only "educators, social scientists, and political leaders." From the point of view of the full spectrum of the liberal arts, this is quite a lopsided amalgam. It runs the gamut of the liberal arts sources of humanistic wisdom from A to B.[12]

The tendency toward subservience on the part of the liberal arts is no new phenomenon. Together with the separatist attitude that the liberal arts hold a monopoly on the human values concerns of higher education, this tendency has long inhibited the healthy expansion of the liberal arts at their interfaces with other academic sectors. If interdisciplinary alliances are to be formed between liberal arts and other fields of study, the liberal arts must retain essential autonomy

[12]For detailed treatment of this topic of absorption versus alliance, see my "Heart Transplants for the Humanities?" *Liberal Education* 54 (October 1968): 456–66; and "The Academic Humanist in a Business Society," *Humanities in the South* (Spring 1975): 4–8.

and integrity, and must enjoy parity of participative weight, of fiscal support, facilities, and organizational status.

Granted the risk, it surely is worth taking. The alliances thus enabled can mean augmented strength, plus augmented contributions to public higher education and to the public good. In this direction, interdisciplinary programs involving the studious and the practicing humanities (the arts) and such programs involving applied science, technological fields, and social action show particular promise.

Some of the most rapid and vigorous growth in American higher education is occurring in the junior colleges and community colleges, and this has significance for the outlook for the liberal arts in the land-grant system. For the students in such programs, those liberal arts courses which have a strong admixture of practice—whether in terms of arts and crafts or in terms of social action and reform—are more likely to have a strong immediate appeal and hence are more likely to prove effective than are liberal arts courses which are exclusively or dominantly bookish. It is significant that, within the current New Humanities Movement, the practice-related interdisciplinary programs show by far the greatest energy and creative thrust, and that those who have it within their scope to develop and expand such programs exert major leadership within the movement. In this regard, it is also significant that the National Endowment for the Humanities has given much publicity to funding of applied humanities projects which are directed toward socioethical action. In projective thinking about the liberal arts in the land-grant system, these trends should be taken into account. They give added thrust to the tendency toward strategic alliances as a promising optative for liberal arts development.

It is also important for newly established college or university units set up to serve the applied needs mentioned immediately above to discover the need to include strong admixtures of the scholarly and the speculative for their own practical efficacy. They need to have liberal studies talent that tends toward research and theorizing not oriented to immediate problem solving or the personal and social urgencies of the moment. This need is being met by outright appointment of full-time scholars within a given action-oriented unit and by appointment of such scholars part-time or jointly with some department in the liberal arts unit of the institution. Both of these methods illustrate the continued vitality of that ongoing dialectic between the liberal arts components and the other units of the land-grant institution and the reasonableness of assuming that they will continue to assert themselves in future liberal arts developments within the land-grant system.

Technetronic Change, the Counter-Culture,
and the Liberal Arts:
Collaboration to What End?

In these current phases of the ongoing dialectic, there is a central irony. The very technological and related change which has given us some of our most critical socioethical problems and issues has likewise stimulated strategic interdisciplinary alliances of the sorts already cited.

Drastic technetronic change, for example, causes many environmental problems. To confront these problems we have mushrooming curricular and extracurricular programs dealing with ecology and the quality of life. Sponsors increasingly recognize that such programs must draw on the accumulated wisdoms and insights, as well as on the fresh perceptions, of such liberal studies as ethics and religion. An example is the volume *Reflections on Ethics, Religion, and Ecology,* which is dedicated to that distinguished land-grant university administrator, physicist, theologian, and philosopher, Dr. Harold K. Schilling. In the opening sentence of his contribution to this volume, "The Whole Earth is the Lord's: Toward a Holistic Ethic," Professor Schilling makes clear the responsibilities of the liberal arts for our efforts on behalf of ecological salvation and renewal:

> Many thoughtful people have come to feel that the pollution and destruction of man's environment are religious and ethical problems that derive basically from irreverent and immoral attitudes toward nature, rather than from technological inadequacy alone. They feel that the solution is not beyond the capabilities of technology—provided it allows itself to be guided by more sensitive religious views and

ethical motivations with respect to nature than now prevail generally in our culture. I share this view.[13]

What goes for such technologically related areas as ecological pollution goes, also, for other areas that feel the brunt of the drastic speedup and pervasiveness of technological and related change. Among these are science, technology and society; technological change, human values, and the individual; cybernation, systems, and the person; systems, and the person; systems, the computer, and the humanities; the mankind idea and humanities teaching; psychosocial- and bioengineering and human values; and future studies (futuristics, futurology).

The interdisciplinary strategic alliances invited by these new foci of liberal arts related programs are likely to have as a common denominator the promise of constructive accommodation to the technological developments largely responsible for the problems or issues dealt with. They may even be committed to a strong positive premise that these very developments which engender the cruxes, issues, and problems—some of them amounting to crises of survival for the individual and society—are rich in promise for the future of man.[14]

On the other hand, these same technological and related developments have evoked a quite contrasting tendency in conventionally designated liberal arts areas and at their interfaces with other areas, both intramural and extramural. This tendency may be loosely and crudely summed up under the designation "counter-culture."[15]

---

[13]Ian G. Barbour, ed., *Earth Night Be Fair* (Englewood Cliffs, New Jersey: Prentice-Hall, 1972), p. 100. (Comment on the Barry Commoner paper.)

[14]See for example, Arnold B. Barach, *1975 and the Changes to Come* (New York: Harper & Brothers, 1962); Dennis Gabor, *Inventing the Future* (New York: Knopf, 1964); Alice Mary Hilton, ed., *The Evolving Society* (New York: Institute for Cybercultural Research, 1965); John R. Platt, *The Step to Man* (New York: Wiley, 1966); Donald A Schon, *Technology and Change: The New Heraclitus* (New York: Delacorte, 1967); Don Fabun, *The Dynamics of Change* (Englewood Cliffs, New Jersey: Prentice-Hall, 1967); John G. Kemeny, *Man and the Computer* (New York: Scribner's 1972); Nigel Calder, *Technopolis* (New York: Simon and Schuster, 1969); Zbigniew Brzezinski, *Between Two Ages: America's Role in the Technetronic Era* (New York: The Viking Press, 1970); and Alvin Toffler, *Future Shock* (New York: Random House, 1970), also *The Futurists*, ed. Toffler (New York: Random House, 1972).

[15]See Theodore Roszak, ed., *The Dissenting Academy* (New York: Pantheon, 1968); *The Making of a Counter Culture: Reflections on the Technocratic Society and Its Youthful Opposition* (Garden City, New York: Doubleday Anchor Books, 1969); ed., *Sources: An Anthology of Contemporary Materials Useful in Preserving Personal Sanity While Braving the Great Technological Wilderness* (New York: Harper & Row, 1972), and *Where the Wasteland Ends:*

As with other alliance patternings that pertain to the liberal arts, those involving the counter-culture are interdisciplinary. They too affirm a central concern for values and the individual, especially his personal and human dignity and the dignity of man—but differ from other alliance patternings because they are severely critical of the liberal arts as conventionally organized and handled. They charge that these have too often been obsequious legitimizers of those power groups largely responsible for the present or impending technology-related crises; that these others have defaulted by too much stress on what they regard as the bloodless categories of scientificism, positivism, and objectivism, or on a correspondingly dry and effete aestheticism. In strong reaction, the counter-culturists favor interdisciplinary liberal studies with the nets down; with maximum emphasis on the extra-rationalistic, extra-scientific faculties or potentialities of man. This means a strong emphasis on the instinctual, the intuitive, and the mystical; on the sensory and the emotional; on fantasy; and on oceanic feelings of love, brotherhood, and cosmic oneness. Other movements lend force and give momentum to this counter-thrust within the ambience of the liberal arts. These include the human potential or sensitivity movement; and, in organized education, the curriculum of *affect,* as contrasted with the strongly cognitive and rationalistic curriculum stressed in the American reaction to Sputnik (1957).

The reverberations of all these currents running counter to the established liberal arts reinforce the affective and other nonrationalistic emphases of powerful components of the New Humanities Movement; and, all together, they cause serious seismic tremors in the liberal arts establishment.[16] Insofar as these tremors serve to

---

Politics and Transcendence in Post-Industrial Society (Garden City, New York: Doubleday, 1972). See, also, the "#1 Best Seller," Charles A. Reich's *The Greening of America* (New York: Bantam Books, 1971).

[16]See my "Freedom, Dignity, and the Telic Intent," *Goal Making for English Teaching,* ed. Henry B. Maloney (Urbana, Illinois: National Council of the Teachers of English, 1973). See also, Gerald Weinstein and Mario D. Fantini, *Towards Humanistic Education: A Curriculum of Affect* (New York: Praeger, 1971); *Educational Development at Michigan State University,* No. 4, Spring, 1972, Office of the Educational Development Program, Michigan State University; and Edward W. Sheffield, ed., *Curriculum Innovation in Arts and Science* (Toronto: Higher Education Group, University of Toronto, 1970), especially W. R. Nibblett's concluding analysis.

loosen and ventilate the encrusted and petrified forms of the liberal arts, these perturbations—disconcerting though they may be—must be recognized as a necessary prelude to freshly reconstituted and invigorated liberal arts in our land-grant institutions.

Yet there are corresponding dangers: The seismic tremors, caused largely by those whom Daniel Bell has called "the apocalyptics," may swell into earthquakes; invigorating perturbations may turn into a St. Vitus Dance or Dance of Death for the liberal arts; the revitalization may so perforate the many-mansioned House of Intellect, that, like the Walls of Jericho, it will all come tumbling down.[17] The stirring and fruitful but troubled career and ultimate collapse of Black Mountain College provides an early warning.

Here, then, is likely to be one of the major tests of the stamina of the liberal studies in the land-grant institutions. It is to be a test of their flexibility and elasticity, of their capacity for creative assimilation of new elements, and of their creative accommodation to new cultural sensitivities and environments, to new pulls and pressures.

In addition to those already listed, among these new circumstances and developments are the open university, the university without walls, and, comprehensively, external degree programs. So far as the well-being and advancement of the liberal arts are concerned, each of these signals both potential boon and potential bane. There is the boon of freedom, freshness, openness, variety, adaptation to individual expressiveness, and individual self-actualization. Yet without corresponding lines of responsibility, channels of creative constraint, and holistic designs, these very boons may turn into bane.

While it would be hard to predict the outcome of this boon-bane ambivalence, it should be said that developments of the past several years give realistic grounds for hope. The Walls of Jericho may indeed be shaken, but renewed and flexible patterns of wholeness are serving as versatile forces of creative constraint, taking the place of current petrified programs.

[17]See my "Humanities and the Alienated Adolescent," *School and Society* 95 (April, 1967): 257–61.

Continuing Education:

A Newly Discovered Twenty-Five Year Old Force

So far as the optative of strategic alliances for the liberal arts in the land-grant institutions is concerned, it has nowhere been better demonstrated than in that area of land-grant endeavor which only recently has come to enjoy the central attention and recognition it has so long and so richly deserved. This is the sector which, for the past twenty-five years, has more and more widely come to be known as continuing liberal education or continuing liberal studies. It is a sector sparked, in the fifties, by such agencies as the Fund for Adult Education established by the Ford Foundation and led by such agencies as the FAE-funded Center for the Study of Liberal Education for Adults (CSLEA). Its contributions rarely recognized, it has run interference for more recently publicized external degree programs in liberal studies and has actually provided a wealth of instances and full case histories of methods for implementing external degree programs in liberal studies. It has also provided comprehensive concepts and safeguards binding particular forms and procedures together into viable wholes.

The very term continuing suggests at once that liberal learning should be a vital continuum from kindergarten through graduate school, through the prime career into the geriatric years. The very term suggests that at any given state in one's education preparations should be made for one's continued competent learning, that a major motivation to continuing liberal studies should be heuristic. It should not only prompt the student to be a lifelong learner, but should give him the power to be a self-fueled learner (as with a fire that utilizes green wood in its upper layers) and should give him the intellectual skills needed for such self-committed and self-propelled learning.

From the start, as FAE leaders Scott Fletcher, Robert Blakeley, and John Osmun developed the concept; as such CSLEA leaders as John Diekhoff, John Schwertman, Alexander Liveright, Peter Siegle, and James Whipple, and Morton Goodon, developed it; as Cyril F. Hager and his associates developed it at Penn State—this new continuing liberal education has been holistic. It has stressed the interdisciplinary. From its inception, as regards both degree and nondegree programs, it has stressed enfranchisement from the trammels of conventional requirements and hardened curriculum forms and procedures. It has stressed the distinctions between satisfying requirements and achieving competence and quality, between working for grades and gaining a valuable liberal education. It has stressed such things as tutorials, liberal studies programs tailored to the needs and interests of particular groups and even of individuals, independent studies (independent studies now increasingly being used instead of correspondence courses, home studies programs, or external degree programs), and combinations of home studies and group counseling or group seminars under lay or professional leadership. In liberal studies, however set up and conducted, it has stressed the central role of the Socratic dialogue, even while it has refused to ignore the lecture when prepared and presented by one competent in this highly complex and exacting art and when appropriate to the particular teaching-learning needs of a given situation, group, or subject.

Further, as these have become available at acceptable cost, this continuing liberal studies movement has stressed the importance of utilizing technological adjuncts for teaching-learning: open and closed circuit TV, telelectures, films, audio-cassettes, audio-visual cassettes, computer-aided instruction. Most recently it has been looking ahead toward utilization of laser-enabled halography. Not only has it urged emancipation from various hurdle requirements of the conventional degree curricula, but it has also urged credit toward advanced standing and credit for life experience. A great deal of its emphasis, indeed, has been on nondegree programs.

Hence, it is not far-fetched to suggest that much, if not most, of the current terminology, rhetoric, and programming associated with the external degree derives from this continuing liberal studies movement of the past twenty-five years. It is well known, for example, that, before the British Open University was launched, representatives of its leadership traveled widely in this country studying our American continuing education programs—at such land-grant institutions as the University of Wisconsin and The Pennsylvania State University.

It is therefore not surprising to find that, in many quarters and for a number of years now, the continuing liberal studies unit at a given land-grant institution has served as change agent—toward greater openness, flexibility, variety, and ingenuity—in the other sectors of the institution. Indeed, the application of the concept of external degree programs to the "traditional" or undergraduate sectors of the land-grant institution is but an extension of a seminal concept that has been at work, for more than two decades, in the area of continuing education. Moreover, the implementation of the university without walls is but the extreme, perhaps the *reductio ad absurdum,* of a concept that has been at work for more than two decades in the continuing liberal studies movement.

It was therefore quite fitting that, in its budgets of the early seventies, the National Endowment for the Humanities allocated about forty percent of its total to continuing humanistic education. This is an index of the role that continuing liberal studies should be expected to play in the coming developments of the liberal arts within the land-grant system.

To be sure, here as elsewhere, we have the boon-bane ambivalence. When externalism extends so far as to get detached from the central core or when all the creative marrow is drained from the core to the peripheries, then promises for good in externalism become prescriptions for bane. Then the university without walls becomes so open that it has no inner vital form and essential wholeness becomes hodge-podge. There is hardly any rationale, program, practice, format, proposed procedure, mode of testing and tallying, pedagogic device, or management and fiscal handling associated with externalism that is not liable to serious abuse.

Starting out as adjuncts, technological instrumentalities may become ends in themselves and badly distort or deflect the liberally educative process. Starting out as a means of comprehensive unification, the systems approach may become a sanctioning agent for deindividualizing coercion and for dehumanizing authoritarianism.[18] Starting out to give due recognition to the liberally educative poten-

18See my *Cybernation, Systems, and the Teaching of English: The Dilemma of Control* (Urbana, Illinois: The National Council of Teachers of English, 1972); "Cybernation: The Dilemma of Control," *The Spectrum* 7 (1967): 12–14; 44–47; and "The Structure and Problems of Human Values: 2000 A.D.," *Symposium II: Technological Education in the Twenty-*

tialities of nonacademic, extramural life experiences, credit for life experiences may and has often become a farce. Such credit, and degrees based upon such credit, may be granted to individuals simply by virtue of their having survived to a certain age and having occupied themselves with more or less gainful and more or less useful activities. Already, by the early seventies, the American Council on Education was expressing concern about at least one institution, chartered in England, that was eager to provide degree diplomas on just this basis.[19]

In connection with the continuing liberal studies optative for the land-grant system, we have to exercise other safeguards as well. Thus, for at least two decades, we have been hearing and talking much about the wonderful challenges to liberal studies by the increasing blocks of open time that technological and related changes are allegedly providing in various quarters of business, industry, and the home. We are urged to do our share to wean our fellow Americans from the so-called Protestant work ethic to a leisure ethic. Within this ethic of education for self-actualization, skill in arts and crafts; skill in scientific, humanistic, and other intellectual endeavors; and skill in the arts of social relationships and social service will replace our traditional market economy, dollars-and-cents drives.

Yet often externalism takes the lure of premature planning and programming, wrongly assuming that future possibilities are already here as actualities. Education for leisure is a case in point. Often ignored reservations about this, as put forward for example by Donald Michael, apply to those in the professions or in positions of managerial, administrative, and executive responsibilities; and to those engaged in scholarly, scientific, artistic or other creative enterprises demanding high professional competence and unlimited per-

---

First Century (Center for Technological Education, San Francisco State College, 1967), pp. 69–98. See also, Parry D. Sorensen, "Colleges Without Walls: No Ivy or Moss," The National Observer, December 2, 1972; Joan Sillech, "Britain's Bold New Electronic University," World (December 5, 1972): 28–32; my "Externalism and the Independent Liberal Arts College," Humanities in the South (Spring and Fall 1973); and Robert L. Jacobson, "Colleges Are Not Meeting Needs of Adults," The Chronicle of Higher Education, (February 5, 1973) pp. 1; 6–7.

[19]See "Summary of Recent Developments," my Continuing Liberal Studies: Degree Curricula Especially for Adults, rev. ed., (University Park, Pennsylvania: The Center for Continuing Liberal Education, 1971; originally issued in 1964), pp. 1–3.

sonal application. According to Dr. Michael, such individuals will not enjoy these new large blocks of open time. Rather, they may be working up to sixty-five hours a week, if they are willing—the need of their skills and competencies being so far ahead of supply.

Again, it is quite clear that often these large, new blocks of open time will come as involuntary consignments to so-called leisure—for recent high school and college graduates, for the handicapped and the aged, for ethnic and other minority people. Nor will the professional classes be exempt, as indicated by the widespread layoffs of highly trained aerodynamics and space technologists several years ago; and by the massive layoffs of the "stagflation" into the seventies. To talk of liberal studies in leisure fulfillment for such people is both unrealistic and callous, lacking in empathic imagination. This John Ruskin discovered when, in nineteenth-century England, he launched his program of fine arts for British factory workers and slum dwellers. The gospel of the fine arts, he came to see, is blasphemy for men and women lacking the subsistence needed for survival, to say nothing of elemental decency and dignity. For the person worried about meeting his mortgage and car payments, leisure-time continuing liberal studies programs are a luxury he can not afford.

Open Structure or PPBS?

In recent years, certain technological developments have given added impetus to the pressures toward positivistic, quantitative yardsticks for measuring educative success. Among these are cybernational developments, particularly as related to the computer. The computer has played such a role in at least two major ways: (1) As an extraordinarily fast, versatile, and sophisticated adding machine, it has facilitated the storage and retrieval of vast quantities of statistics. (2) As a supposedly economic teaching machine, it has been exceedingly attractive to some educators. As a teaching machine, it has called for behavioral objectives put into numeric and quantifiable terms. Both of these capabilities of the computer and computer-related systems have, in turn, contributed momentum to efficiency advocates, who are trying to apply to education the equivalent of some of the Taylorian concepts favored by industrial efficiency experts: accountability in terms of unit costs, cost effectiveness, and so on.

In his *The Future of the State University,* Russell Thackrey has exposed the limitations of this approach to evaluating educational success. In so doing he aids the liberal arts component of the great ongoing dialectic in the land-grant system. He does so in his treatment of the attempt to apply PPBS (Program-Planning-Budgeting System) to higher education. While he gives credit to the useful effects of PPBS, Thackrey, so far as education is concerned, exposes its negative effects. This assessment is all the more important, because Thackrey cannot be accused of holding a vested interest in the nontangible, nonquantifiable values of the liberal arts. Thackrey's criticism of PPBS is not emotional, nor is it based on theory or on lofty tributes to the good, the true, the beautiful. It is pragmatic. It should provide, for the future of the liberal arts in the land-grant system, an effective safeguard against threatened stultification by imposition of alleged objective and numeric tests upon intrinsically nonquantifiable processes and outcomes.

In effect, Thackrey declares that while PPBS is admirably suited to military enterprises bent on "getting more bang for a buck," and for a "wide range of other public policy areas . . . it is being widely applied, or attempted, in many areas in which it doesn't make sense." When and where PPBS is inappropriately applied, there is a strong tendency to ignore factors not amenable to quantifiable handling. In such circumstances, the dictum certainly applies: Out of sight, out of mind. "Benefits or consequences of the highest social, cultural, and economic importance tend to be excluded from consideration because data are impossible to get, difficult to get, annoying, or don't fit into the directive."

In making his point, Thackrey gives as an example "one distinguished economist [who] is reported as saying that the economic and social benefits to *society* are undoubtedly great, but, until they can be measured in dollar terms, education should be viewed solely as an economic benefit to the individual." To underscore the irony of this example, Thackrey puts forth a rhetorical question that shows the bearing upon the well-being and advancement of the liberal arts of the recent governmental-bureaucratic and educational-bureaucratic fixation on PPBS: "Who, for example, can measure dollar value to society of understanding the concept of equal justice before the law?"

This concept is in the realm of human values, of socioethical values; and these have long been a central concern of the liberal arts. Hence, without stretching Mr. Thackrey's point or doing violence to the line of his argument, we may cite this rhetorical question and its embodied example as showing the relevance, for the future of the liberal arts in the land-grant system, of a rigorous and realistic negative critique of PPBS and other so-called objective tests and measurements as applied in American higher education.

Mr. Thackrey is at his most telling in a satiric, imaginary conversation. As Abraham Lincoln and his fictional PPBS staff prepare their brief against the proposed Land-Grant Act, the latter declare: "We have no basis on which to predict the future economic return from this give-away, if any."[20] At this moment the country was in the midst of a tragic and costly war, inflation was rampant, the budget horribly out of balance, and the condition of the Treasury so stark that printing press money would soon be issued. Nevertheless, Lincoln took the risk. The Land-Grant Act was an act of faith: in the future of the nation, in the young people of the nation. It took forty years, some say fifty, before it clearly began to pay off. The payoff was in a revolution that was not only agricultural and technological, but also cultural; and it was upon this composite revolution that our emergence as a great nation was substantially based.

Lincoln made his momentous decision without benefit of quantified data and projections. Nor could the worth of his decisions be determined through quantifiable techniques. Into this decision went large but nonmeasurable increments of faith and hope. It was part of the larger national investment as embodied in the American Dream. It is this same sort of faith and hope by which we have largely justified our society's investment in the liberal arts in the land-grant institutions. For the goals of the Land-Grant Idea, of the American Dream, and of the Liberal Arts have all been the same— personal and human dignity within the ambience of the dignity of man.

[20]Russell I. Thackrey, *The Future of the State University*, pp. 55–56.

So far as the liberal arts, specifically, are concerned, the land-grant investment has been a transformational venture in democratizing and universalizing an earlier aristocratic liberal arts education for a highly select group. This process has been a yoking of opposites to achieve a new vital composite. At times the two components of this process have tended to such opposed polarization as to threaten to destroy the dialectic mechanism and to nullify the dialectic dynamic. At other times, the two have worked synergistically. They have worked for the end-purpose of enabling each student generation, in its own idiom and symbolism, and in terms of its own problems and potentials, to identify and achieve its own sense of personal and human dignity within the matrix of the dignity of man, within the context of the constitutional commitment to life, liberty, and the pursuit of happiness.

This dialectic pattern is in the grain. It's constructive continuation should be assured. It is to be found in the very wording of the Morrill Act itself, as seen, specifically, in the following phrases: "the liberal and practical education of the industrial classes in the several pursuits and professions in life"; and "without excluding the classics." The first of these phrases embraces an historical contradiction. Historically, the man to be educated liberally was *not* a member of the industrial (working) classes. He was one of an elite of blood and position and/or wealth or a member of a professional elite: physicians, lawyers, theologian-preachers, scholars. "Practical education," as applied to artisans, shopkeepers, laborers, workers, had nothing at all of this gentlemanly intent.

In spite of this historical and logical contradiction, however, the paradoxic "liberal and practical" works in actual operation. It has proved an effective formula for implementing the great historic venture to which American higher education committed itself, namely, to combine the personal and social strengths and benefits characteristic of an aristocratic society at its best with the corresponding strengths and benefits characteristic of an egalitarian society at its best. The paradox is summed up in the Jeffersonian ideal of a natural aristocracy of character and intellect, an ideal which, through the early twenties, was still operable in that socially democratic school of culturally pluralistic students, the Boston Public Latin School. For this working combination, there were certain common denominators of shared values: integrity, freedom and responsibility, reason and common sense, justice, and mercy.

As with the phrase "the liberal and practical education of the industrial classes," so a contradiction is imbedded in "without excluding the classics." It is the contradiction between the evasive "without excluding the classics" and the positive "including the classics." It is weak. "Without excluding the classics" is at best a permissive phrase, at worst a sop. So far as the liberal arts within the land-grant matrix are concerned, it could lead to disciplinary and budgetary tokenism and the relegation of these studies, in spite of rhetoric about the democracy of the disciplines, to second-class academic citizenship.

True, in interpretive statements subsequent to the passage of the Morrill Act, both Senator Morrill and other artificers of the act sought to shore up the more permissive overtone of the "without excluding the classics." They did so by widely publicized affirmations about the peer status of the liberal arts within the circle of subject matter, disciplines, and organizational units of the land-grant institution. Thackrey says: "Could a land-grant institution offer the classics? Of course, said Mr. Morrill, it could not only offer them but had an obligation to do so. Didn't the act say that other scientific and classical subjects should not be excluded? This meant, of course, that they must be included."[21] Earlier, Jonathan Baldwin Turner had defined the industrial classes of the time as "95 percent of the people," charging that existing colleges served only the five percent constituting the literary and leisure classes. He had no objection to serving the five percent in his new universities, if the needs of the ninety-five percent were met.[22]

Such statements paved the way for the emergence, by the twenties of the present century, of sometimes dominant colleges of arts and sciences among the more progressive land-grant institutions.[23] But

[21]Ibid. pp. 9–10.

[22]Mary Turner Carriel, *The Life of Jonathan Baldwin Turner* (Urbana: University of Illinois Press, 1961), pp. 68 ff.

[23]See Herman B. Allen, *Open Door to Learning: The Land-Grant System Enters Its Second Century* (Urbana: University of Illinois Press, 1963). For a detailed discussion of the quality-quantity crux in land-grant and other American higher education, see my "Quest for a Unity of Knowledge," the invited American contribution to the UNESCO-sponsored *The University*

within land-grant idea and practice, it is much like Emerson's circus bareback rider who undertook to ride two horses, galloping around the ring. He maintained his precarious balance by leaping back and forth from horse to horse. So with the ongoing dialectic of the liberal arts in the land-grant movement. Over 100 years ago, we committed ourselves to a both-end experiment in higher education. In this we sought to combine the virtues of the traditionally aristocratic and conservative liberal arts with the virtues of progressively democratic social idealism and practice. And, like the bareback rider, we have so far jollied along successfully. We have provided another example of the triumph, in American life and culture, of practical ingenuity over logical contradictions and theoretical impossibility. We have grounds for hope in the successful continuation of this dialectic of the democratization of the liberal arts in the land-grant milieu through the critical years ahead. An enduring optative for the liberal arts in the land-grant system is a major role in reclaiming and making good the American Dream.[24]

Today: Its Role and Place in Society—An International Study (Geneva, Switzerland: World University Services, 1960), pp. 247–252.

[24] See Marcus Cunliffe's review of Michael Kammen's *People of Paradox* (New York: Alfred A. Knopf, 1972) which reports the author as taking "paradox to be an early and enduring American response to the multiplicity of existence." The review is captioned "America as a Dialectic Without a Synthesis," *New York Times Book Review,* October 1, 1972, p. 4. See also, Kammen's *The Contrapuntal Civilization: Essays Toward a New Understanding of the American Experience* (New York: Crowell, 1970).

Chapter 8

SOCIAL AND BEHAVIORAL SCIENCES
IN THE 1970s*

RENEE C. and ROBERT S. FRIEDMAN

SOCIAL, political, and economic change have occurred in the United States at an accelerated rate since the federal government sanctioned a national system of state-supported institutions of higher learning more than one hundred years ago. The land-grant concept was developed with the notion that a group of colleges and universities ought to be responsive to the needs of society. When the Morrill Act was passed, these needs focused upon agricultural and industrial development. Today the United States is the most developed industrial society in the world and, consequently, universities have shifted their emphasis to an urban, post-industrial society.

To some extent the larger political system has already begun to restructure itself to cope with this transformation. Recent court decisions and their implementation in most states guaranteeing "one man—one vote" have altered the distribution of power in the legislatures in the direction of urban and suburban constituencies. Policy changes are not yet clear, but it is very likely to mean, for example, less emphasis in the future upon agricultural interests like rural highways and more accent upon urban interests including public transportation systems.[1]

Our society's requirements are closely linked to the urban, post-industrial condition, and while science and technology have much to offer, the needed breakthroughs are to be found in the social and

---

*The definition of what disciplines comprise the social and behavioral sciences varies with the funding agency, but in this text the authors define them as anthropology, economics, geography, linguistics, political science, psychology, sociology and the applied versions, business administration, public administration, rural sociology, and agricultural economics.

[1] As one critic asserted almost ten years ago, "The principal university of a major manufacturing state spends more each year on 4-H clubs than it does for its entire program of research and teaching for literally millions of industrial workers and their highly important organizations." Frederich Heimberger, "The State Universities," *Daedalus* 93 (Fall, 1964): 1092.

behavioral sciences. This is true whether it is racial equality, which the public concedes is the province of the social scientist, or environmental pollution, which may not yet be fully recognized as having social science implications.

The failure of the society at large and of many universities to recognize fully the relevances of social and behavioral sciences stems from a combination of features involving both the external and internal environments in which social scientists function. Among the most significant external phenomena are the limited perception of the relevance of the work of social scientists to the needs of society and, above all, the politically and socially disquieting characteristics of many findings in social science research. Among the features of the internal environment that result in difficulties for the social sciences are stylistic aspects of the conduct of research and the crudeness of social and behavioral science data by comparison with the hard sciences.

This chapter will attempt to place in perspective the mission of the social sciences in land-grant universities in terms of (a) the history of their role at such institutions, (b) the external and internal environmental problems that they encounter, and (c) a prognosis of their development in the next decade.

History of Social Science Research at Land-Grant Universities

Research was not among the first orders of business for the newly created land-grant colleges. The research function began in earnest with passage and implementation of the Hatch Act of 1887, which established the agricultural experiment stations at each of the land-grant institutions. Prior to this time there was neither a substantial body of knowledge or theory on which practices in agriculture rested, nor were the natural and physical sciences incorporated into the educational curriculum. The engineering experiment stations soon developed, although they were not created through national legislation. Herbariums, museums, laboratories, and observatories were gradually added, but these were tools for teaching and research rather than direct subsidies for the latter.

Interestingly enough, a few social science institutes could next claim modest research support at land-grant universities. Institutes with a political science focus were established to perform services for state and local officials. According to the *Research Center Directory,* at least two such centers have been in continuous operation for more than fifty years: the Institute of Governmental Studies, University of California (Berkeley), founded in 1921, and the Municipal Reference Bureau, University of Minnesota, established in 1913.[2] Such units often provided training for undergraduate students, continuing education programs for public service, and research of an applied nature for segments of the public sector.

Counterparts to aid the private sector were started in the form of bureaus of business and economic research. The Center for Business and Economic Research, formerly the Bureau of Business Research, has functioned at Ohio State University since 1923. Similarly, the Bureau of Economic Research, Rutgers University, has been "encouraging, facilitating and conducting research related to both basic and applied aspects of business and economic life in New Jersey" since 1927.[3] These units tended to be less actively engaged in the teaching function than the institutes serving public officials, but they conducted comparable studies for their clienteles. In the formative stages the professionals involved undertook primarily descriptive or normative research assignments, but in recent years many of the original bureaus have undergone metamorphic changes.

Critics of institutes and centers have suggested that the successful academic entrepreneurs have either set up "housekeeping" or remolded and reworded long-established units to capitalize on what was most salable to sponsors. In fairness, however, the progression in title from Bureau of Governmental Research to Bureau of Urban Research and, presently, Research Center for Urban and Environmental Planning, may signify more than a change in nomenclature. It can be viewed as a state-of-the-discipline message, a public acknowledgement of the complexities in the social setting, an advertisement of new research techniques and alliances, and a meshing of

---

[2]Archie M. Palmer (ed.), *Research Center Directory* (Detroit: Gale Research Company, 1972), pp. 357, 367.
[3]Ibid., pp. 129, 131.

basic and applied research. The social and behavioral scientists have inputs to the solution of such contemporary public policy issues as pollution control or delivery of health care services in the core city.

There is ample precedent for the involvement of the social sciences in matters of national concern. During the early New Deal period, President Roosevelt relied heavily on the counsel of social scientists for policy directives and legislative proposals. Roosevelt's use of Keynesian theory in his economic recovery programs helped economics gain acceptance as a theoretical and empirical science. The Full Employment Act of 1946 formalized the creation of the Council of Economic Advisors. Since then every president has consulted regularly with professional economists in dealing with problems of economic policy.

Conditions created by World War II established a new set of national priorities. While social and behavioral scientists offered their personal services and contributed their advancing skills in survey design, tests, and measurements, their colleagues in the "hard" sciences upstaged them. The enormous successes scored by science were followed by formal recognition of the scientific establishment by the national government. Shortly after World War II, the National Science Foundation was established, and in 1957 a science adviser and science advisory committee were installed as part of the White House staff.[4]

In the decade between 1945 and the commencement of space exploration, mission-oriented scientific research was firmly ensconced in the university setting. However, cold war diplomacy and its repercussion—Senate-conducted hearings into the loyalty of government policy makers and leading academicians—may have been contributing factors in leading social and behavioral scientists to turn inward. In addition, they were vulnerable because the utility of social science research had not been demonstrated as scientific research had been in medicine and engineering. Public policy research was ignored entirely. Research energies were expended on refining methodologies and developing the quantitative skills that would enable social sci-

---

[4]It is not yet clear what impact the abolition in January 1973 of the Office of Science and Technology will have on the role of scientists in policy making.

ence disciplines to compete with the natural sciences in resource allocations.[5]

The social legislation passed during the Johnson administration reaffirmed the persistence and urgency of the domestic crises engulfing us: poverty in rural and urban America, the plight of our cities, and racial tension. Campus turmoil, fueled by the continuing war in Vietnam, and environmental pollution expanded the list of national concerns. Of crucial importance, however, is how much the American public is willing to invest in the prevention or alleviation of such problems.

Little financial support has been available to the social sciences in land-grant universities. This lack of support has generally prevailed throughout the private and public sectors as well, with a few notable exceptions. Orlans has pointed out that:

> Long established agencies like the Departments of State, Commerce, and Labor have traditionally conducted the bulk of their social and economic research with their own staffs, whereas agencies and programs established during and after the Second World War, like the Air Force, and the National Institutes of Health, the Office of Naval Research, the National Science Foundation, and the Office of Economic Opportunity, have had most of their research conducted by universities and non-profit and profit-making organizations.[6]

While data collected by the Bureau of Census, in the Department of Commerce and the Bureau of Labor Statistics, in the Labor Department, have long provided valuable assistance to social scientists by serving as catalysts for research activity, these are leavings compared to the vast research grants and contracts available to engineering and the physical and life sciences. Even the finances for the social sciences emanating from NSF and agencies like the Office of Economic Opportunity are relatively small. This is amply demonstrated by federal expenditure figures for 1968 as shown in Table 1.

---

[5]For a more detailed historical review, see Harold Orlans, "Social Science Research Policies in the United States," *Minerva* 9 (January, 1971): 7–31 and Stanley O. Ikenberry and Renee C. Friedman, *Beyond Academic Departments* (San Francisco: Jossey-Bass, 1972), pp. 63–82.
[6]Ibid., p. 22.

TABLE 1
Federal Obligations For Basic Research, 1968

Subject Area	Funds Available (in thousands)	Percentage
Life Sciences	638,265	30.3
Physical Sciences	731,174	34.8
Environmental Sciences	356,887	17.0
Mathematics	66,516	3.2
Engineering	190,881	9.1
Psychology	54,534	2.6
Social Sciences	61,506	2.9
Other	4,073	0.2
TOTAL	2,103,836	100.1

SOURCE: Michael S. March, *Federal Budget Priorities for Research and Development* (Chicago: The University of Chicago Center for Policy Study, 1970), p. 16.

The minuscule financial support for social and behavioral sciences as late as 1968 is attributable to the nature of the social and behavioral sciences as well as to a number of characteristics of the social and political system in which we live. The discussion that follows attempts to pinpoint some of the key factors associated with lack of support for these disciplines.

Zones of Conflict: The External Environment

The following statement summarizes the goals of social and behavioral science research.

The objectives of behavioral and social scientists are essentially the same as those of other scientists: to establish a body of fact and theory, demonstrable and communicable, that contributes to knowledge and understanding that will permit man to manage his affairs with greater rationality.[7]

Unfortunately, in fulfilling these objectives, social and behavioral science investigation can be perceived as threatening to the society

[7]National Academy of Sciences and Social Science Research Council, *The Behavioral and Social Sciences: Outlook and Needs* (Englewood Cliffs, N.J.: Prentice-Hall, 1969), p. 20.

it purports to serve. Fervent and politically influential believers in some of the myths surrounding such topics as race and distribution of wealth make suspect any social scientist who debunks what John K. Galbraith has termed "conventional wisdom." Compared to the humanities and the natural sciences, the social and behavioral sciences are in their infancy, without the protective coverings or the ameliorative effects of time. While the social and behavioral sciences strive to be value-free, the public frequently assumes a linkage between social science and politics, and between policy and social ideology.[8] Furthermore, a proposal like the guaranteed income plan is redistributive in nature, and the haves do not usually willingly accommodate the have-nots.[9]

In an essay written several years ago, Frank Pinner makes a distinction between "consensual" and "dissensual" disciplines that is useful in understanding the nature and acceptance of the social and behavioral sciences. He terms consensual all those disciplines whose scholars' competence and motives for research are accepted by the public without reservation. He cites mathematics, the natural sciences, and such applied fields as engineering or veterinary medicine as examples of consensual disciplines.[10]

According to his definition, the social sciences, along with philosophy, music, literature, and the fine arts are dissensual:

> Few people in the community will express doubts about the research findings and teachings of a chemist, nor will they ever question his motives and wonder about the values underlying his work . . . The findings and teachings of philosophers . . . do not elicit similarly general confidence. The public tends to wonder about the worth of these scholars' work, it tends to look for hidden motives, and it easily discounts the teachings and even the data of dissensual disciplines either by directly opposing or by conveniently forgetting and ignoring them.[11]

[8]Robert S. Friedman, *Professionalism: Expertise and Policy Making* (New York: General Learning Press, 1971), pp. 7–8.

[9]For a discussion of the meaning of redistribution, see p. 10 below.

[10]Frank Pinner, "The Crisis of the State Universities," *The American College*, ed. Nevitt Sanford (New York: John Wiley & Sons, Inc., 1962), pp. 940–70.

[11]Ibid., p. 943.

Within the dissensual disciplines, there are areas of study that do not engender hostility, and in fact enjoy favorable publicity. In the previous section, we described the activities of the early government bureaus in the land-grant institutions. So long as the areas researched by political scientists dealt with such topics as the organization, administration, and operations of local government, the public acknowledged their expertise. This is in sharp contrast with the reception a Congressional committee recently accorded a proposal to study the political socialization process among school-age children.[12]

Conversely, the consensual disciplines are not impervious to criticism. Much depends on the research specialty. The experimental chemist who develops new synthetic fabrics reaps the applause of an appreciative public. The organic chemist who may have begun to unravel the mystery of creation and can reproduce the beginnings of life in a test tube may be personally and professionally ridiculed.

Even those scientific theories a knowledgeable public no longer questions did not win immediate acceptance in their time. Ptolemaic notions about the solar system suited medieval religious doctrine much more than Copernican heliocentric theory. What furor Copernicus, the father of astronomy, must have generated in fifteenth-century Europe! Perhaps the Scopes trial was a temporary aberration, but if Darwin's theory of evolution could still evoke such wrath in twentieth-century America, imagine the impact on Victorian society.

Eventually society has come to accept many scientific theories originally perceived as alien to its traditions and values. There are other issues, however, that also contribute to the lack of widespread public acceptance of social and behavioral research outputs. One of these is the redistributive character of much of the applied work of social science in the policy system. That is, decisions coming out of the work of social sciences—new approaches to a welfare program, new approaches to a tax system, new housing policies—have a tendency to benefit some elements in the society while depriving others. Even when the validity of a policy proposal is conceded, its im-

---

[12]Dean Schooler, Jr., *Science, Scientists, and Public Policy* (New York: The Free Press, 1971), p. 86.

plementation is not assured if those who are deprived are the socially and politically advantaged and powerful.

The social scientist is also confronted with the widespread belief among individuals in governmental circles and the society at large that social science has not been able to provide us with any solutions to problems. In fact, there is a point of view that social science is not science at all, and even when findings are buttressed by strong statistical validity, doubts persist. Physicians can bury their mistakes, but the fiasco surrounding the prediction of Thomas Dewey's presidential election still haunts students of electoral politics. Witness the public statements made by political candidates disputing the validity of findings in the area of electoral behavior and the forecasting of elections. If the public at large had full confidence in such findings, no political leader would dare dispute them.

An unfortunate aspect of the lack of confidence is that it has a kernel of truth. Much of the social planning and social policy generated in the United States in the 1930–1960 era resulted from interaction between public officials and social scientists. Many of these programs and policies were failures in achieving their ends or have continued to exist despite their obsolescence. In both cases, there is a great tendency to blame the social scientists for lack of solutions to social problems.

Zones of Conflict: The Internal Environment

Several of the exogenous factors have been enumerated with which the social scientist must cope if he desires to be more than a describer of society and its institutions. His role is further complicated by the nature and style of the social science disciplines, their lack of consensus about goals and methods, and constraints imposed by the human dimensions of social science research.

When a social scientist becomes involved in an area of research, it is usually not at the request of a client seeking a solution to a particular problem. More often, it is because the social scientist himself has become involved with a problem that is of intrinsic interest to him as a researcher, without any consideration of its social policy payoff.

Although stylistic changes are beginning to occur in the direction of team research, social and behavioral science research styles have tended to parallel the individualistic character of scholarship in the humanities. This means that the individual scholar expects and is expected to perform the myriad of tasks necessary for meaningful research. This concept is inculcated into the embryonic social and behavioral scientists during the graduate school socialization. In addition, the departmental reward structure has tended to recognize singular achievement but to downgrade "teamsmanship." Just as universities and their political allies must not fixate on the needs of a bygone era, social and behavioral science departments must not remain rigid in their standards. The knowledge explosion has made it impossible for very many of us to be Leonardo da Vincis or Thomas Jeffersons.

The fixation on individualism in scholarship has a tendency to fan the problem within and between social sciences of a lack of commonality in research goals and methods. Economists, sociologists, psychologists, and political scientists dealing with similar phenomena frequently "talk past each other." Yet each is a critical participant if social problem solving is to be based on the findings of the social sciences.

Consumers of social science research should not be misled into thinking that the millenium will arrive if only social scientists will change their habits and learn to work together in groups across disciplinary lines. Under the best working conditions the intellectual problems of the social and behavioral sciences are far more difficult than those of their science colleagues. The complexities of the disciplines, the numbers of variables that must be accounted for, and the limitations in methodology restrict the utility of any research findings in the social sciences. Furthermore, much of the "science" of the social sciences is screened in public; there is no laboratory shield to conceal mistakes. The net effect is a cloud of doubt around the findings.

Other internal difficulties plague the social sciences because of their subject matter. All scientific inquiry impinges upon human values, but it is most apparent and has greatest impact in the activity of social sciences. Recent rumblings among younger elements within the various social science disciplines have strongly suggested a conviction among them that leaders of their disciplines have encouraged

methodologies designed to coincide with their ideological commitment to the status quo. (Ironically, during the McCarthy period,
some of the very same leaders were accused of fomenting revolutionary change.) The issue, of course, is not who is right or wrong, but
the conviction by professionals within the social sciences that some
of their most distinguished colleagues are less scientific and more
political than they had said they were.

As this discussion suggests, the dissensual character of the social
sciences has consequences inside of academe as well as in the larger
polity. The current research of psychologists Arthur Jensen and
Richard Herrnstein on race, heredity, and intellectual capacity is
illustrative. The research itself might or might not make a contribution, but the researchers have been accused of racial prejudice. As
a result, their findings are tainted in the eyes of many of their associates.

Because the social and behavioral sciences deal directly with human beings, the investigation of problems places numerous constraints upon the social scientist. He cannot use a human subject in
the same way that an object of inanimate origin can be used, nor can
he expect the constancy that prevails with inorganic substances.
Issues of privacy are also at stake. Even if they must lose valuable
data in the process, most social scientists support the recommendations made by a panel established by the Office of Science and Technology:

1. Participation in behavioral investigations should be voluntary
and based on informed consent to the extent that this is consistent
with the objectives of the research.

2. It is fully consistent with the protection of privacy that, in the
absence of full information, consent be based on trust in the qualified
investigator and the integrity of the institution under whose auspices
the research is conducted.

3. The preservation of confidentiality, once consent has been obtained or institutional justification for the research received, is the
responsibility of the investigator.[13]

[13]National Academy of Sciences and Social Science Research Council, *The Behavioral and
Social Sciences,* p. 130.

Social Sciences in a Land-Grant Setting

Much of the needed input of social science research to social problem solving will be conducted in land-grant institutions. Although these universities are committed to applied research, they must undertake such activity without compromising their commitments to the pursuit of truth and the creation of knowledge.

Specifically, the university research unit is not an advocate for its clients. It may provide information, research, and advice, but it must avoid direct advocacy. In the public policy sphere this is regarded as the province of the private consulting firm. Peter Rossi has pointed out that the integrity of the university's research has generally been supported in courts of law where testimony from university researchers has been given credibility because of their non-conflict of interest.[14] The line of demarcation, however, between information, research, and advice on the one hand and advocacy on the other is quite fuzzy. During the student unrest of the late 1960s and early 1970s, charges were made that universities were the tools of the establishment and, therefore, advocates for existing governmental policy. In fact, university research units are likely to undertake projects partly defined by clients, and clients who are regarded as "legitimate" are usually also associated with well-established organizations—if not actually part of the "establishment" itself.

A second constraint on the role of the social science units is that, while university research in the social and behavioral sciences may suggest the appropriateness of policy change, the university itself is not a change agent designed to create a particular sort of political and social system. University organizations in the social and behavioral sciences are equipped to train individuals to be change agents, whether this means city managers, extension workers in the agricultural area, or social workers, but the university officialdom and researchers do not go out as agents themselves to operate cities, to provide social work facilities, or to advocate a rearrangement of social institutions on their own.

[14]Peter Rossi, "Researchers, Scholars, and Policy Makers: The Politics of Large Scale Research," *Daedalus* 93 (Fall, 1964): 1142–1161.

In most instances clients and social science research center officials have a similar understanding of the appropriate limits of the activity of such units. However, sometimes they suffer from a time lag in knowledge of developments in the social science disciplines and in the benefits of social science research. For example, references have been made to the long-standing relationship between local government officials and institutes with a political science and/or public administration orientation. Initially, this arrangement proved satisfactory to both parties. Students of municipal administration were concerned with the formal arrangements under which local affairs were conducted, especially the administration of services and ways in which these services might be provided more efficiently.[15] The consumers—municipal authorities—depended on these units for consultation and the recruitment of young professionals.

Gradually, a shift in emphasis has occurred as part of the expanding methodology of political science. "Attention moved from the administration of services to the management of conflict, from how government works to 'who governs,' " and from the formal and legal arrangements to the informal and extralegal distribution of influence.[16] Some public officials have either failed to recognize or refused to accept the new look in political science and public administration and have expected the same working relationship as existed fifty years ago. University training programs and research are eventually likely to have their impact on public agencies but only through the infusion of new outlooks in public service as a result of employee turnover and the absorption of the findings of research.

In some instances segments of the society are aware of a need for help from the social sciences without being able to articulate fully the nature of the need. There is currently a clamor from all over the society for social and behavioral science involvement in numerous applied problem areas. Perhaps the best illustration of this is in the area of environmental policy. Recent interviews by one of the authors with state and local officials in environmental protection agen-

[15]James Q. Wilson (ed.), *City Politics and Public Policy* (New York: John Wiley & Sons, 1968), p. 1.
[16]Ibid.

cies demonstrated their great desire for social science research. A number of them stated that they had adequate research materials on the technical side but that they lacked the social science data necessary to carry out needed environmental changes. One official remarked, "We know how to do away with coal-burning stoves in our city, but we do not know the attitudes of residents toward the problem." The official involved recognized that it is one thing to have technical knowledge and even to obtain authority to compel change in habits of the use of energy, but it is quite another to obtain societal support for social policies. In this case, the official not only understood that a technical change would improve the environment but also recognized that the change itself had to be acceptable to the public. He correctly saw this as a problem about which advice could only come from social science knowledge, but he was not clear about what the advice might look like. More likely than not, he assumes an ability of the social sciences to deliver a product far more easily and precisely than the state of the social sciences will actually permit.

Political scientists, economists, sociologists, and psychologists receive inquiries almost daily from consumers and individuals in the physical and life sciences regarding ways in which the social and behavioral scientists can help solve a vast array of problems in the environmental field. Many scientists and engineers assume that, since they have solved the technical problems, social scientists have only to tell them how to bring these problems to the attention of the populace and the problem will readily be eliminated. This is not true: no social science theory or its application can solve social problems; it can *only* provide a basis for policy makers to solve these problems.

Power and allocation of resources are decisions of the polity. Social science methodology is not so well developed that it can provide easy answers in all instances. And, as illustrated by the coal-burning example, even where a social science methodology does provide an answer, in a democratic society, or one that calls itself a democratic society, the ability to deliver is not so easily granted. Very often what is sought of the social and behavioral sciences is not basic knowledge, clarification of the issues, or identification of the factors, but a mechanism for achieving fulfillment of technical policy change. In effect, the social scientist is asked to help gain public support for a change. This, of course, misconstrues his appropriate role as he has defined it.

In the past, some of the technical people have not only failed to recognize the limits of the role of the social sciences, they have also failed to understand the social science components of the problem on which they were working. This has been changing in the past decade. Highway building is a prime example of this phenomenon. Engineers have begun to realize what was apparent to social scientists many years ago: alterations in land use can have far-reaching social consequences. Even a simple change such as designating a street one-way can transform the social and economic structure of a neighborhood. Unfortunately, even now millions of dollars are earmarked for road improvement and expansion and only a pittance is allocated to solve the attendant social consequences.

Slowly and perceptibly, change has occurred in funding social sciences. The award of grants to a number of land-grant universities in the environmental field and other problem areas with social dimensions has in recent years required that some of the funds be specifically earmarked for activities in the social and behavioral sciences. Opportunities are available, and therefore the responsibility is shifting to the social scientists to demonstrate their commitment to participate in the solution of social problems.

Need for New Approaches

If the social and behavioral sciences in universities are going to contribute to the solution of social problems in the 1970s and 1980s, a number of changes in style and organization will be necessary. These include organizational innovations, changes in the reward system, and appropriate funding arrangements.

As stated earlier, social and behavioral science research, in style and organization, has tended to resemble the humanities rather than the basic or applied sciences. If a contribution is to be made to the solution of social problems, more team research must take the place of individual research.

An obvious requirement for effective applied social science is that it become multidisciplinary. In theory, this is often the rationale advanced for the creation of research institutes and centers, but in practice few organized research units can legitimately claim to have achieved this goal.[17] The failure may in part be due to the wrong emphasis. Samuel Klausner has put it succinctly with regard to environmental problems:

> At this state in the development of socio-environmental studies, each discipline is in baby shoes and needs initial independence to work out the logical conclusion of its frame of reference with respect to this field. Creative interaction can follow later. Before there can be interdisciplinary knowledge, there must be disciplinary knowledge.[18]

One model that should be encouraged and that may speed the process of moving from disciplinary to multidisciplinary activity is illustrated in the operation of two kinds of research centers—those studying geographical regions of the world and those studying policy fields. In the former, scholars from the languages, history, social and behavioral sciences interact in area study programs. In the latter, as exemplified by transportation institutes, scholars from engineering, physical and life sciences and social and behavioral sciences cooperate.

In the fulfillment of their tasks, these units provide a setting where graduate students being trained in a particular discipline have an opportunity to exchange ideas with faculty and students from diverse disciplines. Such arrangements do not diminish the disciplinary focus but encourage collaborative working relationships.[19] The multidisciplinary character of the output stems from solid training of young scholars in an established discipline at the same time that they are learning to interact with peers in other areas working on similar problems.

The inevitable development of multidisciplinary research centers presents opportunities and problems. Traditionally, the disciplinary departments and programs have served as the base for rewards and

[17]Ikenberry and Friedman, pp. 44–48.

[18]Samuel Z. Klausner, *On Man in His Environment* (San Francisco: Jossey-Bass, 1971), p. 176.

[19]This point of view has been expressly stated by Thomas Larson, director, Transportation Institute, The Pennsylvania State University.

sanctions. So long as multidisciplinary work remains in its infancy, a continued disciplinary predominance is critical for purposes of quality control. At the current stage of our knowledge it would be unwise for a civil engineer to make primary judgments about the work of sociologists. However, if there is to be a major thrust in the social sciences in dealing with social problems, there must be some readjustment of the traditional criteria of evaluation. In the past, highest value has been placed on theoretical work that has broken new ground in basic research. In the future, the reward system must be altered so that equal attention is paid to applications of theory that have a payoff in terms of contributing to the solution of social problems. This shift will be accepted reluctantly, in part, because of the inherent conservatism of the academic community, but also because in the past much of the applied social science work has made only a meager contribution.

Some funding agencies have shown increased interest in recent years in the social sciences. Nevertheless, resources remain scarce. If these resources are to be used wisely, the logical approach to their distribution is to award resources regionally on the basis of two criteria: (1) emphasis upon institutions with adequate staff and facilities and (2) location near the source of the problem. If the granting agency is interested in demographic studies, it is essential that the funding go to a relatively small number of institutions; otherwise, the resources will be inadequate to achieve results. Wisdom dictates that the money be placed where scholars of distinction and promise within the field of study are located and where facilities and commitments are adequate to achieve results. The second part of the statement implies that it would be foolhardy, other things being equal, to place an urban study center in a rural state.

Although social scientists are not likely in the near future to command the prestige or research support accorded to physical scientists, there are signs of recognition of the contribution to be made by social scientists in the solution of societal problems. In recent years respected scholars such as Daniel Moynihan and Henry Kissinger have exerted considerable influence in the political arena, applying their social science knowledge to the solution of major domestic and international policy questions. While their influence may be partly attributable to their style, some of their success is related to an increased acceptance of the work of social and behavioral scientists. There appears to be an increasing number of individuals, both in the federal establishment and in our states, who have an understanding of the complexities of the social sciences and of our social problems. They recognize the limits of the research findings but are willing to commit funds and resources to social scientists in universities because this may be the only hope of alleviating distressing problems facing society. They are not naive about what social science can do, and they are prepared to be patient with the tortuous process that will be necessary to achieve the kinds of results in social sciences that have been attained in engineering, the physical sciences, and the life sciences.

A final gentle reminder to social science colleagues. Modesty behooves us to make no claims beyond what we can accomplish. Social science has often been snubbed in the past because of a lack of confidence by the larger society in what social scientists can deliver. Some of this lack of confidence is derived from advice and claims by social scientists that have proved faulty. It is reasonable for social scientists in the 1970s to say that the major problems of the day rest in the social and behavioral science areas. It is not reasonable to say, "Trust us and all will be well with the world."

Chapter 9

THE LAND-GRANT UNIVERSITY
AND ENVIRONMENTAL AFFAIRS

RICHARD D. SCHEIN

COLLEGES and universities are not quickly responsive in adapting their faculties and programs to concerns of society. Theoretical scholars often foresee problems long before society feels or comprehends them (e.g., the world population crisis), but after societal perception occurs an additional time lag occurs before university programs reflect society's concern. University scholars long ago predicted the environmental crisis our society now perceives. Now colleges and universities are in the second lag period, struggling to ascertain appropriate responses.

Do colleges and universities have a special role in society in regard to the environment and, particularly, do land-grant universities have a distinctive role? I believe so, as do many in such schools.

The public multiversities and, particularly, the complex land-grant universities, evolved in interdependence with society and its problems. They now have an immense potential to apply themselves to society's needs in the amelioration of man's impact on the natural and social environment. Land-grant universities were initiated with the idea of giving special educational service to certain components of American society and they have extended themselves into almost every area of that society.

At the moment, each land-grant university is grappling with the problem of ascertaining its role in what society perceives as a new "environmental crisis." The institutions feel compelled to mobilize their capabilities to specific ends, but are faced with difficult problems. Universities are not institutions meant to deal with crises or to operate with a crisis mentality. Mobilization of the universities' capabilities and programs in environmental areas is extremely difficult. Environmental problems so overreach the boundaries of standard disciplines, and so transcend the existing internal organization of land-grant universities, that new university operations philosophies, policies, organizations, and mechanisms will be needed to bring about efficient and intelligent activities.

Each land-grant university must identify, define, and delineate its specific ends or goals. It must clearly determine the role of the university in the environmental crisis while not allowing itself to be diverted from well-developed, justified, and long-standing goals in resident education, research, and public service. Having defined its goals, each university must develop strategies of goal accomplishment.

Perspectives

Despite recent popular interest, the environmental crisis is not new. Conservationists, naturalists, environmentalists, and scientists, many of them in land-grant universities, have been trying to tell us for decades that our industrial society was set on a course which would sooner or later irreparably damage the ecosystem and that our own activities would become the major limiting factor in the future welfare of our society. Ecology is not a new word. It has been a branch of biological science for one hundred years. Recent popular concern is confused about this, and that confusion is reflected in the university as students, faculty, and administrators alike attempt to carry their concern for environmental and societal well-being into university programs with only partial understanding of the complexity of the problems involved. Too often the assumption is made that since the crisis is new, the problems must be new and therefore the university has not been and is not now involved in appropriate programs. Such is not really the case.

The word ecology, coined almost exactly one hundred years ago, is derived from the Greek term having to do with the study of the house or the household. In biology, ecology deals with the interrelationships between living organisms and their environment; significantly, the environment is seen as having two interrelated components—the living environment and the physical environment. This branch of science is based on the understanding that these interrelationships are complex and in the aggregate form an obligate system of energy transfer and utilization upon which all levels of life, including man, depend. Ecologists are engaged in determining the nature and dimensions of these mechanisms and the impact of man's manipulations and disturbances of the ecosystem on the total life-support system. A significant part of the development of the science of ecology has taken place in land-grant universities in past decades.

We might briefly point out that the word economy has a similar base and has to do with the management of the house or household. The idea of household is extended to include various aggregates and subsets of society. We have developed ways of managing the economy to serve certain stated needs or wishes of society or components thereof.

Persons who today express deep concern for the ecology may be belying the layman's lack of understanding of the nature of the problem. Society's concern is more akin to husbandry, to the wise and thrifty management of the household. More and more people perceive the household as the whole surface of the globe, the biosphere, which, together with the thin layer of air and the thin layer of soil, contains those complex and obligate interactions of living things and their environment which we call the ecosystem. Good husbandry is often based on strong, albeit intuitive, understanding. Good husbandry of the biosphere must somehow combine the scientific understanding of the interrelationships (ecology) and the planning and management of human affairs.

Perhaps this concern for husbandry can be useful to us in considering the land-grant university's role in environmental affairs. If the husbandman is one who manages with concern, with understanding, with economy, and with frugality, then it is husbandry which is wanting in our industrial, technological society. Environmental husbandry will come with greater understanding within society of the complexities of ecology, economics, social and behavioral systems, and the whole range of technologies. These are all areas where the land-grant university has considerable knowledge and is giving society better tools, both of which are necessary to the practice of good husbandry.

Only by accepting responsibility as husbandman of the earth can mankind in the long run really accomplish anything for the human condition. An environmental ethic or attitude, if one can be achieved, will be worldwide in concern and application, and hyperopic in outlook.

All colleges and universities, because of their responsibility to educate a wiser citizenry of the future, have an immense role in developing the national attitude within which will be framed national policies and actions aimed at ecosystem preservation. But land-grant universities have a unique capability of focusing a wider spectrum of the necessary disciplines on specific or general environmental problems. This is largely due to these universities' origin and history. Each was founded for the purpose of giving instruction in agriculture, and each soon developed agricultural research and public education capability. In addition, most contained faculties of engineering from the very beginning and so have had a strong role in the development of American technology and technologists. Further, many, because of the importance of mineral resources in their states, from the earliest days have had faculties whose specialties involved the earth's crust and its utilization. And then, in the last few decades of their existence, land-grant universities have increased their competence in the various social sciences and the applications of these to society. Few other universities have on a single campus experts in all of these fields.

In ecological terms agriculture is the manipulation of the ecosystem, the management of energy flow in that system to maximize outflow in forms usable by man, principally food and fiber. A great deal of ecological insight is needed to produce agricultural advances. And so faculties of agriculture have the potential of great ecological orientation. Agriculturalists have not seen themselves this way until recently, agriculture having been man-centered and not ecosystem oriented. Now that agriculturalists are beginning to view their own activities in terms of the long-term health of the ecosystem, they have a large potential to assist in making tremendous changes in our attitudes and methods of exploitation which will be necessary if human life is to endure with the quality to which we aspire.

Land-grant universities are usually rich in technological skills, and these faculties are now more willing to admit the short-sightedness of their previous views. Engineers know that the systems, processes, and hardware they produce have long-term, long-distance effects on the ecosystem which formerly were not considered. Academic engineers are developing an environmental attitude more in keeping with the maintenance of a healthy life support system than with the exploitation of it.

Those land-grant colleges with strong faculties in the earth sciences have the opportunity to teach about the earth's crust and the atmosphere, their use and preservation. They have played and will now play an even more important role in the environmental education of students in many fields. These three areas, agriculture, engineering, and earth and mineral sciences, included as they are in land-grant universities, together form a substantive base of environmental capability seldom found so aggregated in other universities. This unique combination and base suggests that the land-grant university has a special function in responding to society's environmental concerns.

But the problems are not as simple as many would make them out. The simple application of technology will not cause the environmental crisis to go away. Our society has some seemingly opposing goals. On the one hand is our intensive quest for comfort, which we euphemize as the standard of living or quality of life (and these are not the same things). In earlier days America showed great success—actual improvement in the standard of living—and made these improvements broadly available. Improvements in housing, health, sanitation, etc., were extended deeply and quickly into our society. In the last quarter-century, however, we have perhaps been more concerned with increasing comfort than standard of living. An increasing proportion of industrial output may provide additional convenience to our broadly affluent society without giving sufficient attention to true standard of living increases to some of the forgotten elements, particularly the rural and urban poor.

Attitudes and behavior in regard to creature comfort have created a collision course of environmental concerns on one hand and comfort concerns on the other.

Each environmental problem can be sectored into areas which

require expert insight and understanding on the part of physical, biological, engineering or social and behavioral scientists. Attention here is drawn to the last sector. No environmental problem is without important components based on attitudes, political realities, economics, traditions, distribution of people, etc. No environmental problem, created as it is by man's activities and his quest for comfort, can be solved without an intense understanding of the social forces which generated the problem, which sustain it, and which must be modified if the problem is to be ameliorated. Thus, not only do environmental problems in their consideration demand the attention of the physical, biological, and engineering sciences, but the attention of the social and behavioral sciences as well. Environmental solutions will be more than just technological solutions. There is, therefore, an important and new role of the social and behavioral sciences in environmental affairs. Not until we understand the social, behavioral, and economic obstacles to proper use of resources can we hope that public understanding will bring about national husbandry.

As the old land-grant colleges have become the land-grant universities, they have developed competent faculties in the social and behavioral sciences. Land-grant universities that have faculties in the four areas mentioned earlier have long been effective in environmental matters and today, because of the recent changes in perceptions, must be ready to make greater contributions to ensure a better society. Add to these various other faculties, one or more of which various land-grant schools have, in the humanities, design fields, the arts, medicine, law, business administration, and education, and one can view the land-grant university as an institution of unique capabilities in regard to environmental problems. It is perhaps the only institution of our society which possesses expertise in most, if not all, of the areas critical to the understanding and solution of environmental problems.

Land-grant universities are like a sensitive, extremely complicated, multi-purpose electronic instrument needing only appropriate fine tuning and focusing to bring out superior performance. How do we put this machine to work on environmental problems? It helps in going after this answer to first explore another question: What is the appropriate role of the university in environmental affairs?

The Role of the University in the Environmental Crisis

Even if persons in land-grant universities were to agree with the above conclusion, they still have the problem of determining the proper role of the university. To do that, it is necessary to give consideration to the long-term goals of the university in environmental affairs and then to proceed to determine what changes in posture, structure, and operations might be needed to fit the university for its task.

The new environmental consciousness seems to have come across the land at about the times of Earth Day in 1970 and the Santa Barbara oil spill. That was also a time when universities across the land closed their doors early in the spring semester or offered special programs in the face of student and (often) faculty demands for relevancy and action in regard to the nation's Southeast Asian and domestic affairs, including the environment. University after university departed from its traditional calendar and tasks and accommodated in ways that most students and faculty eventually deemed inappropriate. But in the residuum, there remained a feeling that the university should enter the environmental battleground, that it should take positions and become a party to environmental controversies. Happily, American universities disdained to do this; and, now, after five years of relative quiet on the campuses, we can once more face our tasks from a proper distance and with a proper perspective.

Universities have not been and should not be action agencies in the sense that they become party to internecine controversies in society. Universities are committed to the organization and transfer of man's knowledge about himself, his activities and skills, and about the natural world. The same scholars who are engaged in these tasks tend to involve themselves in research, in probing the unknown, and thus add further knowledge and understanding that must be organized and transferred to succeeding generations.

Scholarship, in its finest sense, is as abstract as man can make it. The task of the scholar is to determine the truth and expose it to society for its assimilation and use. It is from this root that the ivory tower aspect of universities and traditional scholarship stems. That necessary detachment of the scholar which causes him to expound the truth whatever its consequences, also causes him to be impugned by some who say he is so detached from society he has no concept of the realities of life. Land-grant universities have traditionally taken a middle course in this controversy and from the outset have said that they would indeed teach, do research, and publish in highly relevant areas of concern where it might be expected to see rapid application to needs of society. The Wisconsin Idea of over sixty years ago was a plan to use the scholars of the land-grant university in the service of state government. By tradition, then, land-grant universities do not eschew practical work but nonetheless maintain certain other traditions of pure scholarship. A large proportion of research is done by students pursuing graduate degrees, and there is general agreement that university research programs should be such as to generate appropriate graduate degree research theses. Appropriate in this case means adherence to standards of scholarship defined by the graduate faculty of the university—which definition does not include crusading on street corners or lobbying in legislatures. Universities' long-term effects are not to be had from those courses.

The universities' environmental role is one of preparing for the future—carrying out programs of education, research, and public service so as to continually prepare a citizenry and a society for wiser environmental decisions and actions. In each of these areas we must attempt to predict what will be needed and discern which functions are properly the universities' and which are more appropriately the province of other areas of society.

Toward the Future

In *The Uses of the University* Clark Kerr left us with the intuitive conviction that somehow the modern multiversity muddles through and renders a great service to society. This may be a reflection of the biological principle that in diversity there is strength. Generally, land-grant universities are organized in a rather nineteenth-century and encyclopedic manner, with each discipline in its place (a department). Faculties and their activities are collected in these departments and then further collected in colleges or schools. Education and research responsibilities may be segmented into over a hundred units within the larger land-grant universities. But, as said earlier, environmental problems, because of their size and complexity, over-reach these administrative and disciplinary boundaries. There appears to be little chance that whole universities can be redesigned for simplicity; indeed, such redesign is arguably not even desirable. But large universities, like all large institutions, have disintegrated (in the literal meaning of that word). While great cost and effort have been devoted to developing techniques of vertical communication, horizontal communication has suffered badly. There is usually little mutual concern and understanding between faculties in the humanities and social sciences on the one hand and the sciences and technologies on the other. We are divided into colleges and departments, into professional schools and academic ones, so laced in by disciplinary self-concerns and the faculty reward structure that it is almost impossible to agree on what should be taught by whom and how to make the program go. We are good in specialist education and research. But if we are to gain the benefits of cooperation among our faculties and other resources, we are going to have to develop new organizations and management schemes to attract the attention of the different faculties and to bring them together to work mutually in environmental problem areas, including undergraduate and graduate education.

If environmental problems overreach responsibilities of individual departments and even colleges, then the organizations and management schemes must work at a level above these. But, because university faculties are wary of pyramiding administrative structures, these organizations must not become super-colleges. They must have the administrative backing necessary to encourage people from different departments and different colleges to work cooperatively, but they must do this without threatening the rights and privileges which departments and colleges, and department heads and collegiate deans, see as theirs.

The pattern for this has been set in the last fifteen years as land-grant universities have established multidisciplinary research institutes. At Penn State during this decade and a half, procedures have evolved which acknowledge these problems. Intercollege research institutes are generally overseen at the vice presidential level within the university. They are not allowed to become para-academic operations in competition with existing units and their responsibilities.

From that experience comes my recommendation concerning the organization of the university for attention to environmental affairs. Because environmental problems transcend our structure both horizontally and vertically, there should be an office in the university at such a level that it can encourage and bring about cooperation among different colleges and, indeed, among the units responsible for education, research, and public education. Whether or not this office has significant administrative weight and is built directly into the hierarchy, or whether it is off-line serving a staff function for the senior academic officer of the university, is a problem to be solved at each school. In Penn State's case the Office of Environmental Quality Programs is a unit of the provost's office and serves in a staff rather than a line function. In his various activities, the director of the office acts as a second to one of the vice presidents. When bringing about intercollege cooperation for undergraduate education, he acts for the vice president for undergraduate studies. Similarly, for research and for continuing education, he acts for and with the responsible vice president. Environmental intercollege research is encouraged and fostered through the vice president for research in the intercollege research institutes and centers which are organized through his office. The director of Environmental Quality Programs is in close communication with the directors of the institutes and centers, sometimes attempting to bring about a broadening or focusing of their programs and at other times helping the directors to achieve goals they and their staffs have perceived.

Not all universities have rationalized the problem in this way. Some have established intercollege environmental research or education institutes which do not have the prerogative to provide services in all functions of the university. In some cases divisions which are in reality multidisciplinary departments, hovering somewhere in the hierarchy between departments and colleges, are being tried.

In any of these cases the complex multiversity will have to overcome the same problems we have seen destroy other transcendent programs in one place or another, such as those in "communications" or "international understanding." Single-discipline departments do not at first encourage faculty members to participate in such programs and hesitate to recruit for such peripheral programs. When salary and tenure considerations arise, departments initally tend to negatively judge participating faculty. When supra-departmental units are erected, they must attract associated faculty from the departments. Failing in this, they tend to recruit their own, most of whom are judged less than superb by the departments. There is a risk of expensive redundancy in allocating jealously sought-after faculty development funds for faculty of lesser competence. Departments hesitate to cooperate with new units because in academic fiscal affairs more mouths to feed often means only less to eat for all.

Such impending problems must be overcome if large universities are to be fully productive in environmental affairs. I believe they can be overcome if the universities will develop flexible organizations and management schemes at an operational level above that of the colleges. Beyond that I cannot go, feeling strongly that local idiosyncrasy and the academic infra-structure must dictate the specific approach at individual universities.

The Benefits

With this approach I see the following benefits. Departments will remain strong and will be able to offer those classic environmental majors which we have developed over the years, producing for society the specialists-in-depth who will be needed to tackle our problems. Further, however, the scheme I propose provides a way for the university in its totality to constantly search for and develop new ways to bring together its competence in diverse areas—forging new undergraduate and graduate programs and more complex, highly interrelated, and socially responsible research programs. And, corollary with this, the university will be able to develop a program of continuing education which will more adequately serve the environmental education needs of its constituency.

From these all-university activities will flow greater public understanding of the breadth and complexity of environmental problems.

And, as environmental education becomes more firmly established in the public schools, we will play a complementary role in the development of that new environmental attitude or ethic which is necessary if our nation, and the world, is to survive the environmental crisis it is inflicting on itself.

Chapter 10

LAND-GRANT UNIVERSITIES
AND THE BLACK PRESENCE

SAMUEL D. PROCTOR

ABRAHAM Lincoln's Emancipation Proclamation, issued September 22, 1862, required that states holding slaves should free them on January 1, 1863.

Higher education was experiencing an emancipation at about the same time. Jonathan Baldwin Turner's agitation for agricultural colleges established with federal funds had culminated in the land-grant legislation fostered in 1856 by Justin I. Morrill of Vermont. The Morrill Act, signed by Lincoln in 1862, after having been vetoed by President Buchanan in 1859, stipulated that income from public lands given to the states was to finance agricultural and mechanical colleges.[1]

However, many states did not admit blacks to these new institutions. (This exclusion was not *de jure* but a *de facto* reflection of the times.) Populism and the new equalitarianism, both of which reacted against classical education, stopped short of encompassing the needs of the new black citizen. In 1890, the Morrill Act was revised to provide paltry sums for black schools, but the major benefits of land-grant college growth bypassed blacks.[2] Thus, in the mid-nineteenth century, the country missed a great opportunity when it allowed the land-grant institutions to exclude blacks and Indians.[3] Today, a century later, attempts are being made to correct this error after its effects have accumulated for a hundred years.

In the West, the reverence for learning, the universal invitation to

[1]August Meier, *Negro Thought in America 1880–1915* (Ann Arbor: University of Michigan Press, 1963), Chapter VI, "Rise of Industrial Education in Negro Schools," p. 87.

[2]John S. Brubacher and Willis Rudy, *Higher Education in Transition* (New York: Harper & Row, 1968), p. 79.

[3]Christopher Jencks and David Riesman, *The Academic Revolution* (New York: Doubleday, 1969), p. 422.

engage in inquiry and search for the truth, somehow never reached beyond those who were already socially and economically privileged. This has been one of the ironies of the ages—that men with emancipated minds never allowed those whom they deemed to be inferior a chance to prove themselves otherwise. The *a priori* assumption that blacks and Indians were a subspecies eventually bore a resemblance to the truth due to limited opportunities.

This denial of opportunity to blacks by the land-grant schools in the 1860s and 1870s was consistent with the attitudes of the majority community toward blacks at the time. Some of the most pathetic conditions accompanied the slow movement of blacks from slavery to a new status of something less than real freedom. With no money, no names, no cultural legacy of their own, distant from their African roots and barely transplanted into a totally Anglo-Saxon ethos, the blacks were pitifully orphaned in this land of opportunity.

Blacks became the object of political vengeance, and the literary and fine arts community considered them fair game for the most insulting and demeaning humor, creating a vicious stereotype that fed racial prejudice for a century. It is, therefore, little wonder that educators, never known for iconoclastic activity, allowed themselves to become party to the scheme that denied new black citizens a right to the training offered by the agricultural, industrial, and mechanical colleges.

Not only were blacks barred from these institutions of public higher education, but by 1878 there had begun a deliberate attempt to define the blacks as inferior and deny them the citizenship that the Constitution had guaranteed them through the Thirteenth, Fourteenth, and Fifteenth Amendments. When the troops were taken out of the South under President Hayes, a rampage of vengeance and hatred was released on blacks that virtually cancelled out all of their gains from the preceding decade.

The churches were the only hope the blacks had. The Episcopalians, Baptists, Methodists, Presbyterians and Congregationalists sent missionaries into the South to work with blacks in building institutions of higher education.[4] With the exception of Hampton Institute

[4]Brubacher and Rudy, *Higher Education in Transition,* pp. 77–78.

and Tuskegee, these colleges began sending out preachers and teachers, trained in the classics.[5] The need of the blacks for the agricultural, mechanical, and industrial training that government funded land-grant colleges provided was denied to them.

Every state had several fledgling colleges when the Morrill Act in 1890 provided funds to establish more black schools for agriculture and industrial arts. Unfortunately, these funds were a mockery, a mere gesture.[6] Black people were so politically impotent by 1890— witness Booker T. Washington's 1895 Atlanta speech and the 1896 Pleasy vs. Ferguson decision—that they had to accept these poor offerings. This was the time when racial segregation laws were being passed in torrents and the blacks had to endure a flood of anti-black political behavior.

The escape was the black church and its ally, the liberal arts campus with its emphasis upon religion and human dignity. Thus, the entire period was not lost, despite the exclusionary land-grant movement. Blacks, nestled in the psychological comfort of their own schools, nurtured by their own intellectuals like DuBois and, encouraged by their thundering orators like Frederick Douglass, somehow managed to survive and to see hope grow.

Blacks on the Move since 1960

The relatively sudden increase in black enrollment in higher education will prove to be the most effective instrument of change that blacks have seen since the 1954 Brown decision. Higher education is the swiftest and most trustworthy method of upward social mobility. Although labor unions can provide quick mobility for masses of people, higher education is a more effective vehicle for blacks. One can be born and reared in squalor, but if he finishes high school and sweats through an A.B. degree, then everything changes for him and his progeny. He makes a clean break with his past, economically and socially.

All of America's ethnic minorities have had this history; in one

[5]Ibid.
[6]Ibid., p. 79.

generation they trade in their push-carts for degrees, their "mom and pop" stores for law shingles, their hack licenses for the M.D. Even though they leave a lot of their relatives behind, they find the ladder; hard work is rewarding and there is always room at the top.

The blacks who have succeeded have followed this route. Their numbers were small and they had to attend black schools; they built on poor, segregated secondary school preparation, and their opportunities after graduation were limited. But a small, educated professional black middle class did develop as a consequence of the opportunities for higher education in the early 1900s. Still, college was expensive and it required a self-identity that was lacking; it called for credentials that were out of reach for most and contacts that were missing. In other words, before World War II and the G.I. Bill, college was for very few fortunate blacks.

Of course, to say that higher education is a fast route out of poverty is not to applaud or even to accept a system that makes this necessary. The squalor and poverty from which one must extricate himself, leaving many masses behind him, are unpardonable failures of our economic system. We have grown too accustomed to having a large segment of the population bordering on extinction from economic oppression, bad housing, poor health care, deficient nutrition, and psychological despair. And among blacks that number is disproportionately high.

Because of this fact, it seems anomalous to urge a handful of blacks to seek college degrees; it appears too privatized and individualistic. However, it is a fact that change will require blacks to be conspicuous in the professions, in management, in research, in politics, in jurisprudence, and in the media. All of these jobs call for higher education. These are the levels at which policy is made, where racism and its effects will have to be dealt with before it is dealt with at the level of the masses. Blacks must be on one to one level with those who run the country's institutions.

Most blacks who come to higher education today come from the thoroughly separate society that developed during Reconstruction. Time has not permitted the development of a black social class that is really unfamiliar with poverty and the black ghetto subculture. Even most professional blacks today have parents who were domestics or farm hands; those from other roots are rare. The small black professional class stands in sharp contrast to the black masses whose lives are dismally bleak in the centers of the cities. Blacks are one generation from a condition close to slavery.

Consequently, the university experience has quickly created two classes in the black community. With no aristocracy of money or family tradition, the blacks can have only an aristocracy of education. Education, therefore, is no ordinary choice for blacks. It means freedom from squalor and poverty but alienation from family and other blacks. It means credentials with no ready acceptance in junior-level positions in business and few advancement possibilities in industry. In the craft unions, there is bold, racial discrimination. But, without college, movement is slow.

The campuses of the major land-grant universities have enrollments of 20,000 to 40,000, but blacks only number 5.9 percent of these students.[7] They are found in small clusters, here and there, leaning on each other for support, all but lost in a world they must enter but which has been and remains slow to welcome them.

Changing Complexion of the Student Body

The big year for the revision in policies toward blacks for many land-grant institutions was 1968. That spring, black students made their plea for more black students, more black faculty, more black-oriented courses, and greater concern for the black community on and off campus.

Let us consider first the matter of more black students. In 1968, blacks represented about 4 percent of the college-going population, one half of which was in black colleges.[8] Thus, in order to increase the number of blacks on major campuses, there had to be an increase of blacks in college altogether, and that increase, in proportion to their percentage of the population, would have to be 300 percent, at least. But, since half the total number of college blacks were in black colleges, the major campuses would have to reach a 500 to 600

[7] *The Chronicle of Higher Education,* October 4, 1971, p. 5.
[8] Ibid., p. 1.

percent increase before achieving their proportionate share of blacks. In other words, if Minnesota had 30 blacks out of 30,000, it would have to increase to 1,500 black students in order to reach 5 percent black enrollment.

Some land-grant institutions tried to reach such increases. They hired black recruiters and sent their black students to black high schools, community centers, and anti-poverty agencies. The result was that, by the time school opened in 1968, the numbers of black students had increased significantly on most campuses.[9] These new blacks landed on large campuses that were almost entirely white and discovered for the first time, outside of their ghettos, just how white the country was.

The schools were poorly prepared. They had no black staff to help students bridge the gap between the expectations of their communities and the expectations of a college geared for white middle-class students. In addition, the colleges had no black persons of visible standing on the campuses. Moreover, these students arrived at college when higher education was already under attack by bored, middle-class whites, the values of the society were in flux, and major black agitation for equality was in full force.

What could the schools do? Fail. And they did, one after another. Not only did the students find the general climate inhospitable but, in addition, they found overt racism, some malicious and some innocent. Administration, faculty, and students knew nothing about the black experience in America. They only wanted blacks to join up with their—the majority—culture and be measured by those norms. This implied the denial of a black student's own identity, rejection of his values, and the docile acceptance of a white definition of inferiority. Instead, black students demanded the reverse—black studies, black counselors, black living quarters, a funded program in black extracurricular activities, more black faculty and students, and a clean break on the part of the university with activities and movements, near and far, that promoted racism and oppressed Third World peoples.

[9] U. S. Department of Health, Education, and Welfare, *Digest of Educational Statistics,* 1970 Edition, p. 72.

This new population presented more than an ideological and programmatic challenge. Academically, they presented another challenge. They were bored; they did not care enough about graduation to endure the discipline and sacrifice that it took to overcome academic deficits, and the atmosphere did not provide the support and encouragement needed.

In order to succeed with larger black enrollments, the land-grant schools must do the following:

(a) Recruit black faculty and staff in numbers and volume approaching the proportion of blacks in the population.

(b) Distribute blacks up and down the entire staffing pattern, giving clear evidence of open and fair employment and an eagerness to correct previous abuses.

(c) Devise methods of determining the readiness of minority students to cope with the challenge of college and graduate study. This involves going beyond traditional testing programs that have failed to discover potentially excellent black students because they reveal more about one's past opportunity than about one's present potential.

(d) Expand the school's program, formal and informal, to include opportunities for black students to authenticate their own intellectual growth and to share in the knowledge and experience of the black world here and in Africa.

(e) Relate the research and extension activities of the university to the needs of the total population of the state including the urban blacks, Puerto Ricans, Chicanos, Indians, and poor whites. Somehow the notion that this public benefaction known as a university must serve all of the people has to be reinforced.

New Faculty for New Needs

The representation of blacks on land-grant faculties today is minuscule. Most institutions with a faculty of about 2,500 do not have more than 25 blacks: 1 percent or less.[10] This is one of America's

---

[10]Ibid., p. 81, Table 108.

most shameful statistics. The exclusion of black faculty reflects the indifference of land-grant universities toward the recruitment and training of promising young blacks.

Some schools have claimed that they have tried to find blacks, but unsuccessfully. Blacks, in turn, have alleged that the job offers to the best black scholars have been at low ranks, with low salary, and without tenure. Further, blacks feel that the schools have sought after a few prominent blacks, offering to pay top salaries for them, and then stopped recruiting: tokenism. Few schools have followed normal procedures for entering faculty: hiring young, promising teachers; putting them with strong, mature, senior faculty; and letting them grow.

Some universities added insult to injury by hiring unprepared blacks as an appeasement to militant students. The schools permitted segregated classes, for blacks only, and in the name of Black Studies allowed anything to be taught. This was a demeaning chapter in American higher education and, thankfully, it is rapidly ending. Today, Black Studies programs are staffed by some of the best-equipped persons, and the curriculum is well developed and represents a truly significant movement.

Apart from development of Black Studies, the land-grant schools face other challenges. The nation is beset with mounting urban problems that will require a specially trained manpower. The critical problem areas include:

(a) housing for the poor
(b) assistance programs to aid families with dependent children
(c) improvement of health care services
(d) assistance in the creation of alternative schooling for those unable to cope with public schools
(e) technical assistance, offered with sensitivity and real concern, to community-based organizations designed to meet needs identified by local groups.

The land-grant institutions have an obligation to recognize the stream that migrated from declining farms to the teeming center cities and to respond, as far as a university can, to their needs. But this requires new personnel. There must be persons in social work, counseling and guidance, government, child care and family life, community health, recreation, urban planning, and a dozen other areas, who know the cities, who care about the people there, who know the historical process of the decay of the cities, who are sensitive to the black experience, who know of the pervasive nature of racism. These persons do not normally find their way to a faculty: they have to be sought out by an administration dedicated to correcting past inequities and bringing the university to grips with minority problems.

Helping College Students to Succeed

After the campus learns how to admit another kind of student and develops a new thrust in programs, there is still the problem of making college meaningful enough to encourage these new students to succeed. The most common criticism heard about students who enter under special programs is that they get bored and attend class irregularly.

There is no substantial experience on which to base any conclusions, but some hypotheses seem to merit a try:

(a) There is a need for a transition program tailored to meet individual student needs.

(b) There is a need for intimate counseling during this transition.

(c) There should be a special emphasis on research and use of the library in the transition year.

(d) There should be some organized effort, on the part of students, and encouraged by the faculty, to engage in some type of community project, even if it is a small one and miles away.

(e) There should be courses that relate immediately to the experiences of the student and the world that he knows best.

Racial segregation has compelled blacks of all classes to live close to one another. The very fact of racial exclusion, overt or covert, forces blacks into a social unit that obscures their individual differences. Therefore, the very nature of prejudice is to look upon all blacks alike. But they are not all alike, and their academic capacities are not related to their racial consanguinity. When new blacks enter the university under a flexible admissions program, counselors should have the skill to determine who is ready for open competition and who needs a bridge experience. Some students may be ready for regular freshman math but wanting in English. Others may be far advanced in the verbal area and deficient in science.

Counselors cannot abandon students at this point to the bureaucracy. Many well-prepared blacks have left strong schools because, at the mercy of the bureaucracy and the alien white ethos, they were smothered and their academic interest stifled. It must be recognized that America has not equipped the white college-going population to deal with aspiring and assertive blacks. In the very nature of things, there will be confrontation, large and small, which must be resolved, day by day, week by week. Along with confrontations, there will be insults, loneliness, defeatism, futility, and the general "cum laude malaise" which may be interpreted as indices that the students are not ready and should therefore be dropped. But wise counselors will be sensitive to this and provide support. In a few years, all of this should level out, ending the need for further special help.

The special developmental courses needed to meet the needs of students in the bridge experience—one summer to one year—should go beyond recounting familiar rhetoric and experiences. Great care should be taken to plunge students into the discipline of independent study and awaken them to the joys of self-directed learning. Spoon feeding destroys initiative, but stupid assignments that are merely quantitative course requirements likewise destroy initiative. In sum, it is deplorable that the developmental courses offered minority students do not develop anyone. It is never enough simply to make things easy and simple. College work ought to keep students reaching and finding out what their maximum capacities are.

In addition, it would be highly desirable to incorporate a field experience, a "hands on" project that provided relevant service-oriented responses to ghetto needs, to counter the artificiality of dormitory life. Many black students feel that college is a waste, a white man's trick to separate blacks into two opposing classes. This frustrates them and makes concentration difficult. However, working five hours a week in a day care center, a community health center, an Urban League office, a settlement house, a tenants' organization, a voter registration group, or in a welfare rights organization would be something relevant and immediate. Young blacks should not be made to feel that college has exempted them from community service; instead, such work should be encouraged and assisted.

Such a program should include courses that take advantage of natural curiosity. These students know the world of poverty and oppression even through all are not really poor. They know the world of racism and of the ghetto. Therefore, mathematics should deal with the reality of consumer fraud, interest rates, rents, welfare budgets, etc. Social science should deal with politics, poverty, colonialism, Pan-Africanism, courts, jail, and capitalism. Natural science should deal with abortion and dope, pharmacology and cardiology, geriatrics, and epidemiology—all topics that relate directly to the poor.

Extension in the City

Again, relevance to urban problems has to do with meeting students' curriculum needs more effectively, but the land-grant colleges have to augment community services. Traditionally, they have been a rural enterprise, but the small poor farmers, especially the blacks, have moved to the center cities.

To provide these services, schools will have to alter their course. They will have to offer majors in urban ecology, community health, urban planning, criminal justice, social welfare, etc. Then, the way to serve is to have an on-site teaching situation in a problem area. Put a faculty member off campus. Allow students to get a large portion of their instruction in the field.

For example, when community multiphasic health centers are constructed, who will staff them? Since there has never been anything like it before, the state university should assess the need, organize a major, recruit students, and place them at the centers on a rotating basis for on hand experience. In this way, when they graduate they will not need a six-week seminar on the disadvantaged. They will have worked with them.

Students of social welfare could be exposed to organizations that the local people create: model cities and welfare rights groups, and some tenants' councils. It would be instructive to learn how the people feel, how they arrive at a certain posture, and how a white person can be helpful without being embarrassed or intimidated. This kind of risk taking is highly educative.

What to Do with Black Colleges

There is one issue that the land-grant movement must come to grips with and that is the black, public, land-grant college or university. It is clear that they are all—in thirteen southern states—coming under the aegis of the university system, just as all other schools are. But should they be liquidated as black schools?

We live in a moral, social, political, and economic continuum. We pick up where the last generation left us. Now, if we are going to inherit the legacy of racism from the nineteenth century, we must also inherit the instruments created to cope with it. Black colleges were invented because white colleges refused black students. This was a mere part of a total pattern of racism. And black colleges gave more than degrees. They gave dignity, overlook, overview, perspective, and fortitude. Therefore, they should be abolished no faster than racism leaves the land. For as long as racism exists, the colleges serve an important service.

So, just as we have colleges of many sorts, Catholic, fundamentalist, women's, men's, military, urban, rural, public, private—all reflecting the mosaic of American life—let us be honest about that mosaic and say that since the needs of the majority are well met with public funds, let us meet the needs of the minority that is still so largely discriminated against and who have so much to overcome from the slave legacy. It is a moral response to moral failure.

Therefore, instead of allowing these schools to atrophy, we should be making them stronger, to do better the task they have undertaken. In time, even without any precedent, we know they will become average colleges. But, they will have met the need.

Brain drain? Should all black bright teachers and students go to white schools and leave the less bright to populate black schools? This will happen if black schools are weakened. If they are strengthened, people will distribute themselves according to taste, proximity, and opportunity. Without loading the choice by weakening black schools, the situation will take care of itself.

If a white school has student blacks, they should have blacks on the faculty. It is silly to talk of recruiting black students and then cringe in moral outrage about recruiting black faculty. The fact is that schools should feel guilty taking black faculty while producing none! So, to feel safe and moral, a land-grant university should send at least five black Ph.D.'s back to black colleges for every black Ph.D. it takes from these schools. That formula will provide for the future of both schools.

Community in America

We are talking about more than simply the swelling of the academic procession. We are dealing with the issue of equalizing opportunity and securing for blacks, Puerto Ricans, Chicanos, and Indians a viable place in the American scene. Sentimental rhetoric must be supplemented with concrete programs for change; and while other programs are taking shape, the land-grant universities can proceed to include them in their ranks and move them forward with skill and competence. Then, whatever new programs develop, personnel will be ready for service.

With this type of movement the American Dream can become a reality. This nation holds out the promise that there can be a society with a high standard of living, justice for all, and equality of opportunity. It promises, moveover, that these can be accomplished in an atmosphere of freedom, with representative government, with an open franchise, without restraint or intimidation, and with the government completely subject to the governed. The contradiction in all of this has been the treatment of minorities who did not belong to one of the major European ethnic blocs.

The idea that all men are created equal implies that any arbitrary stratifications are unjust and unfair. This is clear in our Declaration of Independence and in our Constitution. What is less clear is the responsibility that one generation has for the unjust treatment of persons by a previous generation.

Whatever the legal condition, the moral condition is this: we live in a moral continuum. We are the heirs of certain moral benefactions inherent in the culture—practices and customs, laws and prohibitions. We benefit from them and take them for granted.

In the same continuum, there are the consequences of misdeeds, moral failures, and the inhumane treatment of persons. Likewise, certain institutions, like slavery, have a moral influence that is almost indelible. We have inherited this influence just as we inherited decent plumbing and the smallpox vaccination. It is all a package and this generation must deal with the total legacy, accepting the good and eradicating the evil.

Equality before the law means that no law should exclude anyone from the enjoyment of rights and privileges that others enjoy. This is exactly what the Fourteenth Amendment to the Constitution attempted to guarantee. Of course, there is a way of pretending that the failure to enjoy such privileges is due not to a civil denial but to the want of other prerequisites.

Such pretense would be convincing if the condition did not have a racial concomitant. The fact is that even when laws change and when full legal redress has been made, the habits of people, the social dynamics, and the peer structure all conspire to deny the enjoyment of full equality.

If a university community patterns itself after a racist community that surrounds it, no black could be comfortable there even if every legal right were assured. Therefore, what is needed is vastly more than the removal of a legal restriction; we need a climate of acceptance, an openness and a congeniality that encourage one to take full advantage of every facility the university has to offer. In this way, the university becomes a microcosm of the societal ideal that it teaches its students.

This is the real leadership that America needs to offer the world. China, Russia, or any other nation can come forth with a super bomb and frighten smaller nations into submission. But we claim to have something else. We say that in addition to our higher standard of living we have a better definition of life, living in an atmosphere of freedom.

Such a notion is so foreign to the way billions of people live that it would be a striking contrast to what most major powers can offer. In most societies there is rigid stratification with all sorts of symbols to regulate movement. Even when no overt rules govern, the way people behave tells those on the bottom that the chance for movement is nil.

Our democracy came into being with the sponsorship of three of the most powerful syntheses that man has seen, the Christian, the

Greek, and the Roman. Ethical monotheism and human universalism came from Christianity, freedom of inquiry and the democratic rule from Greece, and equality under the law from Rome. These all filtered through the British experience, freedom of speech, religion, assembly, and the press. With this legacy, we should prove to the world what the human race is capable of becoming. We should be proud to show that institutions created in this society are strong enough and committed enough to come to grips with an issue like racism and give it the treatment that it deserves, seize it wherever it appears, alter its effects, reverse its movement, cancel out its consequences, and neutralize its influence in the most decisive way that can be devised.

Chapter 11

FEDERAL CITY COLLEGE:
A MODEL FOR NEW URBAN UNIVERSITIES?

DAVID C. NICHOLS

THE history of higher education in the District of Columbia can be traced back over two hundred years to the frontier wilderness chosen as the site for the Federal City. President George Washington proposed the establishment of a national university and himself donated $25,000 in bonds to get it started. Nothing ever came of this proposal, although over the years several private universities were established in the District, the principal ones being American University, Catholic University, Georgetown University, George Washington University, and Howard University (which is nominally private, although it receives a substantial share of its operating funds from the federal government), and several smaller institutions.

These universities and colleges were, and still are, primarily national institutions and for all practical purposes are unavailable to most of the residents of the District of Columbia. They are too expensive for the vast majority of the District's residents and their standards are such that only the brighter students are admitted. The opportunity to attend a low-cost, public-supported university, available to most citizens in every state in the nation, was not available to the citizens of the District. This fact was ignored until recent years, and it was assumed that the private universities and colleges, together with the public D.C. Teachers College, effectively met the demand for higher education in the nation's capitol.

Beginning in the mid-1960s, both Virginia and Maryland began developing community college systems that now ring the District. Also, the University of Maryland is only a few miles away, providing additional access to higher learning of high quality. (According to the American Council on Education's 1969 survey of graduate education, the University of Maryland offers the largest single concentration of academic excellence in the Washington metropolitan area, with a commanding lead over the other institutions.) Even with the addition of these institutions to the list of universities and colleges in the Washington area, opportunities for public higher education for the residents of the District were still severely limited, since the Maryland and Virginia colleges primarily serve the residents of those states.

Legislative History of Federal City College

Over the years, at least six bills to establish public higher education in the District were introduced in the Congress. All were rejected, partly on the grounds that the federal government had no business supporting public higher education.

Direct action to found Federal City College began in 1963 with a commission appointed by President John F. Kennedy to study the condition of public higher education in the District. The study, directed by Francis Chase of the University of Chicago's School of Education, was published in 1964 and became a basis for action. The Chase Report called for the establishment of two public institutions in the District, one a liberal arts college awarding degrees through the master's level, and the other a community college giving technical and vocational training.

Wayne Morse of Oregon, the powerful chairman of the Senate's Subcommittee on Education, introduced legislation in that body in 1965 to authorize establishment of the two institutions specified in the Chase Report. The next year, similar legislation was introduced in the House of Representatives by Ancher Nelson of Minnesota; both bills were passed without real opposition. The final legislation, signed into law by President Lyndon B. Johnson in November 1966, created a Board of Higher Education and a Board of Vocational Education for the District of Columbia and authorized them, respectively, to take the steps necessary to establish Federal City College and Washington Technical Institute, the community vocational college called for in the Chase Commission's Report.

Initial Planning for the College

Soon thereafter, the Board of Higher Education selected the college's first president, Frank Farner, a professor of education who was then associate dean of the Graduate School of the University of Oregon. Farner chose his administrative team, which included as vice president for academic affairs and provost, David W. D. Dickson, a Bowdoin and Harvard-educated Milton scholar, then at Northern Michigan University; as vice president for finance and management, Murray Kandle; and as community education dean, Eugene Wiegman, who later figured strongly in the behind-the-scenes drive to achieve land-grant status for the new college. Harland L. Randolph, who succeeded Farner in the presidency, first served as his assistant and later as vice president for planning.

Federal City College was planned as a university for urban America—relevant to its urban constituents (a large percentage of whom are black and poor), equalitarian, aggressive, and dynamic in reaching out into the community. Such a university would be a first step toward achieving a modern teaching, research, and public service equivalent of the vast ensemble of some sixty-eight institutions (with the political support of the U.S. Department of Agriculture, the Federal Cooperative Extension Service, and formal supporting state and local organizations) which made up the national land-grant university system. Former Senator Morse, the principal promoter of FCC in the Congress, thought the college should be distinctly urban and innovative. He said in September 1968, as the college opened, "Educators can sit aloof in the ivory towers of academia—or they can be a vital force in bringing all segments of the community to bear on our urgent urban problems. The faculty and administration of Federal City College are committed to educational innovation—and to educating for innovation. It is with this spirit that the Federal City College begins its job."[1]

The job chosen by the college was admittedly a difficult one, since the District of Columbia amply demonstrates the complex difficulties of urban life. There was solid expectation (encouraged by the college

[1]Wayne L. Morse, "A Federal City College," *American Education* (September 1968).

itself) that the college would do something about these crises, and if not resolve them, at least make a substantial difference. The Board of Higher Education adopted the following statement on March 12, 1969:

> In its role as a state university for the District of Columbia, Federal City College proposes to serve all the residents of the nation's capital. It will seek to excel in the traditional functions of education, service, and research; and in response to the new demands that are being placed upon institutions of higher education, it will also use the micro-community of the College to demonstrate productive models of human interactions. It will seek to employ the resources of the College both to advocate programs for individual and community development and to generate action projects which bring the benefits of higher education to bear on pressing urban problems.[2]

It would not be easy to draw up a more ambitious mandate for any university, especially for a small new one, not yet really a university at all. The college proposed to serve all 800,000 District of Columbia residents. If taken literally, it was an impossible mandate, but supporters of the college, as a developmental strategem, relied on the rhetoric common to the time and to the land-grant universities. A broad mandate is also useful in making a plea for public funds, which in the District of Columbia means largely a plea to Congress. Until very recently, the Congress directly appropriated funds for the municipal agencies, including Federal City College. Although the federal government provided but fifteen percent of the city's budget (the remainder came from taxes in the District), it virtually controlled the official functions of the city through its power over the purse. Congress, in turn, has been largely dominated by its own committee structure in which the chairmen wield enormous power. Since many chairmen (because of seniority) are whites from Southern states, it was felt that racism was long a factor in keeping District residents from gaining a larger measure of control over their public institutions, or outright statehood, and one reason why the Congress does not vote more funds for the District government. In and of itself,

---

[2]Board of Higher Education, Resolution No. X-48.

Congressional control has been a considerable factor for the college to reckon with, paralleled in some degree by many of the state universities in their historic dealings with legislatures. Since 1973, the District has had a measure of self-government, and this situation may change even more.

With the Congress looking over their shoulder, President Farner and his administrative team, led by Provost Dickson, set out to recruit a faculty of high qualifications, their intentions boosted by a salary schedule with an A rating from the AAUP. They were moderately successful, and the first year's faculty was studded with a few stars.

The operating budget was projected at $4.8 million in the 1968–69 academic year, and was expected to rise to $12.4 million in the second year, and to $21.3 million in the third. In addition, the college had received land-grant status in June 1968, which carried with it a permanent endowment fund of $7.24 million in lieu of the federal grants of land that were used to set up the other land-grant colleges. Federal City College proposed to translate the historically rural benefits of the land-grant colleges into urban terms. Senator Morse said FCC professors would go into the city "to help people to help themselves, as their predecessors have been doing for so long in rural areas." Extension centers were planned throughout the city to bring the benefits of the college's teaching and research to District residents. In accord with the principle promulgated by the War on Poverty of "maximum feasible participation," District residents were promised a strong voice in the policy of the centers. Community residents were also employed as teacher aides, community extension workers, and as staff for child-care centers to accommodate mothers who wished to participate in the college's programs.

It was decided that the college would open its doors to all applicants, providing they had a high school diploma or equivalency standing, since it was believed that other admissions criteria were essentially elitist and tended to discriminate against the poor. It was also recognized that some form of open admission is practiced by state higher education systems. With this barrier removed, District residents applied in unexpected numbers. While only 900 spaces were available under the first-year's budget, more than 6,000 letters of application were received by April 1968. Hindsight attributes this demand to the near complete lack of public higher education opportunity in the District, and the rush by other-than-recent high school graduates to take advantage of the opportunity. To help accommodate some of this demand, the Congress was persuaded to appropriate additional funds to bring enrollment up to 2,000. A lottery was used to insure impartiality in selecting students for the limited spaces. Actually, this demand was more apparent than real. Of the 6,000 applications, lottery numbers to 3,800 were exhausted to get 2,000 students for the first quarter.[3]

Efforts were made to place the college within the means of practically everyone. Tuition was set at a nominal $25 per quarter, and an assortment of financial aids and work-study arrangements was made available. The library developed a large collection of paperback books, including 200,000 duplicate copies of the book on course reading lists, which it gave away. Flexible academic scheduling permitted students to hold full-time jobs, if necessary.

Initial plans were laid for the college to grant two-year Associate in Arts degrees in urban services, education, nursing, and health; Bachelor of Arts degrees in liberal arts and sciences, business, nursing, and urban studies. Master's degrees would be offered in teacher education, social work, urban studies, recreation, nursing, public health, business, and liberal arts.

Site planning called for permanent facilities for the college in two downtown locations: Mt. Vernon Square, not far from the Capitol, and Ft. Lincoln, on a site vacated by a boys' reformatory which was being planned as a new community-within-the-city. It is a small historic irony that the reformatory was moved to Morgantown, West Virginia (at the intercession of Senator Robert C. Byrd of West Virginia) to be near another land-grant institution, West Virginia University. There it was named in memory of Robert F. Kennedy. The college expected its enrollment to grow to 20,000 students within the first twelve years, and a capital budget was prepared to

[3]Irene Tinkes, "Federal City College: How Black?" *Academic Transformation,* edited by David Riesman and Verne Stadtman for the Carnegie Commission (New York: McGraw-Hill, 1973).

provide construction outlays of $125 million through 1974. Demand for higher education in the Washington area was projected to exceed the national average, and thought was given to opening up a third campus. Temporarily, the college operated (and still operates) in rented facilities.

Planning had also taken into account the growing demand among college students for more participation in matters of policy affecting them, and President Farner opted for a full measure of participatory democracy in the planning of the college. There was to be a decentralized mode of decision making with emphasis on student and faculty participation.

With the faculty recruited, the students selected, classroom space and other facilities available, an operating budget reasonably assured, and the other housekeeping details apparently tended to, the Federal City College was prepared to begin. As opening day approached, the prospects of the college, in educational terms, must have seemed reasonably bright. But outside the college, extraordinary events were taking place that subjected Federal City College to the volatile racial and ideological tensions developing in the city and society at large. The impact of these tensions on the college was initially crippling and led to internal chaos.

To a very real degree, Federal City College was born in crisis. Created *de novo* as the only urban land-grant college in the country, any resemblance to its rural land-grant counterparts was coincidental. Its doors opened in the aftermath of Washington's terrible spring and summer of burning and rioting in 1968 when the atmosphere in the city was charged with racial tension.

A personal recollection fixes the mood of the time. Only a day or two after Martin Luther King had been shot, I was one of the last government workers to leave the main Health, Education and Welfare Building after it had been ordered evacuated in fear of the violence taking place a few blocks away. Nearing an exit, someone told me there were snipers outside. On the streets, the few people remaining in the area were scurrying to their cars and buses for cover. The sky was filled with smoke, police sirens wailed, what sounded like gunshots could be heard in the distance. Uptown, the streets were clogged with cars carrying anxious government workers away to their homes in the Virginia and Maryland suburbs. There were no snipers, of course, but nobody then knew that. Federal City College, temporarily located in the old Securities and Exchange Building, just over the Mall and two blocks from the Capitol, was on the edge of some of the worst burning and looting in the city. This was the urban crisis, full blown. There was nothing academic about it.

The Hidden Agenda

My own connection with Federal City College was entirely casual. During the previous winter and spring, I was the principal staff operative on a task force study ordered by the White House that aimed to find out what colleges and universities could do to help solve urban problems. In the course of this work, we consulted several times with planners of the new college; they, in turn, sought our ideas and support, especially for obtaining Congressional designation of the new institution as a land-grant college.

Among my colleagues, there was strong sentiment that Federal City College should test the hypothesis that the federal government ought to support the establishment throughout the United States of a series of urban-grant universities in some measure similar to the land-grant universities. Unlike the land-grant universities, the new institutions would emphasize not only urban development generally but more specifically the need of urban blacks, other ethnic minorities, and the poor. While there was general agreement that universities should be doing more to help solve urban problems, opinion was divided among staffs at the White House and in HEW about whether whole new universities should be established or, instead, if federal funds should be directed to existing universities, and if so, for what urban purposes.

The basic argument then being advanced for the creation of new urban institutions—comparable to the land-grant system—was that existing universities were so tied down to scholarly concerns that they had neither the capacity nor the commitment necessary to educate disadvantaged city youth. It was further argued that new institutions could forego all the accoutrements of elitism in higher education—academic excellence, accreditation, degrees, graduate peer rankings, scholarly rigidity to disciplines, and so on—and instead devote themselves to the basic needs of urban students; for example, mastery of the English language, career training, and understanding of the responsibilities and rights of citizenship. The new institutions would conduct research on urban problems, and research results would then be applied to the community through extension. Agents would go out to work with people in the cities, teaching them how to manage their resources, offering job and family counseling, consumer advice, and so on. It was thought that the new universities, free of traditional academic constraints, would have all the flexibility they needed to make a difference in the quality of life in the cities. In a memo to President Johnson from one of his aides, this course of action was recommended on the grounds that "a system of urban-grant universities would be quite a legacy for you to leave the country in 1972." (Copy in my files.)

On the other side of the issue were those who thought that new federal funds should be given to existing institutions. It was readily conceded that the higher education establishment (including, ironically, the land-grant universities) would strongly oppose the creation of new universities, if only in view of the necessary redirection of federal funding that such a move implied. More positively, it was also recognized that existing institutions had resources—faculties, libraries, facilities, and the like—that might be redirected to urban concerns through the promise of increased federal spending for those purposes. Cooptation through categorical aid is, after all, an established principle of federal support to higher education.

This dilemma was never resolved in the Johnson administration, although the balance of opinion favored increased aid to existing institutions, together with substantially larger amounts of support for the education of disadvantaged youth through work-study and educational opportunity grants, counseling services, tutorials, and the like. Had the Vietnam War not loomed so large in the scheme of things, bringing with it campus turmoil, eruptions of urban vionence, shrinking federal funds available for education, and the demise of the Johnson administration, more attention might have been given to the establishment of new urban institutions and programs. As it turned out, Federal City College was an exception.

New Yet Traditional

Although it was conceived as a new liberal arts institution in the terms outlined above, FCC also incorporated features of traditional colleges and universities. It sought academic excellence in its faculty, in terms of their demonstrated scholarly productivity, though special attention in recruitment was given to a faculty candidate's interest in teaching, his concern about urban needs, and his ideas for presenting traditional knowledge in innovative ways. The traditional library was incorporated, but its name was changed, in the McLuhanesque mode of the day, to a media center. Instead of organization along traditional lines of the disciplines, the curriculum was divided into four parts: the humanities, social sciences, natural sciences, and professional studies, all under the administrative direction of the vice-president for academic affairs. Team teaching was employed in some courses, field experiences in others, although the course and the lecture were retained as basic units in the educational plan.

Grading was used, but not on the traditional scale; instead, freshman courses carried grades of high pass, pass, and deferred, the last allowing students to retake a course without penalty during the first year. This system was later changed in response to student demands and a traditional college grading system was instituted. The majority of the new, educationally starved students at the college made it clear they considered the high pass, pass, deferred system patronizing. They were less interested in testing new ideas than they were in pursuing a college education which would allow them to compete in a tradition-oriented society.

Befitting the college's land-grant status, extension activity was to be given strong emphasis. And since most of the students were black, black awareness was an important feature of virtually everything the college did. Otherwise, there was nothing radically different about what the college did, romantic rhetoric to the contrary. From the beginning, it sought conventional accreditation, actually achieved on schedule in 1973.

Internal Conflict

In these and other ways, FCC was planned as a blend of old and new academic methods brought to focus on a predominantly black, urban community. But from the beginning, there was conflict between the traditionalists and nontraditionalists in the faculty and administration of the college. This conflict, perhaps normal to new institutions, was compounded by the extreme social volatility of the combined racial and urban crisis of the time and by the absence of any clear lines of authority or organization of the college.

Before the end of the college's first year, President Farner resigned, followed a few weeks later by Provost Dickson, who in November 1968 had startled an audience at the annual convention of the National Association of State Universities and Land-Grant Colleges where in a prepared speech he announced that FCC was being torn apart by racial tension. Farner denied this, but the Dickson speech signaled the end of their administration. Farner, who is white, was quoted as suggesting to the District of Columbia Board of Higher Education that only a strong, black educator could provide the kind of leadership needed for the college. Racial concerns and black power demands were admittedly strong forces figuring in the year's turmoil and in Farner's and Dickson's resignations. In a personal letter to me in 1972, Dickson, now President of Montclair State College in New Jersey, points out that FCC was planned to be interracial in staff and student body, drawing from beyond the District of Columbia. "This latter hope never materialized and led to the emphasis on blackness which in the context of those years became inevitably irascible and militantly nationalistic and put some of us in a most difficult position."

Some observers believe that the mode of participatory democracy in decision making undercut any possibility of organized leadership at the college and gave rise to political factions jockeying for power to control the institution. This jockeying continued under President Harland Randolph, a black, who succeeded Farner. The principal dispute appeared to be the resolution of a power struggle between the president and some of the leaders of the FCC Faculty Organization, who demanded Randolph's resignation as a condition and prelude to serious consideration of needed systems for institutional governance and organization. This faction, which included perhaps fifty faculty members (although sympathizers may have swelled their ranks to almost half the faculty on a given issue), named its own vice president for academic affairs, in the wake of the resignations of seven persons who had officially held the position, and declared in effect that there would be no peace until the board named a president of whom they approved. The Board of Higher Education has had its own difficulty in resolving the issue of leadership. It had three chairmen in 1971–72; early in 1972 the District's mayor replaced five of the nine members, whose terms had expired, with new appointees. This new board summarily fired President Randolph in August 1972 after he refused to step down.

Work in Progress

Before the college had operated long enough to graduate its charter class, it had already awarded 189 degrees to students who transferred into the college with prior credits or who completed programs at the associate or master's degree level. An additional 250 degrees were awarded at the end of the 1971–72 academic year, including the graduation of the charter four-year class. By the 1974–75 academic year, the college had graduated nearly 2,000 students combined at the associate, bachelor's, and master's degree levels.

The output of graduates, important as this is, cannot alone prove the effectiveness of the college's programs. Another measure of the worth of degrees granted is the acceptance of FCC graduates by graduate and professional schools, placement of graduates in professional and technical jobs based on qualifications gained at the college, and, even further, promotions and salary increases for students and graduates already employed. Success in these areas results in both immediate and long-range economic gains for individual graduates and their families, the private business sector in the District, and the D.C. government revenue base. The earning ability of FCC's graduates is important to the District of Columbia and the resolution of urban problems.

Other examples of innovations included: The Office of Experimental Programs of the college has operated four Upward Mobility satellite colleges for low-level federal employees seeking to earn college degrees, upgrade their skills, and qualify for more rewarding jobs. The satellite colleges are located at the students' job sites and offer a standard college curriculum of mathematics, humanities, social sciences, and natural sciences to some 1,500 students who attend classes during their lunch hours, before and after work, or on released time from their employers. The program has been funded initially by a $1.5 million grant from HEW.

Another satellite program of the college is the Lorton Project, which offers a complete college curriculum to inmates of the Lorton Reformatory, the state prison for the District of Columbia located in Virginia. The Lorton Project has been selected by HEW to serve as a national model for educational rehabilitation programs throughout the United States.

In fulfilling its role as a land-grant institution and an instrument of the people of the District, the college also has provided a wide range of services directly to the community.[4] For example, some 250 cases per week have been handled by the faculty and staff of the Graduate Counseling Department in the ward offices of the D.C. Representative in Congress. The Media Services Division of the college provided audio-visual equipment, materials and technical assistance to the Model Cities Program, the D.C. Youth Center, local high schools, and other community groups.

Services to the community are combined by many areas of the college. Two-hundred fifty teacher education students have served as teacher aides in the D.C. schools, without cost to the school system, as part of their practicum experience. Faculty and students in the accounting department have provided income tax consultation services free to inner-city residents. The Natural Science Division has served thousands of District high school students through its Mobile Science Laboratory. The program has been used by FCC students to demonstrate how science can be applied to urban problems. Sixty students in the Urban Studies-Social Planning Department have

[4] I am grateful to Paul Mathless of Federal City College for providing information about current programs as well as for his helpful comments on an earlier draft of this paper.

provided an aggregate of about twenty man-years of paraprofessional services to community agencies.

In many ways the most ambitious activity of the college is directed outward into the community. The Community Education Division of FCC is the continuing education arm of the college, funded primarily through the Federal Extension Service. The division is involved in countless activities directed to social development in the District. It claims to be reaching more than 300,000 residents each year through forty satellite community centers and the efforts of 600 full- and part-time staff. And yet the division has embroiled the college in controversy and even scandal. Late in 1972, the college was embarrassed by a federal audit conducted to investigate the alleged misuse of about $200,000 in Department of Agriculture funds. A spokesman for the college denied any wrongdoing, but the eventual outcome was prosecution for criminal fraud and a lengthy prison sentence for an FCC dean.

Continuing Issues

There are a number of major issues facing the college at this stage of its development. First, the college must find stability through effective and acceptable leadership; a means must be found for the resolution of conflict within the college without this conflict spilling over into the mass media, where it tends to obscure the more important educational business of the institution.

A second issue concerns permanent facilities for the campus. FCC has not received the facilities construction aids that existing institutions enjoyed earlier in the 1960s. A capital budget is stymied in the Congress, and the college is operating out of fifteen or so rented buildings scattered around downtown Washington. Site plans for three campus centers are being prepared in expectation of funding. They link the college's facilities to the cultural resources of the city, and are in line with urban architectural concepts that keep buildings on a human scale, emphasizing urban variety and social interaction.

Third, while the college's operating budget has grown appreciably from the initial $4 million to more than $20 million in 1975, the budgetary process is a bureaucratic nightmare. It involves review and hearings through the District government and the City Council. Until recently, it also involved the several committees of the Congress concerned with District affairs, as well as the executive branch of the federal government. At each stage of the review, the college must defend its budget, line by line, secretary by secretary. Preparation of the budget for any fiscal year got underway eighteen months before the start of that fiscal year, and the funds eventually appropriated typically arrived six months late, well into the next fiscal year. In order for the college to pay its bills during this hiatus, the college had to get from the Congress a continuing resolution permitting continued spending at the previous year's level. At any given time, the president of the college was defending and explaining budgets overlapping a three-year period.

This entire process consumed enormous amounts of the college's administrative resources that might otherwise have been devoted to educational matters. Also, appropriations at FCC, as elsewhere, were never quite enough; and at a struggling new institution, without the internal supports of tradition, new resources are especially critical to its balanced development.

The fourth issue is perhaps the most important. It concerns the kind of institution that Federal City College is to become. Is it to be new, in the sense of doing things differently than existing institutions, being experimental and innovative, and providing new ideas and models for other institutions? Or is it to follow the lines of traditional institutions, perhaps taking a few risks, but becoming in most respects an imitation of other institutions? To answer these questions, one must look more closely at the nature of the student body.

The birth of Federal City College unlocked educational opportunities for many thousands of District residents, who seized upon it for upward career mobility. In its first four years, FCC's enrollment climbed above 9,000. More than seventy percent of FCC students are employed, thirty-one percent by the federal government and twenty percent by the District government. Two-thirds of the working students work more than twenty hours per week. About fifty percent of the working students earn less than the minimum cost of living established by the U.S. Department of Labor for families in the District of Columbia. The average age of the students is twenty-six.

In this population the demand for educational opportunity is overwhelmingly directed toward career advancement. It is anything but a radical student body.

Despite its many setbacks, FCC has tried to develop aspects of excellence in its academic programs, to cater to the overwhelmingly vocational interests of its students, and to tackle community problems on a broad scale. The question remains whether Federal City College will produce anything new or whether it will simply imitate others. Already it is meeting a need and perhaps that is enough. In daring to be different, risks must be taken, politically and intellectually, and yet these risks might destroy a developing institution. In perspective, many of the land-grant colleges struggled for a century to become strong enough to absorb the consequences of real risk-taking. It is probably expecting too much of Federal City College that it do so now.

The University of the District of Columbia

The issue of mission is highlighted by the potentially most far-reaching development yet, one that bodes for well or ill to transform Federal City College, Washington Technical Institute, and D.C. Teachers College into an amalgam. In the fall of 1974 Congress passed legislation to combine the three colleges into a new comprehensive institution, the University of the District of Columbia. However, the legislation passed by Congress contained a remarkable provision, allowing the D. C. Council to change any or all of the act or to repeal it entirely (in effect). The council has taken this responsibility seriously and has come up with a set of somewhat different proposals.

In the main, however, the two sets of proposals are similar. Each would create a university by consolidating FCC, WTI, and DCTC into a unitary university with a new name. FCC would bring the liberal arts core, DCTC would add to the liberal arts while continuing a teaching professionals program, and WTI would bring an emphasis on vocational-technical training.

The proposed university would be governed by a president and a fifteen-member board of trustees, twelve of whom would be appointed by the mayor, now popularly elected under the new form of District government.

Not surprisingly, everyone is not pleased with the proposal. Merge, not submerge, or better yet to leave things as they are, is the position taken by some. The current president of FCC, Wendell P. Russell (who also serves as head of DCTC), is on record as being opposed to a single, unitary university structure.[5] President Russell also is opposed to provisions in the legislation that would require the approval by the City Council of a long-range master plan covering all major aspects of the university's development. According to Russell, "submission of educational master plans for legislative approval is highly irregular."

Conversely, the President of Washington Technical Institute, Cleveland Denard, has advocated the proposed merger. During public hearings on the university bill, Denard urged Congress to pass the measure speedily so that the trustees could be appointed and begin their planning efforts without further delay. Denard has the reputation of being a tough administrator who runs a tight ship (in contrast to the untidiness of FCC), and there has been speculation that he would be named president of the new university.[6]

Nothing is expected to happen until 1977 at least, permitting time for yet another round of studies and hearings on the *why* and *how* of the proposal. President Russell of FCC, in testifying before the City Council, urged that a thorough study be conducted "in hopes that the wisdom of maintaining separate higher education and vocational-technical education institutions might be convincingly demonstrated to the Council."[7] As normal, the debate has entered the news media in Washington with columnists taking sides. William Raspberry, a popular black columnist who writes for the *Post,* has urged that the merger not take place on grounds that vocational-technical education and liberal education cannot effectively take place in the same institution or at least not in the same classroom.[8] No one to date has entered into the argument some lessons from history, which

[5]Letter from the President to all faculty and staff of FCC and DCTC dated June 11, 1975.
[6]"University Project Hits New Delay," *Washington Post,* June 15, 1975, p. 24-A.
[7]Russell's letter to the faculty.
[8]*Washington Post,* June 6, 1975.

show that land-grant universities have been grappling with this issue since the 1860s and have presumably learned something about the chemistry of mixing oil and water. The issue is being debated on ideological and political grounds, not surprising in Washington.

What else concerns the new (now not so new) FCC, whose history may turn out to be brief after all? It will come as no surprise to presidents of the older and non-urban land-grant universities that the president of FCC cites the other problems of the institution in 1975 as follows: recruiting irregularities in the football program, changing back from a quarter system to a semester system, cuts in the budget, improved governance processes, and the advent of collective bargaining.[9] FCC's president sounds very much like his brothers and sisters in the land-grant system. Clearly FCC has arrived. There should never have been a moment's doubt about how the story would turn out.

---

[9]Letter to the faculty.

Chapter 12

LAND-GRANT UNIVERSITY SERVICES
AND URBAN POLICY

DAVID C. NICHOLS

THE Smith-Lever Act of 1914 provided funds for the states to appoint county agricultural agents who were expected to teach farmers how to improve agricultural practices. By utilizing the research data of the agricultural experiment stations, county agents would provide a continuing source of new technology to American farms.[1] The Smith-Lever Act not only added the third leg of federal support to the land-grant colleges, it also firmly established the principle that while elementary and secondary education might remain the responsibility of the states, the national government would aid the expansion of higher learning to the common man. What this has meant for the land-grant colleges, over and beyond being trendsetters, is that they have enjoyed systematic and preferential treatment from Washington compared to other colleges and universities.

Intended Consequences

Undoubtedly, the contributions of agricultural extension to the development of the nation have been substantial.

The remarkable increase in productivity of food and fiber per acre between 1870 and 1960 is owing in some part to the teaching, research, and extension of the colleges of agriculture. Over this period of ninety years, agricultural productivity in the United States increased 949 percent, while productivity for the United States as a whole increased by 453 percent; increases per worker in agricultural productivity exceeded by two or three times in-

---

[1]For the early history of rural extension see Alfred Charles True, *A History of Agricultural Extension Work in the United States, 1785–1923* (Washington: U.S. Department of Agriculture, 1928).

creases in productivity per worker in the industrial sector.[2]

The percentage of Americans employed as farmworkers or farmowners, or in other agricultural pursuits, was nearly sixty percent in 1900. By 1947 the percentage of persons so employed had fallen to fourteen percent, and by 1964 to 6.3 percent. In the latter period alone, 1947 to 1964, the number of farmowners and farmworkers decreased from 8.2 million to 4.8 million, a decrease of 42.3 percent. Such changes indicate the substantial contribution of agricultural productivity to the economic growth of the country and to the transfer of human resources from the production of food and fiber to other industrial and service occupations.[3]

Unintended Consequences

Agricultural educators are understandably proud of their part in the phenomenal agricultural productivity of the United States, although they would agree that it is impossible to quantify the specific impact of the colleges on the total effort. Also apparent is the part of the colleges in the unintended or negative consequences of agricultural development. For example, the vast Cooperative Extension Service, which now consists of about 15,000 employees spread throughout the nation, historically has focused its work on farmers readily receptive to change. The literature on agricultural extension frequently refers to this fact.[4] Although no data are available, it seems likely that this was true as well of the Negro county agents, segregated in the southern states to work with Negro farmers. The extension services, like their parent agricultural colleges, early determined that the greatest payoff came from adding value to relatively prosperous rather than marginal farmers. While the success of this

[2]Lester B. Lave, *Technological Change: Its Conception and Measurement* (Englewood Cliffs, New Jersey: Prentice Hall, 1966), p. 169.

[3]Paul A. Miller, David C. Nichols, et al., *The Professional School and World Affairs: Agriculture and Engineering* (New York: Education and World Affairs, 1967), p. 30.

[4]See, for example, Harry A. Cosgriffe, *The Washington Agricultural Extension Service, 1912–1961* (abstract of unpublished dissertation, University of Chicago, 1966), pp. 23–24. "Those who took part in extension programs were more highly educated than other rural people, had higher incomes, owned larger farms, had more assets, were more active in formal groups and associations, and had a higher level of informal social contacts than did other farm people."

approach is apparent in terms of its impact on the agricultural productivity of the nation, the aggregate impact contributed to the great migration of unsuccessful rural people to the cities. This included large numbers of both Negroes and whites forced off the farms because of their inability to compete in an increasingly sophisticated agricultural market. America's cities have been unable to absorb them all into the middle class, and thus large numbers of the rural poor have remained relatively as poor in the cities as they were on the farm. Well-meaning affluent whites who argue that poor blacks are better off in the cities are not very convincing.

It is a cruel irony, too, that for those who remained on the farms, poverty is close at hand. About one-third of the poverty in the United States is found among rural people. In recent years, some resources of the extension services have been shifted toward the problems of rural poverty, but too few.

The vast system of agricultural education, research, and extension is one of the historic reforms of American education. But the long-term consequences of this reform never have been studied systematically. The rhetoric of reform and commercial success seems to have precluded serious attention to the human factors of technological change.

Although no analytical history has been written of the agricultural extension services, it appears that they have been strongly influenced by organized agricultural interests—agribusiness—who seek the commercial advantages the colleges can provide, and that the colleges, while emphasizing technological improvements, have neglected the social aspects of the rural population as a whole, and the disadvantaged in particular.[5] While the reforms initiated by the land-grant colleges have indeed furthered democratic principles in education, an unfortunate reaction has been the development, over time, of a narrow conception of the people to be included in its programs. It may be suggested that the land-grant colleges were fine so far as

[5]The influence of organized agricultural interests is suggested in Charles E. Kellogg and David C. Knapp, *The College of Agriculture: Science in the Public Service* (New York: McGraw-Hill, 1966), p. 18. More recently and critically, the influence of "agribusiness" is studied in *Hard Tomatoes, Hard Times* (Washington: Agribusiness Accountability Project, 1972).

they went, but they didn't go far enough. And their public service arm—the extension services—sadly neglected human factors and community development.

Urban Extension

It is often suggested that universities should develop urban extension services, perhaps modeled after the successful agricultural extension of the land-grant institution. Seldom is it known that many land-grant institutions unsuccessfully sponsored urban extension even before 1900. Then, as now, the clientele for urban extension is either elusive or adamantly resistant to academic manipulation. Following is a summary of some recent attempts to explore the potential of university urban extension services.

Ford Foundation Project

The heads of several land-grant universities successfully proposed to the Ford Foundation in the mid-1950s that it support their efforts to provide extension services to urban areas within their respective states. With grants ranging up to $1,000,000 each, eight universities —Rutgers, Wisconsin, Delaware, Missouri, Berkeley, Illinois, Oklahoma, and Purdue—experimented with ways of shifting their experience in agricultural extension to urban problems. Most of the institutions participating in the experiment attempted to provide consultative services to urban organizations on numerous problem areas—water pollution, housing, health care, education, and other technical fields. Most were interested in developing collaborative relationships between urban agencies and the experts in university departments, and in organizing community self-help programs. After several years of experimentation, the Ford Foundation reluctantly concluded that the work had not been very successful. They determined, for example, that it is not possible to reduce urban extension to precise definitions, and thus any evaluation of results is virtually impossible.

However, these experiments did help local communities equip themselves for participation in the Johnson administration's War on

Poverty. Neighborhoods in which extension programs operated were better able to organize for the anti-poverty programs than other areas in the same cities. Similarly, the engagement of the universities enhanced their ability to serve state and local governments in setting up community action programs in line with federal requirements. According to the Ford Foundation, the federal poverty programs, more than any other factor, gave shape and purpose to urban extension programs, providing a focus for testing new ideas and patterns of organizations.[6]

Title I, Higher Education Act of 1965

Before the Ford-sponsored experimentation had concluded, President Johnson announced that he would seek new legislation for urban extension programs. He remarked on June 30, 1965, in an address at Irvine, California:

> Now 70 percent of our people live in urban areas. Their needs are immense. But just as our colleges and universities changed the future of our farms a century ago, so they can help change the future of our cities. I foresee the day when an urban extension service, operated by universities across the country, will do for urban America what the Agricultural Extension Service has done for rural America.

This presidential sentiment became Title I of the Higher Education Act of 1965. To date, about sixty percent of the funds available under Title I have been used in urban areas to bring university resources to bear on such problems as housing, poverty, government, recreation, employment, youth opportunities, transportation, health, and land use. The legislation assumes initiative by institutions of higher education within the framework of statewide plans for the identification of key community problems.

Title I projects are built on community-university collaboration. The typical plan begins with a team of university personnel studying the particular needs of a given community. Next, the team deter-

[6] *Urban Extension: A Report on Experimental Programs Assisted by the Ford Foundation* (New York: Ford Foundation, 1966).

mines how the institution's facilities, research capacity, and faculty members can best be used to meet these needs. Finally, a strategy is developed to close in on a special problem. It may involve workshops, classes, conferences, demonstrations, or consultative services —or all of these.

Since the inception of the Title I program, there has been little enthusiasm for its impact on urban problems. To be sure, appropriations have been limited—$10 million or less in each fiscal year. Secondly, considerable fragmentation of the program has occurred because of the formula distribution of funds. The largest amount received by any state (California) under Title I is about $500,000. The state's share is then divided up among participating institutions of higher education, thus further narrowing the scope of given projects. As a result, the impact on urban problems is uncertain; to the federal budget examiners, Title I is a frill in a time of ever-dwindling resources. The net effect of the program is general indifference.

White House Task Force on Higher Education and Urban Problems

In the summer of 1967, some of the White House staff under President Johnson became convinced that additional legislation should be enacted to involve universities more directly in meeting urban needs. This led to the formation of a special task force charged to study the field of possibilities and to recommend action programs. The task force consisted of several college administrators, an urban renewal administrator, the state director of a program for the educationally disadvantaged, a representative of organized labor, and officers of HEW and HUD.

In one of its reports, the task force argued that, as the land-grant colleges had triggered the great technological discoveries which revolutionized agriculture, they now could initiate an educational revolution in urban America if Congress would provide new resources. As an immediate proposal for congressional action, the task force proposed "The Urban Grant Act of 1968" which would have supplemented Title I of the Higher Education Act by providing additional funds for university-based urban research and services, especially those which might improve urban elementary and secondary schools. It also would have established a national clearinghouse for urban technical services, intended to collect informational materials and conduct evaluations of existing urban education programs. In addition, the report asked for the development of a nationwide system of urban specialists, based in the universities, to provide extension services to city agencies and community groups.

These proposals were not accepted by the White House. One reason for rejection was the inability of HEW, HUD, and OEO—the three legislative divisions involved—to agree on a division of labor among them for operation of the proposed programs. Secondly, many people remained unconvinced that universities should conduct extension programs in the cities in any way comparable to rural extension programs. Undoubtedly weakening the entire case was the suspected impotence of Title I of the Higher Education Act, the proposed legislative vehicle for the new program. But, finally, budgetary considerations in late 1967 prohibited new initiatives. The task force had argued that unless the new programs were funded at a level of $200 million by 1973, they should not be implemented at all. The task force rejected any hint of tokenism by declining to suggest promises for urban development that the federal government was incapable of keeping. With escalation of the Vietnam War, and rising pressures on the budget generally, almost all new initiatives were rejected for the 1969 budget.

The task force also studied, but categorically rejected, the idea of federally sponsored urban-grant colleges analogous to the historic land-grant institutions. Instead, it argued that the federal government could achieve more significant results with less money by providing additional aid to community colleges, municipal universities, and other existing urban institutions for new community services.[7]

---

[7] These reports were only made public in 1972; they are collected in the Presidential Archives in Austin, Texas.

Teaching, Research, and Public Service Instead of Extension

Examining the evidence, one may conclude that "extension" is an obsolete concept in an urban society. In an agrarian period, there may have been need for an elaborate bureaucracy of extension experts and field workers to apply the results of agricultural research on individual farms; but it is impossible to picture that same system in operation in the cities. What would they do that professional people are not better equipped to do? John Bebout, former director of Rutgers' Urban Extension Program, remarks: "A universal urban extension service staffed with locally-based urban agents on a scale proportionate to the Cooperative Extension Service suggests the image of a bureaucracy of do-gooders truly terrifying in its potential for mischief."[8]

In contrast to extension activity, there are more obvious avenues by which universities can address the needs of an urban society. These avenues extend from the traditional university functions of teaching, research, and public service. For example, the college teaching process is gradually accepting experiential learning. Although the passion of students to serve the inner city seems to have ebbed, a growing number of institutions permit, even encourage, students to stop-out for service experience. Affective learning, as well as cognitive, is in every man's vocabulary. While it is taking a long time to die, rote learning seems to be giving way to less formalized relationships between professors and students. New concepts in continuing education are needed to help people continue their own learning, wherever they live. Cable television, adequately developed, offers greater potential for continuing education than an army of community service workers. Continuing education is coming of age at a time when distinctions between "urban" and "rural" are becoming meaningless.

A large number of universities are involved in research projects with urban implications. At last count, over 200 universities had established urban research centers. Many of these centers are only

[8]John Bebout, "Urban Extension," *The American Behavioral Scientist,* February 1963, p. 26.

a few years old and are supported by government grants.[9] Most institutions are trying to develop research programs useful to their immediate communities. Some twenty universities have used funds under Title I of the Higher Education Act to help plan Model Cities programs, now a defunct enterprise gone the way of most Great Society programs. Others are focusing on given areas of a city in an attempt to set priorities for research and to involve graduate students directly in community problem solving. Financial resources to support the development of urban research, per se, are limited by modest funding through the relevant federal statutes, but there are extensive funds available in health research and other technical areas.

But even if resources were available in greater quantity, the problems would still remain of how to relate appropriate research topics to the interests and competence of the faculty. Also, the clients for urban research are impatient for useful and quick results. The academic style of leisurely study is ill-suited to the task. Frequently, the academic researchers know less about a given problem than professionals routinely involved in managing urban agencies. In this context, the nature of academic expertise, the credentials prerequisite to inquiry, is uncertain. Given the production of research in the rather narrow areas of academic disciplines, how are these studies to be related one to another to produce a composite framework for urban development? The complexity of the city defies comprehensive interdisciplinary research, and problem-solving technology is of limited use. The university, not unlike municipal agencies, responds to specific aspects of a given crisis rather than to longer-term strategies of urban development. This is only partly owing to immediate pressure; it is also because of inadequate information about how the city works.[10] The apparent recourse is to make specialized inputs, "do" studies, and hope the city somehow improves. But even if adequate information were available, how would one choose, much less imple-

---

[9] *University Urban Research Centers* (Washington D.C. The Urban Institute, 1969).

[10] Elden Jacobson of the Washington Center for Metropolitan Studies has proposed the establishment of "urban observatories" throughout a given metropolitan area which would help to develop composite information to feed into a centralized ecosystem analysis of the city. Elden Jacobson, *Higher Education and Urban Affairs: An Approach for Metropolitan Washington* (Washington D.C.: Center for Metropolitan Studies, 1969).

ment the appropriate policy alternatives? The university is not in the business of making or implementing public policy. Few deny the enormity of the task; fewer still feel competent to assume its responsibility. Small wonder that the universities have moved into the arena at snail speed.

A somewhat more manageable concern on the part of the urban university is its relationship with the immediate neighborhood. One important case is the University of Chicago. In recent years the university has taken the initiative in conserving its neighborhood as a more desirable place for students and faculty to live. It has joined efforts of local groups to provide educational and health services for low-income residents of the area and has adopted a neighborhood elementary school for experimental purposes. Its medical and law schools provide services for local residents. Through these innovations, low-income residents of the area have discovered that the university provides access to services that they scarcely could obtain on their own. While residents are not wholly satisfied with the extent of the services they have received, the university recognizes their need and is taking deliberate steps to meet it.

Another important case is Harvard. A faculty committee, reporting its recommendations on steps to improve the relationship between Harvard and Cambridge, argues that what the university does in the community is constrained by what it is. "The university—any university—has a distinctive competence, a special nature: that competence is *not* to serve as a government, or a consulting firm, or a polity or a pressure group, or a family, or a kind of secularized church; it *is* to serve as a center of learning and free inquiry."[11]

Following this declaration about the limits of university participation, the committee explored a host of issues about Harvard's presence in Cambridge and concluded: (1)that the university's presence has an adverse effect on Cambridge's supply of housing, and that Harvard should help to ease the impact; (2)that the university should increase the number of blacks in its employ; and (3)that the constituent schools of Harvard have dramatically increased their city-related

[11]"Preliminary Report of the Committee on the University and the City," Harvard University, December 1968, p. 2.

programs. Examples include a neighborhood law office managed by law students, a dozen community assistance programs organized by undergraduates, experimental schools developed by the school of education, classes for black businessmen conducted by the business school, and a community health program being planned by the medical school.

Harvard and Chicago, of course, do not stand alone among universities in the growth of community services activity. But they are both distinctly urban in setting, and in this they are far more experienced than the land-grant universities. Virtually every university can report activities of these and other kinds. Partly through student efforts, but also by institutional initiatives, universities are groping for ways to improve relations with the community. UCLA and Michigan, for example, have established university-community councils to seek improvement in these relationships through an exchange of ideas among students, faculty, administrators, and local residents. The president of one of the universities believes that the existence of the council has provided useful guidelines for the institution to follow in employment practices, landlordship, and in conflict resolution between local residents and the university.

Universities everywhere are attempting to find relevant and useful relationships with the local community. There is need for evaluation of these efforts and replication of those that are more successful. New federal legislation may be in order to support them. In any event, it is clear that there is plenty for universities, land-grant or otherwise, to do on and off the campus to ease the workings of an urban society. That they do a better job of what they are supposed to do—educate —is doubtless of highest priority. This they cannot do by mythologizing their accomplishments in the past.

Urban Models

The conventional wisdom has it that land-grant universities provide a model for universities in the city. There are some who would direct the talents of land-grant universities toward urban problem solving. Others have claimed that applied research and extension, or open door equalitarianism, have been the distinctive contributions of land-grant universities, and that these functions and the attitudes favoring them should be grafted onto existing urban universities or be brought into being through massive federal spending. Others think the social sciences and humanities should be supported on a par with the natural sciences and imply that, if they are, this will lead to breakthroughs for urban problems. A "science of the cities" has been proposed, based on the rural precedent of a science of agriculture. All these views are questionable on several grounds.

First, it is doubtful that rural precedents are very helpful in conceptualizing urban complexity. As we have already pointed out with respect to urban extension agents, what was effective in a rural setting has not been very promising when applied to the city. And yet the myth persists that an urban corps of extension workers can do something to uplift the cities, translating the results of university research into useful application. In fact, this function is already being carried out, if imperfectly, by trained professionals—teachers, social workers, physicians, engineers, and so on. They are the modern equivalent of extension agents. If these professionals are not doing as well as they should, and they are not, the university has a responsibility to find out why not and to alter its curriculum accordingly if the faults are grounded in educational failings.

Second, few of the main campuses, meaning research centers, of the land-grant universities are located very near large cities. Even though distances are less important now than they were on the frontier, remoteness from the source of urban problems does not lend itself very obviously to their understanding or solution. Every university, wherever located, has responsibilities for preparing professional people and informed citizens, and every university conducts research with potential implications for improved urban services. It is all well and good for the land-grant institutions to emphasize urbanization in their programs, but it is quite another thing to claim to be a model for urban institutions and to expect to be taken seriously. We already have urban universities by the score, and hundreds of community colleges devoting themselves to the needs of the cities. Their experiences are more obviously productive of urban models than are rurally based institutions.

Third, it is generally agreed that research has provided the basic strength of land-grant contributions to American agriculture. It is quite another thing to propose application of the model to urbanization. The principal urban problems—housing, income distribution, racial conflict, equal opportunity, crime, to mention some of the most significant—are intensely political and economic problems, much more difficult and complex than the application of technology to produce more corn per acre. We know how to build better public housing, for example, since the technology is already available; but for a variety of political and economic reasons, we do not do it. While more research should and will be conducted, calls for massive increases in research funds for the behavioral sciences and humanities as a means to approach the giant social problems are based more on faith than experience. Moreover, the hard sciences are perhaps more likely to make a difference in these problems than are the soft sciences so long as our society enjoys relative democracy and freedom from authoritarian (or academic) manipulation. As far as a "science of the cities" is concerned, it is not clear how this science would differ in content or organization from the knowledge we already have. It would likely become a gigantic academic boondoggle. Continued selective support to competent scientists is a more promising and politically realistic likelihood.

Fourth, land-grant universities have prided themselves on being equalitarian in admissions and outlook so that, in many states, virtually every rural youngster who could afford to lay down the plow had the opportunity to go to college. In recent years, however, many universities have become more selective, admitting to their main campuses only the most academically talented students plus a quota of minority groups who are admitted under different criteria. Meanwhile, the community colleges, statewide systems, and some urban public universities have developed open door admissions, and it is these institutions that have principally assumed the equalitarian criteria. Should the land-grant institutions become more research oriented than they are now, and at the same time continue to raise the cost of tuitions, they will become even more selective. Here again, the land-grant model is more myth than reality.

Rural Policy

One may wonder if land-grant institutions do not have their work cut out for them at home, rather than trying to assume large responsibilities for urban development, responsibilities that other institutions are better equipped to assume. There is poverty in abundance in rural America, together with the associated ills of inadequate housing, health care, racial ignorances, schooling, and the like. Should not more of the land-grant resources be devoted to these problems?

Too, the back-to-the-earth movement in America may be more than a passing fancy of the youth culture. It is deeply ingrained in the American agrarian spirit. In the future, the movement may be expected to gain momentum as more Americans choose this alternative over urban complexity and blight, and over suburban homogeneity and dullness. The land-grant colleges can ease and assist this development, devoting research and extension resources to the needs of the small and part-time farmer, to organic agriculture, rural land-use planning, rural health services, and schooling. These needs are great, but they are no greater than the potential contribution of the land-grant universities.

In the rush to be relevant and urban, we have not very often taken the long view with respect to patterns of living beyond the city. Most people now prefer the lifestyle of suburbia, and many others are rediscovering exurbia. For a more sensible social organization, and to relieve the pressure on the inner city, these alternatives should be enhanced, giving city and suburban residents—black and white alike —the social and technical supports they need to make a rural style of life, once again, a feasible and attractive possibility. This is as great a challenge as urban needs; indeed, it is part of the solution to urban problems.

Chapter 13

UPDATING EDUCATION FOR THE PROFESSIONS: THE NEW MISSION

LARRY L. LESLIE

An Historical Sketch of Professional Education

THE place of education for the professions in the university has been varied. There have been times and places in which the teaching of applied subjects was considered beneath the dignity of learned gentlemen. In such instances, the less obvious the subject's relevance, the higher its status. In mid-nineteenth-century America, President Barnard of the University of Alabama indicated that the craft society and all that was vocationalism would never have a place in institutions of formal learning: "While time lasts, the farmer will be made in the field, the manufacturer in the shop, the merchant in the counting room, the civil engineer in the midst of the actual operation of science."[1]

Such views, however, were not present in the earliest days of the university. The first universities specialized in preparing young men for professional callings. Salerno, founded in the ninth century, and Montpelier, in the thirteenth-century, specialized in medicine. Bologna, established in the eleventh century, stressed the study of law, while the University of Paris, in keeping with twelfth-century piety, educated theologians.[2]

But when the university came to America with the founding of Harvard in 1636, it did not come to prepare professionals. Harvard sought primarily to educate "the men who would spell the difference between civilization and barbarism."[3] Harvard would endeavor also

[1]Walter P. Rogers, *Andrew D. White and the Modern University* (Ithaca, New York: The Cornell Press, 1942), p. 108.

[2]*The Columbia Encyclopedia* (New York: Columbia University Press, 1950), p. 2043.

[3]Frederick Rudolph, *The American College and University* (New York: Alfred A. Knopf, 1968), p. 6.

to prepare a "learned clergy," schoolmasters, and other servants of society but only through the traditional means; there would be no special job training.

The colonial college uniformly adhered to this philosophy. Indeed, when the specific training of civil servants was proposed at the College of William and Mary in 1724, it was rejected out of hand.[4] Although Virginia's leaders and public servants would continue to be educated at William and Mary, no formal statement of goals would confess to such a narrow purpose and no courses would be established to serve that explicit goal. The colonial college would maintain a purist tradition throughout. Thus, until the 1850s:

> Professional training, when available, was to be had only in narrow, dogmatic, and highly organized "schools" or thought and practice, but for the overwhelming majority, lawyers were office-read, physicians, apprentice trained, and ministers, emotionally inspired.[5]

The universities attempted to resist all that was applied prior to the 1850s, although the old, established professions gradually began to gain footholds. Professorships in theology appeared at Harvard and Yale before 1750. Thomas Jefferson established the first law professorship at William and Mary in 1765, the same year in which instruction was first offered in medicine at the College of Philadelphia. For the newer professions, there was no accommodation in eighteenth-century American universities: to prepare these professionals, separate, single-purpose institutions had to be founded. The first civilian technology school was developed at Rensselaer Polytechnic Institute in 1824; a special pharmacy school was established in Philadelphia in 1824; the first professional education of teachers began at a state normal school in Lexington, Massachusetts, in 1839; and the Baltimore College of Dental Surgery opened in 1840 (see Table 1).

The initial foothold gained in the universities by the "old" professions could be traced to the traditions of the colonial college which had concerned itself with educating the elites to be "honorable and

[4]Albea Godbold, *The Church of the Old South* (Durham, N.C.: Duke University Press, 1944), p. 5.
[5]Earle D. Ross, *Democracy's College* (Ames, Iowa: Iowa State College Press, 1942), p. 10.

Preparing the Professionals: The Scope of the Task

TABLE 1

First Independent and First University Professional Schools in the United States

Occupation	First Independent School	First University School
Accounting (CPA)	1881	1881
Architecture	1865	1868
Technology	1824	1847
Dentistry	1840	1867
Law	1784	1817
Medicine	1765	1779
Librarianship	1887	1897
Nursing	1861	1909
Optometry	1892	1910
Pharmacy	1824	1868
School teaching	1839	1879
Social work	1898	1904
Veterinary medicine	1852	1879
City management	1921	1948
City planning	1909	1909
Hospital administration	1926	1926
Advertising	1900	1909
Funeral direction	1870	1914

SOURCES: Harold L. Wilensky, "The Professionalization of Everyone?" *The American Journal of Sociology* 70(September 1964): 137–158; Mary Irwin, ed., *Higher Education in the United States* (Washington D.C.: American Council on Education, 1961), p. 14.

courteous gentlemen" through the study of the classics.[6] The common thread linking these early studies to the curriculum of the old professions (theology, law, medicine) was the focus on liberal studies centering upon man himself. "The new professionalism," however, "studied things, raised questions not so much about man's ultimate role and his ultimate responsibility as it did about whether this or that was a good way to go about achieving some immediate and limited object."[7]

But Jacksonian Democracy, nurtured by the increasingly complex industrial society of the latter nineteenth century and by post-Civil

[6]Frederick Rudolph, *The American College*, Chapter 1.
[7]Ibid., p. 342.

War equalitarianism, not only generated the wide-scale sentiment that all occupations were worthy, but also guaranteed passage of the Morrill (Land-Grant) Act in 1862. With the birth of the land-grant movement, the spirit of vocationalism could no longer be resisted by elitist universities. Indeed, the public universities only feigned resistance; most soon became willing partners in vocational education. Before long (1889) even Yale began offering undergraduate curricula and majors in several professional fields.

The land-grant mission that evolved was service to the people. It was, in the words of Lincoln Steffens of the University of Wisconsin, "Sending a State to College"; it was "teaching anybody-anything-anywhere."[8] The land-grant university was county agents and agriculture experiment stations; it was providing the expertise for anything the people needed or wanted to know. But it was more than just *direct* service to the people. The land-grant university meant preparing all the kinds of expert-professionals the people thought they might need and even those they had not yet thought about. The land-grant mission meant reacting to the immediate needs of the people and anticipating their needs far in advance. Sometimes it even meant doing things the people did not at the time think were good and useful. For this reason, the land-grant mission meant basic as well as applied research, even though the former occasionally might be resisted by a shortsighted public. In short, it sometimes meant assuming the responsibilities that accompany expertness and professionalism—placing the public welfare ahead of political expediency.

The preeminence of land-grant institutions in the preparation of professionals was no accident. At the outset, even their labels testified to their practical purposes and to their break with the dominant philosophy of early American higher education, which was traditional, elitist, and nonpragmatic. Land-grant institutions were called "colleges of agriculture," "colleges of mechanic arts," or "colleges of agriculture and mechanic arts." Their purposes were primarily to educate the farmers and agricultural technicians for increased crop

---

[8]Lawrence R. Veysey, *The Emergence of the American University* (Chicago: University of Chicago Press, 1965), p. 107.

production; to educate the housewife-home economist and her supporting cast for better nutrition, child rearing, and homemaking; and to prepare the engineers and technicians for a soon-to-expand industrial society.

Other universities, both public and private, involved themselves in professional education, to be sure; but they limited their efforts to those professions that could be characterized as learned—medicine, law, theology. The somewhat tainted professions—the mechanic arts (engineering) and especially agriculture and home economics—were almost the exclusive domain of the land-grant institution. Only the land-grant institution housed both types of professions.

Does the land-grant institution still have an exclusive domain in contemporary society? What is the present role of the land-grant institution in performing its assigned mission of preparing the nation's professionals?

Contemporary Demand for Professionals

Both of these questions imply a continuing demand for professionals in American society.

In general, the demand for professionals in the United States is expanding both relatively and absolutely. As demonstrated by the data in this section, the absolute number of professional workers and the percentage of the total work force engaged in professional practice now doubles about every fifteen years.[9]

Although the transition is by no means complete, the United States is rapidly becoming a post-industrial society. Many new businesses staffed by professionals, scientists, and consultants are now serving society by innovating and advising. Specialization is the watchword of the day, and millions of professionals are needed to serve the ever more complex society. In 1950 there were 4.6 million professional workers; in 1960 there were 5.9 million; and in 1970, 10.3 million (see Table 2). The 1950 figure represents 8.2 percent of

[9]The term "professional worker" as used here is from the Census Bureau classification: "professional, technical, and kindred workers." U. S. Department of Labor, *Handbook of Labor Statistics* (Washington: U. S. Government Printing Office, 1969); Idem., *Occupational Outlook Handbook* (Washington: U. S. Government Printing Office, 1968–69).

TABLE 2

Total Work Force; Number and Percentage of Professional Workers By Sex (in thousands)

	Work Force			Professionals			Percentage of Work Force			
	1950	1960	1970	1950	1960	1970	1950	1960	1970	1975 (est.)
Males	40,510	45,686	49,455	2,762[a]	3,430[a]	5,961[a]	6.8[a]	7.5[a]	12.1[a]	
				2,970[b]	4,543[b]	6,917[b]	7.3[b]	9.9[b]	14.0[b]	
Females	15,715	22,304	30,347	1,853[a]	2,428[a]	4,350[a]	11.8[a]	10.9[a]	14.3[a]	
				1,939[b]	2,793[b]	4,644[b]	12.3[b]	12.5[b]	15.3[b]	
Totals	56,225	67,990	79,802	4,615[a]	5,912[a]	10,311[a]	8.2[a]	8.7[a]	12.9[a]	
				4,909[b]	7,336[b]	11,561[b]	8.7[b]	10.8[b]	14.5[b]	19.4[b]

SOURCE: Comparable data are available from a variety of sources. These are taken from Department of Commerce, Bureau of the Census, *Statistical Abstract of the United States*, 1959, p. 220; 1970, pp. 227–28; and 1974, pp. 352–54.

NOTES: The data in these tables are not strictly comparable because the Census Bureau groups professionals with "technical and kindred workers." Therefore, it was necessary to cull the lists by hand, eliminating the technicians. The only exceptions to the culled lists are the 1975 estimates where no lists could be culled. Even the adjusted data, however, are still not completely accurate because the Bureau excluded some large groups usually classified as professions, such as military officers and certain scientists (e.g., chemists and physicists). These problems tend to deflate the figures in Table 1 and to make them quite conservative.

[a]Excludes occupations clearly technical in nature and not generally considered professions.

[b]All professional, technical, and kindred workers.

the total work force; the 1960 figure represents 8.7 percent; in 1970 the percentage had risen to 12.9. (In 1970, 10.3 million people were employed in occupations generally considered to be professions. Another 1.2 million were employed in technical or related occupations for a total of 11.5 million, or 14.5 percent of the total work force of almost 80 million persons.) By 1975 the percentage of workers in professional and professionally-related occupations is expected to have risen to 19.4 percent—almost one-fifth of the total work force.

1970 data revealed the male work force (49.4 million) to be about 2/3 larger than the female work force (30.3 million); only ten years earlier the ratio had been about 2:1; in 1950 the ratio was 7:2. Undoubtedly, the proportion has shifted again since 1970 as the ever-increasing number of women taking jobs has put the female work force nearer its maximum limit. The percentage of male workers in professional jobs (12.1 percent) is less than the female ratio of 14.3 percent, although this gap too is closing (see Table 2). Further analysis of these data by sex provides other insights into the professional work force. Among males, engineers, teachers (including higher education), accountants, and auditors compose almost 6 percent of the total work force and 42 percent of all male professionals. Six professions compose over 50 percent of the total male professional work force (see Table 3).

Female teachers alone make up almost 50 percent of all female professionals and are over 6 percent of the total female work force. About 18 percent of female professionals are engaged in nursing, which is the only other profession that appears to be either attractive or open to women. Teachers, nurses, and the next four ranking professions—writers, artists, and entertainers; accountants and auditors; social and recreation workers; and librarians—attract 78 percent of all female professionals and almost 12 percent of all female workers. A comparison of Tables 3 and 4 seems to provide much of the basis for the women's liberation movement, as it is quite apparent that the older, higher-status professions have remained primarily male callings. Only two professions, teaching and nursing, seem to be receptive to women.

For the combined sexes, only eight professions contain a substantial number of workers. The eight composed over 60 percent of all

TABLE 3
Male Professionals (1970 Census Data)

Occupation	Number Males	Percentage of Male Professionals	Percentage of Male Work Force
Engineers	1,210,000	17.5	2.45
Teachers (all levels)	1,172,000	16.9	2.37
Accountants and Auditors	526,000	7.6	1.06
Lawyers and Judges	260,000	3.8	.52
Physicians	256,000	3.7	.52
Religious workers	228,000	3.3	.46
Total	3,652,000	52.8	7.38
Total Other Male Professionals	3,265,000	47.2	6.60
Total Male Professionals	6,917,000	100.0	
Total Male Work Force	49,455,000		13.99

SOURCE: Statistical Abstract of the United States, 1974, pp. 352–55.

TABLE 4
Female Professionals (1970 Census Data)

Occupation	Number Females	Percentage of Female Professionals	Percentage of Female Work Force
Teachers (all levels)	2,093,000	45.1	6.89
Registered Nurses	819,000	17.6	2.69
Writers, Artists, and Entertainers	241,000	5.2	.79
Accountants	187,000	4.0	.61
Social and Recreation Workers	161,000	3.5	.53
Librarians	101,000	2.2	.33
Total	3,602,000	77.6	11.87
Total Other Female Professionals	1,042,000	22.4	3.43
Total Female Professionals	4,644,000	100.0	
Total Female Work Force	30,347,000		15.30

SOURCE: *Statistical Abstract of the United States*, 1970.

professionals in 1970, with the top three—teaching, engineering, and nursing—accounting for 46 percent. The 1970 data, although not strictly comparable because of varying procedures used by the Census Bureau in compiling statistics, do show large percentage gains in the numbers of physicians and surgeons, teachers, engineers, lawyers and judges, and social workers. Accountants and auditors and clergymen were more stable groups. The larger gains can be partially accounted for by the increasing demands for health care in an increasingly prosperous and egalitarian society (physicians), lower public school dropout rates and a disproportionately large school age population in comparison to the total population (teachers), ever-advancing technology (engineers), the extension of legal services (attorneys), and a more socially aware society (social workers).

The eight professions listed in Table 5 and the six professions listed separately for males and females by no means exhaust the usual list of professions. Dentists, librarians, doctors of veterinary medicine, pharmacists, architects, and certain groups of scientists are almost *always* considered professionals. Administrators, managers, dieticians, home economists, actors, artists, foresters, systems analysts, and journalists are *often* so considered. Technologists, especially in the health and scientific fields, are *categorized* as professionals.

Indeed, this question of professional status has long been an issue among all vocational groups. Vollmer and Mills, for example, avoid the issue by defining a profession as "an ideal type of occupational organization which does not exist in reality."[10] Howard S. Becker does likewise and his definition best suits our purposes here. Becker refers to professions as those occupations which are fortunate enough to have obtained and maintained the title.[11] This definition, which reflects general societal perceptions, is implicitly used throughout this paper, except where noted.

The task of preparing the bulk of the nation's professionals falls largely on the land-grant colleges and universities and on compre-

[10]Howard M. Vollmer and Donald L. Mills, *Professionalization* (Englewood Cliffs, New Jersey: Prentice-Hall, Inc., 1966), p. vii.

[11]H. Becker, "The Nature of a Profession," *Education for the Professions: The Sixty-First Yearbook of the National Society for the Study of Education,* Part II (Chicago: University of Chicago Press, 1962), pp. 32–33.

TABLE 5

Number in Selected Major Professions (1960 and 1970);
Percentages of Total Professional Work Force (1960 and 1970);
Percentage Increase (1960 to 1970)

Occupation	Number		Percentage of Total Professionals		Percentage Increase From
	1960	1970	1960	1970	1960–70
Teachers (al levels)	1,993,000	3,265,000	28.1	28.2	63.8
Engineers	864,000	1,210,000	12.2	10.5	40.0
Nurses	614,000	819,000	8.7	7.1	33.4
Accountants & Auditors	496,000	713,000	7.0	6.2	43.8
Physicians & Surgeons	217,000	256,000	3.1	2.2	18.0
Lawyers & Judges	211,000	260,000	3.0	2.2	23.2
Clergymen	220,000	228,000	3.1	2.0	3.6
Social Workers	123,000	274,000	1.7	2.4	122.8
Total	4,738,000	7,025,000	66.9	60.8	
Total Other Professions	2,352,000	4,556,000	33.1	39.2	
Total Professional	7,090,000	11,561,000	100.0	100.0	

source: *Statistical Abstract of the United States, 1974.*

hensive colleges. Although most professional education occurred in independent schools prior to the land-grant movement, such is no longer the case. William McGlothlin's national study of ten major professions revealed that members of three of these professions are trained exclusively in complex institutions. Only two independent nursing schools and two independent architecture schools offer baccalaureate degrees. Of 126 accredited law schools, 6 are independent, while 11 of 70 medical schools are in this category. Of 210 engineering schools, 35 are independent. The proportion of such business schools is somewhat higher. Of 1,200 teacher-preparing institutions, 125 were titled "teachers' colleges" in 1960.[12] But such single purpose institutions are in general decline for teaching and for most other professions.

Trends in the composition of the work force indicate the magnitude of the task confronting institutions of higher learning in the preparation of professionals. The question remains: to what degree is the preparation of professionals being met by institutions of higher learning in general and land-grant universities in particular?

In 1950 the task was to produce 205,000 first professional degrees of the 365,000 total bachelors' and first professional degrees granted. By 1971 first professional degree output (462,483) was greater than the total bachelors' and first professional degree output had been in 1950, while the total degree output had more than doubled. The 1971 percentage of first professional degrees and of bachelors' degrees that were professional degrees exceeded 50 percent. Hence, on the dimension of degrees granted, the major task of the nation's colleges and universities was professional education. Further, the 50-percent figure was conservative because a sizable portion of the degrees listed as nonprofessional were undoubtedly professional in the sense that their earners took professional employment in the field for which they were prepared. For example, many prospective teachers earn degrees in the area of their teaching specalty in the liberal and fine arts. Many person who receive degrees in chemistry, physics, English, drama, etc., take professional positions as chemists, physicists,

---

[12]William J. McGlothlin, *Patterns of Professional Education* (New York: Putnam, 1960), pp. 169–70.

TABLE 6

Number of Bachelors' and First Professional Degrees Conferred;
Percentages of Total Degrees Conferred (1971)

	Number	Percentage of Total Degrees Conferred[a]
Professional Field		
Education	176,571	20.1
Business	115,527	13.1
Engineering	50,046	5.7
Law	17,966	2.0
Agriculture	12,672	1.4
Nursing	12,199	1.4
Home Economics	11,167	1.3
Communications	10,802	1.2
Public Affairs & Services	9,220	1.1
Medicine	8,919	1.0
Theology	8,799	1.0
Architecture	5,570	0.6
Dentistry	3,745	0.4
Library Science	1,013	0.1
Miscellaneous Professional	18,267	2.1
Total Professional	462,483	52.7
Nonprofessional Field		
Social Sciences	193,206	22.0
English and Foreign Languages	93,067	10.6
Physical and Biological Sciences and Mathematics	81,956	9.3
Fine Arts	30,394	3.5
Miscellaneous Nonprofessional	16,570	1.0
Total Nonprofessional	415,193	47.3
Total Degrees Conferred	877,676	100.0
Total Professional Degrees Conferred (1950)	204,922	
Total Degrees Conferred (1950)	365,748	

SOURCE: Department of Commerce, *Statistical Abstract of the United States,* 1974, p. 139.
[a]All figures rounded.

writers and editors, and actors. Others defer professional employment only until completion of graduate training. In short, most higher education is clearly professional training.

Among the degrees granted in 1971, 20 percent of all bachelors' and first professional degrees were in education and 13 percent were in business. Engineers accounted for another 6 percent. The remaining approximately 14 percent of professional degrees were conferred in 11 other professions.

Society's collegiate institutions have generally responded well—perhaps almost miraculously—to the ever-expanding demand for professional workers. In some cases, they have over-responded and in other cases they have not responded quite well enough. Table 7 shows that if the 1969 rates were to be held constant until 1980, surpluses would occur in some fields and shortages would persist in others. There would, for example, be far too many teachers; indeed, the years since 1969 suggest the 40 percent excess of Table 7 is conservative (note 1971 data). Law school enrollment increases in 1971 suggest an exacerbation of the surpluses in this area. Engineering enrollments in 1971 were, temporarily at least, continuing to rise in spite of an impending glut. On the other hand, there is good reason for some encouragement that steps have been taken to diminish the deficits in the health fields, although there is somewhat less encouragement regarding the production of accountants and auditors and social workers.

A number of tentative conclusions related to the magnitude of the nation's need for and institutional preparation of professionals can be made. Clearly, American society is becoming more complex: the portion of the total work force that is composed of professionals definitely has exceeded 10 percent and may have exceeded 20 percent. A larger segment of the employed female work force is professional than is the case for males, and the total number of employed females is also increasing more rapidly than is the case for males. Accordingly, more than half of all degrees granted are in professional fields: the correct figure may be 60 or 70 percent. Even so, certain professions are plagued by shortages while others are experiencing a definite buyer's market. The role of the land-grant institution in these regards is and will continue to be meeting society's ever-changing demands for enough competent professional workers.

TABLE 7

Comparison of Degrees Conferred (1969–71)
to Annual Average Openings to 1980

Profession	Degrees Conferred[a]		Average Annual Openings 1968–80	Percentage Difference 1969	Percentage Difference 1971
	1969	1971			
Accountants & Aud.	21,556	23,257	33,000	53.0	41.9
Dentists	3,437	3,745	4,900	42.5	30.8
Engineering	60,173	70,127	53,000	−11.9	−24.4
Lawyers & Judges	18,571	18,941	14,500	−21.9	−23.4
Librarians	6,949	8,053	8,200	18.0	1.8
Nurses (professional)	11,773[b]	13,736[b]	65,000[c]	not applicable	not applicable
Physicians & Surgeons	8,082	8,919	20,800	157.0	133.2
Social Workers	8,578	not available	16,700	94.7	not available
Teachers	189,291	228,271	96,300	−49.1	−57.8

SOURCES: *Statistical Abstract of the United States,* 1971, p. 130, and 1974, p. 139; *The United States Economy in 1980,* United States Department of Labor, Bureau of Labor Statistics, Bulletin 1673, 1970, p. 58.

[a] Varies with figures in Table 6 because of large number of graduate degrees in these categories, whereas Table 6 excludes most graduate degrees.

[b] Nurses with four-year degrees or more.

[c] This figure is for registered nurses.

Changing Societal Needs and Their Relation
to Education for the Professions

Complex societies are dependent upon professionals. Professional workers provide the services essential to a society having great diversification of labor. Professionals in agriculture provide the technology which not only allows food and lumber supplies to keep pace with a growing population but also provides recreational facilities to meet rising leisure time demands. Business professionals contribute immensely to the total economic well-being of the entire society; in fact, without their expertise and philosophic outlook, we as a society would not have the luxury of worrying about leisure and refinements of the social order. Architects and engineers make equally essential contributions to the general welfare of the nation. Their expertise is what has assisted America in maintaining its position of leadership in the society of nations. Teachers have been instrumental in the development of an egalitarian educational system which has at the same time retained a character of quality. Social workers have been instrumental in attempting to extend the fruits of the American system to all citizens. The legal profession has consistently acted to defend the accused no matter how unpopular the cause. The health professions have promoted medical science to a point that millions of lives have been saved. Diseases, which only a generation or two ago caused great loss of life, are now little more than entries in the history books.

The professions have indeed had distinguished histories of service. Their contributions to the welfare of mankind defy tabulation. However, the maintenance of a sense of social responsibility by professionals is a task requiring constant attention and sensitivity. Change is the descriptor of this period in our history, and land-grant institutions have a major role to perform.

On at least two dimensions land-grant institutions would appear to have diminished the magnitude of their tradition of service to the people, and thus a rekindling of professional commitment is needed. The first dimension, which is not mutually exclusive of the second, has to do with the changing composition of the work force. No longer is the society predominantly agrarian: only about 8 percent of the population reside on farms. But land-grant universities have not shifted their orientations accordingly; their attention to the urban condition has not kept pace with societal changes. For the multitudes who have moved to the cities, the land-grant universities have not launched an effort comparable in magnitude to the great agrarian-relatedservice undertakings of the past. For the cities, there have been no massive, coordinated efforts to serve the needs of the people. As Clark Kerr tells us:

> Higher education is facing the city for the first time. In Europe—in fact in most of the world—the university is a city institution; the capital city has the most famous university and each provincial city has its own university, usually of lesser note in proportion to the city itself. This has not been the American pattern. . . . Except for occasional studies, as at the University of Chicago in the 1930's, and occasional institutes, as at Berkeley and Syracuse, the city was largely ignored. This neglect of the city paralleled the interests of the population at large.[13]

It may be argued that the land-grant university's relative effort of service to the people has declined and the social distance between the land-grant university and its people has increased. At the very least, the service component of the land-grant mission has declined in relation to the teaching and research components.

The second dimension, which is largely an explication of the first, is a decrease in the relative amount of direct service to the people of the state by representatives of the land-grant institutions. Although there is no sound empirical evidence to support this statement, it would nevertheless seem that the land-grant university of the early twentiety century and especially the 1930s and 1940s was in almost constant contact with the public. This period was the heyday of the agricultural experiment station, the decentralized extension service in areas such as agriculture and home economics, the county agent, the university's public school accrediting teams, and the traveling

---

[13]Clark Kerr, "New Challenges to the College and University," *Agenda for the Nation* (Washington: Brookings Institution, 1968), p. 251.

professor who toured the state evenings and on weekends spreading knowledge and expert assistance directly to the applier of that knowledge—the worker. Perhaps more of this remains than is visibly apparent; but considering the number of persons to be served and the declining portion of personnel responsible for meeting these needs directly, per capita direct contacts must surely be decreasing. Agriculture and home economics services appear to be in relative decline on a per capita basis, and the portion of courses taught away from the central campus must also be greatly diminished. Today, the expert professor of the modern land-grant university dispenses his knowledge largely through his courses on the main campus and through the scholarly journals rather than directly to the people in the field. The public's perception of these changes is clearly that the land-grant university is no longer quite the people's institution it once was. What seems clear is that the land-grant institution has not yet adapted its general goal of service to the people to the needs of contemporary society. What, then, are the specific needs of contemporary society, especially the urban, that are related to the professions?

The list of profession-related needs reads like a catalogue of the domestic social problems of the day. Society is asking such questions as:

Why are teachers seemingly incapable of educating disadvantaged children, while at the same time they are conspicuously successful with white children from middle-class homes?
Why do medical doctors, whose primary motivation as premedical students was to serve mankind, avoid establishing practices in inner cities or in rural areas where their services are desperately needed?
Why are engineers and scientists apparently more concerned with efficiency and product performance than with the long-range effects of those products and polluting by-products, particularly those that result from the growth or extraction of raw materials and the manufacturing process?
Why do social workers seemingly nurture client dependence rather than independence?
Why do lawyers and medical doctors concentrate on treating manifest problems rather than seeking to prevent the occurrence of latent problems?

Current Patterns of Professional Operation

Many such questions could be posed; the above list is only illustrative. Clearly, the present pattern of professional operation is failing somewhere. We can best determine what these failures are and how to remedy them by considering the responsibility of professionals to the society as a function of three interrelated factors:

1) providing an adequate supply of professionals who would
   . . .
2) provide the kind of service society needs, and . . .
3) provide the service in an efficient and effective professional delivery system.

(See Table 8 for application of these to eight major professions.) Failure in any of these three results in a societal problem as shown in the last column of Table 8.

Supply of Professionals

All professions have some serious concern with professional supply—be it oversupply or undersupply. Most have been faced with continuing and usually serious shortages (doctors, nurses, dentists, social workers, conservation-related agricultural occupations, accountants and related business specialities, landscape architects, and most types of engineers). In several other occupational groups, (teachers, lawyers, aerospace engineers, scientists, and mathematicians), the immediate concern is with an oversupply.

In several professions (e.g., medicine, nursing, social work), supplies of workers are directly related to certain other social needs. In fact, shortages of nurses and doctors may be the most serious issue related to the health professions. That many of the poor and geographically remote are without medical service is more serious than the particular quality of the service that is provided elsewhere. Whether the cause for shortages has been an effort by professional school faculties to keep enrollments down, a lack of vigorous recruiting, a lack of sufficient pecuniary rewards for graduates (as may be the case in social work and nursing), insufficient resources for expanded professional school faculty and facilities, or the increasing demand for professional services due to the rapid growth of society's ability to pay, it is the professional schools' responsibility to produce professionals in sufficient numbers. As such, supply may turn out to be a profession's major preoccupation, leaving few resources available for other reforms.

Mode of Professional Service

The professional's mode of service is self-explanatory. The primary mode of professional service for law is defending the accused or resolving conflict; for medicine, it is healing the sick; for social work, it is ministering to the needy; for teaching, it is educating the educable. How these service modes relate to societal stresses will become clear later.

The mode of service for the professions can be sorted into two general types: treatment of a condition (the upper half of Table 8, hereafter referred to as Group I professions) and production of goods or services (the bottom half, hereafter referred to as Group II professions). In the former case, society (clients) receives a direct service, while in the latter case there is an intermediate client (usually an employer) before the ultimate client (society) receives the goods or services (see Table 8).

Although there is general merit in this simplification of service modes, a word of caution is necessary. Whereas it is true that the Group I professions project an image of being concerned chiefly with treating manifest conditions, they are also involved in prevention. For example, much of the attorney's time is devoted to such preventive functions as family counseling, estate advising, and tax consulting. Similarly, the medical profession does devote much attention to medical research and public health. The point emphasized here, however, is the need for some redressing of the balance between condition treatment and condition prevention in order to meet the changing needs and expectations of society. For example, because medical care in this country is coming to be a right rather than a privilege, it will be necessary to streamline delivery systems and to place a greater emphasis upon preventive measures. Only in this way will professionals be able to decrease the incidence of more serious and costly diseases and fully meet the expectations of society.

The nature of the two general modes leads to certain difficulties. First, by emphasizing the treatment of conditions, prevention of conditions is often overlooked. That is, by emphasis upon healing the sick and injured, the well are not prevented from becoming ill or injured. By focusing upon the accused, sources of criminal behavior and causes of civil litigation are sometimes ignored. By responding primarily to the manifest conditions of the needy, dependence is increased rather than reduced. By satisfactorily educating only those who are easily educated, many broader social conditions worsen. The Group II professions respond only secondarily to society; their top priority is to their employers. As such, if the employer's goals run counter to the goals of society—a condition that may often be the case—the general public welfare suffers.

Professional Delivery Systems

Table 8 also defines the professional delivery system. In law, for example, it is the court system; in medicine, it is the hospital, clinic, medical center, or private office. For social work the primary professional delivery system is the government agency, and for teaching it is the neighborhood school. For Group II professions, the primary professional delivery system for agriculture is government and business; and for architecture, business, and engineering, the primary delivery system is the business or industrial firm.

The delivery systems, as well as service modes, of the legal, medical, social work, and teaching professions are directly related to the results or outcomes, i.e., the social issues themselves. Indeed, the relationship of these two elements to the social issues is clearly implied by Table 8. As seen in Table 8, the results of implementing general professional modes through a given delivery system are determined by the values or constraints attached to the modes and/or the effect these values or constraints have upon the delivery system or the delivery system has upon them.

An example applied to Table 8 should aid in its interpretation: The legally accused are defended in the courts on the general basis of their ability to pay. To be sure, the criminally accused can be appointed

TABLE 8

A Framework for Analyzing Operation of the Professions

Professional Area	Quantity (projected)	Mode of Professional Services	Professional Delivery System	Present Societal Results (including by-products)
Group I				
Law	Oversupply	Defend the accused or resolve conflict.	Court system	Drawn-out legal proceedings with no guarantee of a speedy trial; public jeopardy from criminals; high insurance costs; equal treatment of the poor denied.
Medicine	Undersupply	Heal the sick (treat rather than prevent conditions, and only for those who can pay).	Hospital, clinic, medical center, private office	Few physicians in rural areas; shortages in central cities; shortages of family physicians; unavailability to many of the poor.
Social work	Undersupply	Minister to the needy (sustain client dependency)	Government agency	Client dependence; dramatically higher costs; jeopardy of our social institutions—the family, the work ethnic.

DIRECTLY

INDIRECTLY

Teaching	Oversupply	Educate the educable (ignore the difficult to educate).	Neighborhood school	Inferior education for the disadvantaged resulting in lifelong inequality for jobs; segregation; tradition-bound education for all.
Group II				
Agriculture	Undersupply	Provide goods or services.	Business & governmental agencies	Insecticide damage to the ecosystem; destruction of forest resources; damage to leisure life; insufficient recreation areas.
Architecture	Assessments vary	Provide services.	Business or industrial agencies	Loss of aesthetics.
Business	Varies by subfield	Provide goods or services.	Business or industrial agencies	Environmental damage; consumer exploitation.
Engineering	Varies by subfield	Provide goods or services.	Business or industrial agencies	Environmental damage.

*This paradigm was developed from a recent two-year survey of the periodical literature of these eight professions.

legal counsel; but the quality of the defense is generally directly proportional to the client's ability to pay. Further, free counsel in noncriminal cases is not yet widespread, and the accused too often wait long periods in prison or are freed at public peril while awaiting trial. Civil suits often wait years before being heard. Chief villains are the contingency fee system, which encourages lawyers to seek and nurture complaints, and anachronistic court procedures.

Numerous other specific societal problems result from dysfunctional delivery systems. The mandatory need of business or industry, the delivery system of Group II professions, is to return a profit on the goods or services their professional employees help to produce. If the ultimate client, society, suffers, it is only of secondary concern. But there is no inherent reason why professionals cannot faithfully perform their services at a profit to employers and still be protective of the public welfare.

The delivery system of medicine is the doctor's office, where a nurse, technician, and receptionist may be in attendance; but the health team's goal is disease treatment, not prevention. Although the number of health clinics (a needed delivery system) is increasing slightly, the unit of service mode—disease treatment—is not changing significantly. Furthermore, within the given delivery system the poor are neglected because doctors, by and large, do not establish practices among the poor, clinics are not built for easy access to the poor (even though their greatest need is preventive medicine), and the costs of medical service are so great as to tend to exclude the poor from the form of medicine that is available. The overall effect is to make health care to a great extent a privilege of the nonpoor. And yet the solution is obviously not so simple as making physicians socially responsible. The model of medical education and medical service and the system of delivery mitigate against doctor initiatives for reform. But if the medical mode were to become disease *prevention* or a more reasoned combination of prevention and treatment, the delivery system would necessarily change as would the observable social responsiveness of the health worker.

Social workers deliver their services through a government agency system which is both a facilitator and an inhibitor. Without the government bearing the brunt of public criticism, the welfare system might lose much of its ability to cope with the problems. However, agency regulations curb caseworker efforts to act as client advocates and to provide means for eliminating dependency.

The neighborhood school with "egg-crate" classrooms and a system of "musical chairs," whereby students may rotate from one traditional, teacher-centered classroom to another, is the delivery system for public education. The neighborhood school concept has successfully preserved *de facto* segregation for decades, and the traditional classroom has done much to prevent an educational renaissance for a good deal longer.

The net effects of the present pattern of operation of the professions have been considerable exclusion of clients from professional services in the medical and legal fields and jeopardization of those services in all of the Group II professions. Undersupplies of professional workers, nonpreventive modes of service, and outmoded delivery systems have increased the costs of and reduced the availability of many professional services. In other cases, clients have suffered ill effects from dysfunctional service modes and delivery systems, to wit, the welfare and educational systems.

For those professions having society only as an indirect client (Group II professions), employers have dictated the priorities. Byproducts from the production of goods have accumulated to the point that serious damage to the environment has become inevitable. Pesticides from agriculture; water, air, and land pollution from industries and indirectly from engineering; and visual pollution from architecture are causes for societal concern.

Responding to Evolving Societal Needs

It follows logically that land-grant institutions, through their professional schools, can respond to the largely urban-related social needs by themselves exercising professional responsibility in the education of sufficient numbers of professionals and in facilitating the alteration of service modes and delivery systems through their curricular formats. The professional schools are the transmitters, the perpetuators, of prevailing modes of service; thus, there is little hope of bringing about changes without first effecting them. This poses the rather difficult problem of changing the socialization of neophyte professionals in departments run by faculty who are themselves not socialized to the currently needed patterns.

A fundamental aspect of the need for change involves the current problem of undersupply in certain fields. With respect to this problem, the efforts of some professional schools have been to keep enrollments low. Sometimes professional school faculties have good cause for their exclusiveness; however, they often appear to be doing nothing more than maintaining a favorable balance in supply and demand. There can be little defense for this practice. If it could be assumed, however, that applicants in sufficient numbers could be obtained, the challenges of supply would still not be fully met. A part of this problem is that of assuring a supply of professionals having a sensitivity to the changing social demands upon their profession and a willingness to meet these obligations.

Space is insufficient to develop fully the argument here, but it can be demonstrated that the primary locus for altering the values, attitudes, and perspectives—the sense of social responsibility—of neophyte professionals is the professional education process itself.[14] That is, professionals are socialized to certain values in the professional schools and it is almost impossible to change undesirable behaviors emanating from those values. Hence, for example, Group II professionals are taught that their first loyalty is to the employer, although there is no absolute reason why this must be so. In fact, one of the most essential characteristics of a profession is that it have the best interest of society at heart. As Howard Becker maintains in discussing the criteria for professional membership, in a professional-client relationship the client "rests comfortable on the knowledge that this is one relationship in which the rule of the market place does not apply."[15] New student selection criteria are demanded to provide a supply of professionals who will respond to societal needs.

[14]Larry L. Leslie, Kenneth P. Mortimer, and G. Lester Anderson, *Professional Education: Some Perspectives, 1971* (University Park, Pennsylvania: Center for the Study of Higher Education, The Pennsylvania State University, 1970), pp. 46–51.
[15]Becker, "The Nature of a Profession," p. 37.

But the heart of the matter of professions meeting changing societal demands involves more than new selection criteria; it involves also altering existing service modes and delivery systems. It would appear that professionals are so locked into present modes and delivery systems that the basic outlook of individual professionals will have to be modified. The modification of outlook and the resulting modification in service modes and delivery systems may most reasonably take place in the professional schools.[16] The question, then, becomes one of means.

The most obvious and most often employed strategy in the past has been the addition of electives in the humanities and social sciences. However, as Rosenstein noted, the mere addition of electives in these areas, if taught in the normal departmental delivery mode, does not lead to the results required. Rosenstein recommended that the beginning courses in the social sciences and humanities, which are often taught in their respective disciplines as first courses toward the Ph.D., be transferred into the organizational structure of the professional schools.[17] Through this means, Rosenstein felt, elective courses would come to be taught in an applied fashion, drawing the implications of the humanities and social sciences to the socially responsible practice of the profession.

Though a step in the right direction, moving electives into a professional school may not be adequate. It was noted at the Institute of Technology of the University of Minnesota in the late fifties, for example, that when personnel from other disciplines taught within the institute, there was little visible effort to relate these courses to engineering practices. Courses continued to be taught as discrete disciplines even though they were housed in the institute.

It seems essential that courses aimed at increasing social awareness and sensitivity be taught by members of the profession involved, and that these persons be individuals concerned about the various

[16]This conclusion results from an exhaustive consideration of options as given in Larry L. Leslie and James L. Morrison's, "Society and the Professions: Challenge to Education for the Professions," Mimeographed (University Park, Pennsylvania: The Pennsylvania State University, 1972).

[17]A. B. Rosenstein, *A Study of a Profession and Professional Education* (Los Angeles: Reports Group, School of Engineering and Applied Science, UCLA, 1968).

social problems and, if possible, persons with relevant social experience. Examples of such persons would be the socially sensitive physician who has worked in the public health service or in central-city clinics, the comparably sensitive teacher who has taught in disadvantaged schools, and the comparably sensitive engineer who has worked in pollution control. These persons should have graduate training in one of the social sciences, but the critical variables are identity with the profession and socially relevant experiences.

A further strategy would be that of selective internships in agencies geographically proximate to the locus of social needs. This would eliminate the too common practice of internship assignments structured to insulate neophyte professionals from experiences that might be trying and frustrating. Teaching internships, for example, have characteristically avoided the central city wherever possible. The same sort of protected arrangements have been the rule in other fields. The reverse of such practices could facilitate the development of social sensitivity and a sense of responsibility among many young professionals, with the result that prospects for altering service modes and delivery systems would be greatly increased. Such changes are vital if professions are to continue to remain relevant to the collectivities they serve.

There are larger organizational changes professional schools need to make as well. It is probably necessary that formal departments or programs be established in areas such as family and community medicine, urban education, environmental engineering, and so forth. Regardless of the dangers inherent in formalizing such structures (e.g., the problems of working across departmental lines), departmentalization is probably necessary to the legitimation of the basic philosophy which such departments would represent.

Recently, a pilot study testing these ideas was completed in Pennsylvania professional schools that seek to meet precisely the kinds of social needs discussed here. From this limited investigation, several key elements of change were identified.

Important changes seem to occur only where at least two, if not all, of the following conditions are present: (1) a strong external stimulus, usually in the form of a large grant, which dictates the establishment of a new program direction; (2) dynamic, unrelenting leadership that insists on meeting the objectives set forth in the initial proposal; (3) a new organizational structure with new and relatively inexperienced (less socialized) faculty members; and (4) a student-recruiting effort designed to clearly convey the special purpose for which the program was established.

Numerous examples exist of institutions beginning to demonstrate a commitment to meeting the demands of the modern, largely urban society. Yet there is much more to be done. The problems of the late twentieth century American society call for greatly expanded efforts by all of higher education. Yet, no social institution is so uniquely equipped to meet this challenge as is the land-grant college or university, an institution that was created to meet precisely this need and an institution that has had a long and distinguished record of such accomplishments.

Chapter 14

NEW COLLEGES FOR NEW OCCUPATIONS

WILLIAM TOOMBS

The American Work Ethic and the Land-Grant Tradition

THE belief that action is the measure of the man has always been part of the ethos of American life. Lacking the cumulative effects over centuries of land tenure or inheritance, without the symbolic superiorities of blood and tradition, the New World identified and judged men by their acts. As the more regular patterns of industry and commerce replaced the frontier farm, work in the form of occupation became the symbol of action and a key to social position. Public schooling found its justification by linking education to job improvement and, hence, to a richer life and higher social position. This cultural network of education, work, and position has been a social force of unusual potency for a century and a half.

The land-grant movement fitted squarely into this view. In the words of the Morrill Act, education was to be "liberal and practical" with a heavy emphasis upon the "useful sciences" and putting knowledge to work.[1] And the search to fulfill this idea developed a powerful interplay between higher education, the sphere of productive endeavor, and the social structure.

Constant Direction and Dynamic Response

Even in the earliest stages of the land-grant movement the commitment to democratic opportunity was fundamental. Extending educational options equally to a large sector of the population was the central idea that gave constancy to the development of the institution. By itself, however, democratization does not explain the vital-

---

[1]Arthur J. Klein, *Survey of Land-Grant Colleges and Universities* (Washington, D. C.: Government Printing Office, 1930), vol. 1, p. 22; vol. 2, p. 2.

ity of the land-grant movement, which met clear and serious challenges.

At their inception, land-grant institutions faced an array of basic dualities. There were cleavages between the agronomist and the dirt farmer, the mechanic and engineer, the inventor and researcher, between those who sought accommodation with nature and those who would shape nature to man's ends. Educational differences reached even deeper to a continuous confrontation of contemporary views and classical collegiate education. Those who were trained in the older colleges saw knowledge as stable and authoritative, while the challengers perceived it to be tentative, always in a state of becoming. Hardin called attention to the practical difficulties in founding new institutions with faculty drawn from the older tradition.[2] "The faculties of the new Land-Grant institutions were often composed of scholars and scientists trained in the strict and orthodox institutions, and these men often found their own philosophies colliding directly—often rudely—with the needs, desires, and demands of the pioneer societies they were called upon to serve." There was contrast, too, between the classical emphasis upon the educated man and the newer goal of an educated society. These divisions and contrasts were transformed into a source of continuing vitality in the land-grant setting. Although arbitrary selection of one view or the other might have become the basis of policy, none of these dualities could be resolved outright, for each set of views is, at its roots, a paradox. It was the continuous interplay—debate, trial, criticism, and review—that became the source of vitality.[3] Another source of vitality has been continuous contact with the practical world of applied ideas and with people engaged in practice. Such associations provided a feedback that was absent from, and not even imaginable in, classical education. Extension services, experiment stations, and laboratories created a network of interaction that lay close to the process of oscillation between the specific

[2]Clifford M. Hardin, "Address to the Ambassadors" (Washington, D.C.: American Association of Land-Grant Colleges and State Universities, 1969), vol. 1, p. 7.
[3]Klein, *Survey of Land-Grant Colleges,* vol. 2, pp. 1–5. The author recounts how four different views of the arts and sciences were kept under continuous experimentation and debate.

and the general which Whitehead sees as the heart of education.[4]

As a consequence of this dynamism, the land-grant institution has kept very close to the main currents of national life for the last ninety years. The development of science into its applied dimensions of technology; the institutionalization of research as a planned, continuous, and directed group effort; knowledge seen as a developmental phenomenon rather than a structure to be maintained: all this became part of normal operation for the land-grant university. And finally, the concept of learning as an activity appropriate for all the people fitted perfectly with the social strivings of an open society. Whatever limitations may be attributed to this dynamic interplay, one valuable effect has been to render the land-grant institution a servant of public interest and not an instrument of government control.

In summary, the land-grant movement drew its direction from a commitment to democracy, drew its vitality from the exchange of diverse views and from interaction with the daily life of the nation, and found a mission in responding to this complex of factors.

I. The Land-Grant Institutions and National Manpower

Nowhere is the capacity of the land-grant institutions for sensing social change and responding to it clearer than in the development of national manpower resources. The magnitude of this response to a steadily increasing need for new levels of competence is well illustrated by an increasing number of land-grant graduates prepared in the traditional professions, law and medicine, and in the newer professions of engineering and education.

Beyond the professional sector lies the more open landscape of occupations. It is here, buried in the complexity of change, that some of the qualitative factors of the land-grant response can be found, factors that have much to do with the employment of tomorrow's graduates. We note, for example, the role of land-grant institutions in moving occupations into the professional ranks. In response to the

---

[4]Alfred North Whitehead, *The Aims of Education* (New York: Macmillan, 1959), pp. 222–26.

rise of public education, particularly at the secondary level, training at these newer colleges transformed schoolmasters and schoolkeepers into educators and teachers with professional viewpoints, competencies, and status of their own. A similar transition is visible in business, where scattered commercial activities crystallized into the profession of management. The distribution of baccalaureate degrees at several points in time (Table 1) gives some indication of the nature of the land-grant response to the need for new levels of skill and knowledge.

Any attempt to draw a sharp line between the professions and occupations has limited utility, but certain broad distinctions are clear and necessary for a consideration of the future. Professions are usually defined in terms of the competence of the practitioner, often in terms of his personal preparation for a lifetime commitment. He has a large measure of autonomy in his day-to-day practice and is accountable, primarily, to his peers. Technological change may redefine the range of competency of a profession, but it will seldom destroy it.

Occupations are much more a matter of tasks and activities. They are defined in terms of the work unit rather than the person. This distinction of job content from person, fundamental to an analysis of the changing occupational structure, is often obscured by our systems of classification based on conditions of an earlier time when a craft or trade stayed with a person for a lifetime.[5] The classification laid out by Alba M. Edwards for the Bureau of the Census in about 1940 was essentially a socioeconomic typology whose value as an analytical tool declined as technology, the economy, and the social structure changed.[6] Under the impact of technological change the job structure itself exhibited major adjustments, with some occupations disappearing entirely, new ones appearing, and, in many cases, occupations differentiating into a cluster of specialities. For individuals,

---

[5]James G. Scoville, *The Job Content of the U.S. Economy 1940–1970* (New York: McGraw Hill, 1969), pp. 1–10, and Anne Roe, *The Psychology of Occupations* (New York: John Wiley and Sons, 1956), pp. 135–68. Both analysts have proposed modifications of reported data that reflect the occupational structure more adequately than the classical divisions of the Bureau of the Census.

[6]Leonard A. Lecht, *Manpower Needs for National Goods in the 1970s* (New York: Frederick A. Praeger, 1969), p. 123.

TABLE 1
*Distribution of Baccalaureate Degrees Awarded
in Representative Fields at
Land-Grant Institutions*

	1863 through 1928[a]		A/Y 1962–63[b]	
	Number	Percent	Number	Percent
Agriculture	15,314	4.8	3,434	4.2
Education	13,002	4.1	15,301	18.3
Engineering	48,124	15.2	11,599	14.2
Business	4,347	1.4	9,705	11.9
Bachelor of Arts	84,991	26.9		
Bachelor of Science	95,202	30.7		
Social Science	—	—	11,614	14.3
Physical Science	—	—	3,134	3.8
Biological Science	—	—	4,045	5.0
English, Journalism	—	—	4,672	5.7
Other Bachelors	54,563	16.9	17,966	32.4
TOTAL	315,543	100.0	81,470	100.0

[a]Klein, vol. 1., p. 294.
[b]George Lind, *Statistics of Land-Grant Colleges and Universities,* Year Ending June 30, 1963, Table E, p. 6, OE 50002-63.

the shifting occupational structure has career implications that have been accentuated in the past decade. Switching occupations has become such a common mode of adjustment that it is no longer regarded as unusual. One study reported about twelve jobs in a forty-six-year work life as typical of non-college workers.[7] Still, we have not yet learned to deal with this adjustment smoothly, and it is one of the most troublesome by-products of policy changes or new technical systems.

Distinctions between professions and occupations, their essential character and method of adjusting to change, have strong implications for education, and effective planning must take them into account. Increasingly, college graduates will find employment oppor-

[7]Harold L. Wilensky, "Careers, Counseling, and the Curriculum," *The Journal of Human Resources* 2 (Winter 1967):32.

tunities in that sector of the labor force which exhibits the occupational characteristics. The number of persons prepared by colleges
and universities at all degree levels and in most areas of specialization
now exceeds the number required for replacement and forseeable
growth in the traditional professions. Wolfle has noted that the
increased proportion in occupational careers is already evident:

> In 1960, a majority (of college graduates) were employed in fields in
> which most of their colleagues were not college graduates. Census
> records show that 21 percent of the men and 16 percent of the women
> with degrees were in fields in which 90 percent or more of all workers
> were college graduates; . . . 24 percent of the men and 45 percent of
> the women were in fields in which a majority had college degrees
> . . . the other 55 percent of the men and 39 percent of the women
> graduates were in fields in which college graduates were minorities.[8]

Viewed from a slightly different perspective, the trend data indicate that an even larger share of future graduates will find careers
in the occupational categories of the labor force.

> In the 1960s about two-thirds of all college graduates entered the
> labor force as professionals. In the 1970s only about 55 percent of the
> college graduates will be needed to enter the professions; and in the
> 1980s, less than half of the college graduates can expect to find jobs
> in the professions even if we assume that a higher percent of entrants
> to the professions are college graduates (70 to 80 percent).[9]

Such a shift away from careers of professional practice does not
invalidate either personal knowledge or the fundamental competence
provided by college experience. Individuals in the occupational market may change jobs but they tend to stay within their general field
of study. Lecht observed:

> The role of higher education in preparing individuals for careers as
> doctors, teachers, or engineers is generally apparent. It is less gener-
> ally recognized that a large majority of those who have received a

[8]Dael Wolfle, *The Uses of Talent* (Princeton, New Jersey: Princeton University Press, 1971),
p. 45.
[9]John K. Folger, "The Job Market," *The Journal of Higher Education* 63 (March 1972):215.

college education make use of this education in their employment. According to a Department of Labor survey . . . almost 80 percent of those who had completed three or more years of college held positions related to their college major.[10]

Educational planning, especially in those institutions sensitive to public need, will have to assess the full implications of these changes. Programs of study at the college level today are governed by the professional model. Primary emphasis is placed upon the socialization of the individual to a role set well defined in behavior, values, and attitudes to accompany knowledge and technique. The assumptions underlying preparation for occupational roles are quite different. The emphasis falls upon competence and skill for a specific class of activities. The developmental aspect of higher education—personal growth and increased social sensitivity—is no longer intimately bound up in the work role. Internalization and personalization of job values is much lower in occupational fields even where a substantial body of background knowledge is required to support the job skill. Knowledge and skill in the occupational setting is perishable and, unlike the professions, there is no process of continuous updating but rather intermittent periods of retraining.

II. Major Trends in the Labor Force Structure

Two long-term trends are part of labor force history. The land-grant institutions are intimately involved with both. The first is a shift from an economy dominated by agriculture to one in which industrial production is a major force. A second is an alteration in the occupational structure of the labor force away from work of the unskilled type. The first trend has changed the kind of activity required while the second reflects a change in the way work is done.

A. *The rise of industry* is a hallmark of Western civilization and has appeared elsewhere in the world as other nations joined in the revolution of production. Simon Kuznets has documented the nature of this transformation by calculating the change in both national

---

[10]Lecht, *Manpower Needs,* p. 104.

product and labor force composition for eighteen nations over long periods, some reaching over two centuries.[11]

In all countries but one—Australia—the share of the national product originating with agriculture has dropped, and in every country the labor force participation in this sector has fallen. The United States is distinguished by the long duration of the downward trend rather than the steepness of the decline. The dimensions are well known, with agriculture representing less than half the national product by 1897 and dropping to four percent by the 1960s.[12] Labor force participation rates still showed half of the workers involved in agriculture in 1890, but by 1960 they had declined to seven percent. The accompanying rise in industrial production brought forty-five percent of the U.S. labor force into the category by 1950.

In the third facet of this economic transformation—the rising service sector of the economy—the United States presents an exception.[13] Somewhat over 50 percent of our national product has been identified as services; and by 1970 nearly half the labor force was engaged in service occupations. No other country comes within ten percentage points of this high level of economic commitment to service activity.

The service sector and the jobs associated with it have attributes quite different from industry or agriculture, attributes of importance to education. To begin with, activities under this category are heterogeneous, and each responds to quite separate influences. The sector is shaped less by material factors and more by cultural factors—social trends, acts of public policy, matters of taste and preference. This means that changes may be rapid and extensive when they come. It means, too, that conscious choice on the part of the individual consumer through his decisions or collective choice by the citizenry through the enacted public policy will carry new economic weight. It is for this reason that increasing discussion of national goals, priorities, and the central purpose of national life has appeared

[11]Simon Kuznets, *Modern Economic Growth* (New Haven: Yale University Press, 1966).
[12]Ibid., Table 3.1, pp. 88–93.
[13]Richard A. Lester, *Manpower Planning a Free Society* (Princeton, New Jersey: Princeton University Press, 1966).

on the contemporary scene. This discussion has also appeared because the service sector has shown a low or unmeasurable improvement in productivity compared to industry. Incremental additions in services therefore appear to be very costly and, as a consequence, will be a constant target of public debate.

B. *Changes in the occupational structure*—the way work is carried out—have accompanied the major shifts in production. Labor force participation has increased steadily, reaching 59.8 percent of the population sixteen and over by 1968. The distinctive feature of the 1960s has been increased involvement of women, reaching a level of 40.2 percent in 1968.[14] Distribution of the labor force among the professions and occupations has shown a decline in the farm occupations, moderate growth in the blue collar groups, substantial growth in non-household service groups and clerical occupations, and the greatest growth in the professional-technical group. Domestic and personal service has declined while institutionalized services in health and education have increased rapidly. Those services related to trade and commerce expanded at a steady rate, with advertising, finance, and sales keeping pace with industrial production. The most rapid growth has been in public services administered by government, including protective services of police and military, supervisory and regulatory functions, as well as social services. By using a more precise classification of job content, Scoville has given an even more accurate description of the change from 1940–1960.[15] Inspection-supervision jobs in industry grew rapidly, as did the higher paid administrative jobs. In the service sector he identified the rapid increase in health-related jobs but also pinpointed the growth in protective services and entertainment. The new service occupations are "knowledge based" rather that "experience based," and much of the knowledge must be gained by training.[16]

Another long-term trend in the occupational structure has been an increase in the number of job categories, a phenomenon so marked that new subdivisions had to be invented for twenty-two areas of

[14]Sophia C. Travis, "The U.S. Labor Force: Projections to 1985," *Monthly Review,* May 1970, Table 1.

[15]Scoville, *Job Content of the U. S. Economy,* pp. 41–45.

[16]Peter F. Drucker, *The Age of Discontinuity: Guidelines to Our Changing Society* (New York: Harper & Row, 1968).

work when the *Dictionary of Occupational Titles* was revised in 1965. Part of this change, of course, reflects the differentiation of tasks into more specialized work patterns, a characteristic first observed by Adam Smith. There are also wholly new job categories generated in recent decades by television, computer, and space industries. The long-trends in the traditional format are shown in Table 2. Projected growth rates are compared in Table 3.

For a long time it was believed that increased levels of education in the labor force produced higher quality job performance, thereby contributing to a steady upgrading of the occupational structure. It is clear that many occupational areas have had substantial increases in educational levels, the most obvious being managerial, sales, teaching, and technical. The infusion of education takes on even more significance when we note that the amount of schooling time represented by those levels had also risen from 121 days of attendance in 1921 to 158 days attended by 1950.[17] Whether all this education is put to use has now come under debate. As the role of college trained people has been examined more critically over the last few years, an important distinction between job performance and educational requirements has appeared. Indications are that educational requirements have gone up much more rapidly than performance requirements. Once entry requirements in terms of education become a screening device rather than a reflection of competencies necessary to the job, such consequences as job dissatisfaction, high transfer rates, and low return on education appear.[18] This question of where college graduates upgrade the occupational structure and where they simply inflate entry requirements is both new to the American scene and crucial for the next decade. More than one-third of the college graduates in the 1970s will be available to upgrade job performance after the replacement needs of professions and technical fields have been met and they must be directed to jobs where education has value.[19]

---

[17]Clarence D. Long, *The Labor Force Under Changing Income and Employment* (Princeton, New Jersey: Princeton University Press, 1958), p. 49.

[18]Ivar Berg, *Education and Jobs: The Great Training Robbery* (New York: Frederick A. Praeger, 1970) also "Education and Performance: Some Problems" *The Journal of Higher Education* 63 (March 1972).

[19]Wolfle, *Uses of Talent*, pp. 46–47.

TABLE 2
Percentage Distribution of Occupational Groups

Selected Occupational Group	1900	1910	1920	1930	1940	1950	1960	1970	1980
Professional, technical, and kindred workers	4.3	4.7	5.4	6.8	7.5	8.6	11.0	14.2	16.3
Farmers and farm managers	19.9	16.5	15.3	12.4	10.4	7.4	3.7	3.0	2.7
Managers, officials, and proprietors, except farm	5.9	6.6	6.6	7.4	7.3	8.7	8.1	9.5	10.0
Clerical and kindred workers	3.0	5.3	8.0	8.9	9.6	12.3	14.1	17.4	18.2
Sales workers	4.5	4.7	4.9	6.3	6.7	7.0	7.1	6.2	6.3
Craftsmen, foremen, and kindred workers	10.6	11.6	13.0	12.8	12.0	14.2	13.6	12.9	12.8
Operative and kindred workers	12.8	14.6	15.6	15.8	18.4	20.4	18.9	17.7	16.2
Private household workers	5.4	5.0	3.3	4.1	4.6	2.6	2.7	3.1	3.5
Service workers, except private household	3.6	4.6	4.5	5.7	7.1	7.9	8.5	9.6	10.0
Farm laborers and foremen	17.7	14.4	11.7	8.8	7.0	4.4	2.3	2.0	1.7
Laborers, except farm and mine	12.5	12.0	11.6	11.0	9.4	6.6	5.2	4.7	3.7

SOURCE: Data obtained from *Occupational Trends in the United States 1900 to 1950,* Report No. 5, David L. Kaplan and M. Claire Casey. Washington, D.C.: United States Department of Commerce.

Data from 1960 obtained from the *Census of Population,* Volume 2.

1970 and 1980 data obtained from *The U.S. Economy in 1980* (Washington, D.C.: Department of Labor, Bureau of Labor Statistics, 1970), Bulletin 1673.

TABLE 3
Rates of Change
For Major Occupational Groups
1960–1980

Occupational Group	Number Change		Annual Rate of Change	
	1960–70	1970–80	1960–70	1970–80
Total Employment	12,849	16,473	1.8	1.9
Professional and technical workers	3,671	4,360	4.1	3.4
Managers, officials and proprietors	1,222	1,211	1.6	1.4
Clerical workers	3,952	3,586	3.5	2.4
Sales workers	630	1,146	1.4	2.1
Craftsmen and foremen	1,604	2,042	1.7	1.8
Operatives	1,959	1,491	1.5	1.0
Service workers	1,689	3,388	1.9	3.0
Nonfarm laborers	171	−224	.5	−.6
Farmers and farm laborers	−2,050	−526	−5.2	−1.8

SOURCE: *Manpower Report of the President*

Mobility, both geographic and occupational, has traditionally acted to prevent overstatement of job entry requirements. Most professions and many highly skilled occupations respond to a national, even international, labor market, with the result that the highly educated have been the most mobile segment of the population. Movement from field to field has had a number of social benefits, not the least of which is the diffusion of new technology. One outcome related to mobility, but not exclusively so, is the capacity of the American labor force to fill a newly created job type rapidly and effectively. No skill shortage has persisted very long. Wolfle cites remarkable data on solid state physicists.

Although there were only 86 Ph.D.'s in solid state physics in the 1964 Register, there were 1,894 Ph.D. holders who were working as solid state physicists. . . . This is a striking example of the fact that a new field can expand rapidly by drawing into itself people who have some of the necessary knowledge, skill, habits of thought, and methods of work, even though their formal training and previous experience lie in other fields.[20]

Among the more recent but persistent trends in the occupational structure has been the rise of paraprofessional occupations. Variously titled as semi-professions or quasi-professions, they hold in common only a few distinct characteristics. A degree of specialized training at an advanced level is required; practitioners have a degree of autonomy in their work, and it takes place in an institutional setting. Activities of paraprofessionals are often associated rather closely with a traditional profession. Beyond these similarities are differences so vast that each paraprofessional setting must be examined by itself. In some cases the appearance of the paraprofessional is a direct consequence of technological development and their activities are an extension of the techniques of the profession. In the health fields, a large number of narrowly defined, high-skill occupations, ranging from biomedical engineering to hospital administration, have evolved within a tightly structured organization. In other circumstances the need for paraprofessionals arises because a professional institution—school, hospital, social service unit—must extend its services to a segment of society that requires special understanding, interpretation, and communication. Hospitals, courts, and schools in Spanish-speaking areas or black ghettoes have developed trained paraprofessional intermediaries. Instead of levying new requirements of social sensitivity and cultural understanding upon the roles of judges and physicians, it has been possible to introduce paraprofessionals as social catalysts and liaison members. Thus, the institution rather than the profession responds to social requirements.[21]

Public understanding of paraprofessional practice stems from conditions in engineering and science where technical aides increase the efficiency of professionals by relieving them of less demanding or routine tasks. We know now that paraprofessionals can be and are becoming much more than aides. A structural change in the way occupations are interrelated is underway in large segments of the

---

[20]Ibid., p. 131.
[21]Alan Gartner, *Paraprofessionals and Their Performance* (New York, Frederick A. Praeger, 1971).

labor force but particularly in those occupations which are performed in an institutional setting. Perhaps the closest one can come in a brief statement is that the delivery system for medical care or for justice is becoming the principal unit for occupational analysis instead of the traditional institutional unit like the hospital or the court.

C. *the Future: Visible and Invisible.* A search of all these trends and indicators for factors that will shape the policy choices of land-grant institutions turns up some interesting contrasts. Clearly visible, on the one hand, are the continuing effects of the trends we have seen in the past. But our instincts and intuitions signal in dozens of ways that this nation and its people are at a major point of change; whether this deserves to be called a "cultural revolution" or the emergence of "Consciousness III" remains to be seen, but there is evidence enough to support Peter Drucker's idea of the "age of discontinuity." The future of land-grant institutions will be drawn partly from the visible trends, but the greater influences will come from the less visible forces and the policies based upon them.

First, the visible future to 1985: The trend away from agriculture has not yet run its course and we can expect continued decline in that share of national product and labor force related to it. Whether industry or the service sector will pick up most of the increase is more a matter of public choice than ever before. Production activity and service activity both have a capacity for growth, but national policy will determine which one takes the lead. As Lecht has pointed out, a decision to reconstitute the urban environment with mass transportation, housing, and devices to insure purity of air and water would produce an upsurge in production. Subsidized ventures into world markets, or massive scientific programs in space, have demonstrated the same capacity. Choices in the direction of human services—improved health care, a reconstituted system of protection and justice, the development of preschool and adult education—all these would bring further rapid growth to the service sector.[22] Succinctly, both industry and service will continue the growth trend, but policy choices, not intrinsic forces, will accelerate one or the other.

The labor force will grow less rapidly because there will be fewer

[22]Lecht, *Manpower Needs for National Goals,* Chapter 5.

young entrants. Persons in the age class 25–34 will "increase at a dramatic rate, growing by 800,000 a year compared with an average of 175,000 in the earlier period (the 1960s)."[23] This is a mobile, ambitious, vigorous age group that will produce a high demand for adult education in all forms.

With respect to the supply of college graduates, the most important single fact is that the supply of degree holders will be well above the number needed for replacement in the traditional professions and occupations.[24] This condition has obtained since the mid 1950s, but an additional factor has appeared since 1965. Up to that time, much of the college-trained talent went into upgrading professions like teaching, engineering, and social work. Now this kind of option is closing, and new opportunity lies in occupational fields where concentrations of college graduates are lower. In its first stages this occurrence has given an appearance of crisis, but as colleges and universities adjust to the new semiprofessional and occupational job market, reactions of uncertainty and disillusion will decline.

Where in the occupational structure will these employment opportunities lie? In business activities, notably sales and administration; in government positions with state, local, and federal agencies; in fields such as fiscal management, and regulatory and protective activity; and in social work and health agencies. Technical and scientific employment will appear more frequently in non-profit enterprises as well as in industry. For groups that are now underrepresented in the professional and occupational structure—women, blacks, Chicanos, and other minority groups—there will be a much broader range of employment choices.

Continued mention of occupations as the area of opportunity may carry a false impression of low pay and prestige. Scoville has demonstrated that for the 1940–1970 period the upper pay levels of growing

[23]Sophia C. Travis, "The U.S. Labor Force Projections to 1985," *Monthly Labor Review*, May 1970, p. 3.

[24]The U.S. Department of Labor takes a conservative position: "The supply and demand for college graduates is expected to be in relative balance during the 1970s." Bulletin 1676, *College Educated Worker 1968–80*, Bureau of Labor Statistics, 1970. Independent analysts emphasize that there will be a surplus of college graduates for traditional fields, and adjustments must be made to find new places of employment.

occupations grew most rapidly.[25] College graduates can expect to move into occupational roles at salaries that are comparable to or better than the professions but with less prestige.

III. Occupational Directions and Response of Higher Education

Land-grant institutions can be expected to respond to the changing occupational structure as they have to every major development of the last seventy-five years. How rapidly the response develops will depend upon the assessments of new developments that are beginning to emerge. The paragraphs below, speculative but not fanciful, summarize some of the educational outcomes that are likely to be part of that response.

A. *National–International Interrelationship.* The land-grant colleges and universities are well on the road to becoming national, even international, institutions. A variety of events promise to accelerate the change. The labor market for educated people is clearly a national one, and geographic mobility is a condition of occupational growth. There is a new mobility developing for young people out of legislative and judicial decisions that define them as independent adults and negate restrictions based upon residency in a state. The effects of federal sponsorship of research, construction, and student assistance have also extended institutional horizons beyond state borders. Patterns of cooperation and exchange constructed around special institutional competence—the Committee on Institutional Cooperation is an example[26]—will give land-grant institutions across the nation the qualities of an interrelated educational system.

B. *Application of Knowledge and Research.* In two areas of established land-grant strength, the application of knowledge to life and the linking of research to policy, there is a fund of unfinished business. For the natural sciences there is a whole range of applications in restorative, preventive, and control activities that lie beyond the exploitative emphasis of the past. Most of these applications will generate occupational rather than professional positions. Exem-

[25] Scoville, *Job Contents of the U.S. Economy,* p. 75.
[26] Committee on Institutional Cooperation includes the Big Ten plus Chicago.

plified by the soft technology movement that seeks to hold the needs of man in balance with the essential structure of nature, this approach levies new requirements on scientific education. Robin Clarke described the effort: "We laid down what in scientific terms we could call a series of boundary conditions. . . . One rule is that we shouldn't use technologies that mortgaged the future of unborn generations, using resources that are not renewable."[27] For the behavioral sciences there are bridges to be built to the human service occupations from the growing body of sound research. In the arts, which touch an increasing share of the population in a mass media culture, there are opportunities for linking the communication sciences with new levels of esthetics and design. Throughout, the new element in the application of knowledge is an introduction of the human modifier.

C. *New Industries.* A number of new industries are just ahead, and they promise to replace agriculture and steel not only in importance but in the form and scope of their organization. Peter Drucker has identified the rootstocks for some of these: the "information industry," which is central to a society whose key resource and critical factor of production is knowledge; the "oceans industry," which touches the last major undeveloped resource area; the "materials industry," which begins with a set of requirements and constructs a specific material to meet them; and the "megalopolis," which promises a structure of government, services, and relationships beyond anything yet experienced by man.[28] Again, the weighting of employment opportunities in new industries tends to be occupational rather than professional.

D. *New Educational Models.* The qualities of modern occupations do not fit well into the traditional university and college curricula which purport to offer ultimate preparation of the whole person for a lifelong career. An emphasis on knowledge and skills that have immediate application but change rapidly, an orientation toward a specific task, and a tendency toward interdependent systems of jobs —all these occupational features suggest new structural forms for the

[27]John L. Hess, "Researchers 'Commune in Wales to Promote' Soft Technology," The *New York Times,* June 9, 1972.
[28]Drucker, *The Age of Discontinuity,* Chapter 2.

university. Prototypes, not nearly so experimental as one might expect, are already in operation. The John Jay College of Criminal Justice in the City University of New York is an educational institution designed to prepare and keep continuously upgrading individuals who currently have careers in the justice system. A full range of degrees is offered, Associate in Arts through Ph.D., but these are incidental to the main purpose, which is to allow individuals to develop individualized careers in the broad field of justice administration. The educational unit that serves this purpose is nothing less that the college itself. It can develop any kind of program from pre-college to in-service seminars from its staff and resources. Disciplines are secondary to the principal focus, which is nothing less than the whole system of justice.

Another prototype is the College of Human Services. "The College for Human Services, chartered by the Regents of the State of New York in May, 1970, is an experimental educational institution offering an Associate of Arts degree to those low-income adults completing the subsidized, two-year work-study program. The curriculum prepares students for careers as 'new professionals' in the human services."[29] Here the emphasis is on the development and maintenance of skill and understanding necessary for work in the whole range of human services from neighborhood block workers to psychiatric social work. Dr. Audrey Cohen, one of the founders of this college, has pointed out that our notions of age-bound education fail to take advantage of that interplay of experience and personal development which characterizes the most alert and able people in the society. The principal effort at CHS has been to remove every barrier to that development through individualized programs, financial support, a liberal policy of interruption and return, and flexible requirements. It is a college in which a wide range of student abilities and special interests can be developed around a common focus.

The attributes of these institutions suggest certain new features of the land-grant college aimed at occupational preparation. Graded levels and formal curricula will give way to an agglomeration of

[29]College for Human Services, 121 Varick Street, New York, New York, (Mimeo description) November 1970.

courses open to all. Prerequisites, when they are needed, will be defined in terms of skill and knowledge and met by independent study, tutorials, or instructional technology rather than by courses. Admissions will be entirely open and the student composition will be heterogeneous in age, ability, and experience, homogeneous only in its common interest in the field. Fields will be defined by systemic boundaries rather than disciplines. There will be few cohorts or classes of students moving through a "program" as a group. To borrow a simile from Marshall McLuhan, learning patterns will be individual mosaics rather than linear accumulations.

E. *Separation of Work from Lifestyle.* Heavier participation by college graduates in occupational areas of employment will force redefinition of the traditional concept that education, work, and social position are contingent upon each other. Work and style of living will come to be less closely related. Separate purposes of education, now linked into a single value set, will gain significance in their own right. Job training and the background information for mobility in the field will represent one segment of study. Understanding the world of nature and man as an aid to full social participation will be another. Quite separate will be those studies which enhance the quality of personal life ranging from the creativity in the arts to an understanding of group processes. This has been called "education for consumption" by some analysts to emphasize the immediate and personal value of such learning. There is clear but fragmentary evidence that this differentiation of work from intelligence, education, and lifestyle is in progress. Wolfle cited studies that show that, in occupational areas, "brightness" is positively related to earnings, but education alone is not.[30] Folger and Nam have recorded a long-term decline in the strength of the correlation of educational level and occupation.[31]

Land-grant institutions have built an unusual capacity for responding to social trends and economic events. The educational

[30]Wolfle, *The Uses of Talent,* p. 84.
[31]J.K. Folger and Charles B. Nam, *The Education of the American Population* (Washington, D.C.: Bureau of Census, 1967), p. 169.

aspect of this response has fitted into the traditional moves of mobility which emphasize that the sacrifices made for higher education are compensated by prestigious employment at income levels that support an elevated social position. However, over the next two decades many of the employment opportunities for college graduates will appear in the occupational structure. Work roles are likely to be segmented from personal, family, and social roles. An educational response to this condition will require restructuring of the values of higher education with new emphasis on its intrinsic significance for personal development and social participation as well as for career preparation. Part of this response will come in the form of new patterns of organization within the land-grant institution. Only the outlines of these forms can be seen now, but they will be filled out as the land-grant colleges and universities begin to read the strong signals of the social environment.

Chapter 15

EXTERNAL DEGREE PROGRAMS:
THE CURRENT EDUCATIONAL FRONTIER

KENNETH P. MORTIMER and MARK D. JOHNSON

ONE of the most dramatic developments in postsecondary education in the early 1970s has been the move to award degrees through off campus, nontraditional, or external programs. Statewide efforts to develop opportunities to gain degree credit for off-campus learning are being developed in California, Connecticut, Florida, Illinois, Massachusetts, New Jersey, New York, Ohio, Pennsylvania, Rhode Island, and Washington. As of 1972, at least 386 institutions offered nontraditional or external degree programs. The current number is undoubtedly higher.

The purpose of this chapter is to examine the nature, scope, issues, and problems of the external degree movement as it has taken shape since 1970. It is important to note that many aspects of the external degree movement are not new. Indeed, the idea of providing post-secondary educational services for the nonresident student has its roots, in both Great Britain and the United States, in the 19th Century.[1] The activity of the 1970s, however, appears to involve a number of important departures from past practice. Perhaps most important is a widespread acceptance of the belief that the adult learner should have access to a degree entirely through part-time study. Toward this goal, new practices and procedures in instructional delivery, curricular design, and the evaluation and certification of learning are now being tested on a wide scale. This experimentation has confronted the educational community with some important questions concerning the past practice and future direction of higher education, particularly with respect to the needs of nontraditional clienteles.

---

[1]Cyril O. Houle, *The External Degree* (San Francisco: Jossey-Bass 1974), p. 7.

The Current Scene: An Overview

It is difficult to estimate the number of external degree programs currently in operation. One of the major problems has been a lack of consensus over terms and definitions. Another has been the sheer difficulty of keeping track of new programs and obtaining detailed information about them. The most comprehensive survey of new programs to date is the study conducted by the Center for Research and Development in Higher Education at Berkeley in 1972. Although somewhat dated, the survey provides a sense of the scope of activity and some of the problems involved in defining the external degree.[2]

In the spring of 1972, the Berkeley staff sent a questionnaire to all accredited colleges and universities in the United States, requesting information on "any specially designed programs based on new or unconventional forms of education free of the time or place limitations of traditional classroom instruction." These programs might be unconventional in *any* of the following ways: the type of student enrolled, the location of the learning experience, or the method of instruction. The content might be either different from or the same as conventional courses or programs.[3]

The survey yielded 1,185 usable responses from a population of 2,670. After analyzing the data and eliminating programs that did not meet any of the above criteria, the staff concluded that there were at least 641 nontraditional programs in operation at 386, or 33 percent of the responding institutions. Sixty-two percent of these programs were less than two years old and 86 percent were less than five.[4] Seventy percent were designed for nontraditional students and 67 percent were carried out at nontraditional locations. Nontraditional methods of instruction (57 percent) and nontraditional program content (48 percent) were somewhat less frequent. Only 20 percent (127 programs),

[2]Janet Ruyle and Lucy Ann Geiselman, "Non-Traditional Opportunities and Programs," *Planning Non-Traditional Programs,* K. Patricia Cross, John R. Valley and Associates. (San Francisco: Jossey-Bass, 1974), pp. 53–94.
[3]Ibid, pp. 67–68.
[4]Ibid, p. 84.

however, were described as nontraditional along all four criteria.[5]

It is probably safe to say that no two people with access to the original data would arrive at the same count of external degree programs from among the 641 nontraditional programs identified in the Berkeley study. In the absence of more current and definitive data, the present authors can only suggest that external degree programs number in the hundreds.

External Degree Programs Among Land-Grant Institutions: Information available from the National Association of State Universities and Land-Grant Colleges (NASULGC) and the Office of New Degree Programs at the Educational Testing Service (ETS) indicates that in the spring of 1975 at least 16 of the 72 land-grant institutions were conducting nontraditional degree programs specifically designed for nonresident students. An additional 13 reported active consideration of such programs in a 1973 survey conducted by the NASULGC. It should be noted, moreover, that there are now a number of statewide external degree programs in which the land-grants participate by virtue of their relationships with state systems of public higher education.[6]

There are several external degree programs among land-grant institutions which have received considerable national attention. The Universities of Massachusetts, Minnesota, and Wisconsin are participants in the University Without Walls Program, sponsored by the Union for Experimenting Colleges and Universities. The University of Maryland and Rutgers University have participated in a project to test British Open University materials. And the University of California has just completed the pilot stage of its Extended Degree Program, to be discussed in detail below.

One of the more recent contributions of the land-grant universities is the work being done at the State University of Nebraska. Following a three-year period of planning, market surveys, and course development, the SUN program enrolled its first students in fall, 1974, with initial course offerings in introductory accounting and psychology. Courses in computer science and consumer affairs were

[5]Ibid, p. 71.
[6]Education Commission of the States, *Higher Education in the States,* 4 (1974): 291–92.

added in spring, 1975, and a number of additional courses were planned for fall, 1975. The courses are designed for completely independent study, supplemented by educational television, newspaper articles, and instructional materials kits. The program currently has four learning centers, located in urban areas, which serve not only as counseling centers for students enrolled in SUN courses, but also as information clearinghouses on all postsecondary educational facilities and opportunities in their respective regions.

Widespread interest in the SUN program in the Midwest has led recently to a consortial arrangement among the University of Nebraska, Iowa State University, Kansas State University, The University of Kansas, and The University of Missouri, known as the University of Mid-America (UMA). While each institution will determine its own policies and procedures for implementing its programs, initial management, course production, research and evaluation, and delivery system development are to be provided under a subcontract with the University of Nebraska. Under this arrangement, UMA expects to produce a total of fifty courses by 1980. At this point, however, there has been no public announcement of plans to develop a full degree program.[7]

Elements and Models

Any effort to examine systematically the nature and scope of external degree activity must start with an important caveat: there is no such thing as a typical external degree program.[8] It is nevertheless possible to identify some basic elements and models which have characterized the external degree movement to date:

Elements: Of all the elements that characterize external degree programs, the most prevalent is the objective of serving a new clientele. In general, both the actual and potential clientele of external degree programs are adult learners—i.e., those beyond the tradi-

---

[7]Information concerning the SUN, UMA, and other programs was obtained from descriptive literature, telephone conversations, and/or correspondence with program administrators, unless otherwise cited.

[8]Fred A. Nelson, "Has the Time Gone for an External Degree?" *Journal of Higher Education* 45 (March 1974): 175.

tional college age (18–22) who have for one reason or another missed the opportunity to begin or complete a traditional, campus-based college education. The Berkeley survey suggests that the largest constituencies of nontraditional programs are housewives, working adults, and special occupational groups (including military personnel).[9]

Another major potential clientele is the traditional college student who may be dissatisfied with or unable to continue a resident education. Although aggregate enrollment figures are unavailable for this constitutency, many of the newer nontraditional programs are being designed for the college-age student as well as the adult learner. Of the nontraditional programs identified in the Berkeley study, 42 percent allow traditional college students to enroll in their courses.[10]

In addition to a new clientele, external degree programs also make use of a variety of nontraditional instructional delivery systems, including independent study, off-campus learning centers, community-based resources, direct experience, and classroom instruction at off-campus locations. Many of these instructional delivery systems are not new of course, but they are now being employed on a scale designed to promote full degree program opportunities for nonresident students.

A third aspect of the external degree movement is the application of unconventional approaches toward the definition, control, and evaluation of the learning experience. Traditionally, the faculty defines a curriculum that leads to a degree. The student may or may not have a certain amount of flexibility in selecting from a predetermined set of treatments. Some external degree programs simply move these treatments to a new time and/or place, transform them into a programmed text format, or condense classroom time, placing greater emphasis on independent study. Typically, in such cases, the traditional program structure is left intact. Other programs, however, allow the student substantial latitude in designing his own program of study which may include a variety of learning experiences. Programs of this sort vary in nature and content with each

[9]Ruyle and Geiselman, "Non-Traditional Opportunities," p. 73.
[10]Ibid, pp. 73–74.

individual student. The faculty member, however, still maintains a semblance of control over the nature and sequence of treatments selected to achieve certain knowledge or skills.

In still other cases, the faculty member may play little or no role in the definition or control of the learning experience. The emphasis is placed not on the learning process, but on what the student knows and how to measure it. The student may be required to pass a series of written or oral examinations or to document his knowledge by submitting a book he has written, a work of art, or another product of his past efforts. In this type of arrangement the faculty member's role is changed from teacher to evaluator. In addition, this arrangement facilitates the development of credit-granting agencies which may differ substantially from the traditional educational institution.

The fourth basic element of the external degree is the content of the curriculum. Course and program content vary substantially, of course, in student designed programs. Many external degree programs, however, follow the traditional practice of faculty control over the curriculum. Almost half (42 percent) of the 641 nontraditional programs identified in the Berkeley survey include or consist entirely of the same content as the traditional curricula of the institutions. The trend among newer programs, however, is toward occupational programs. Sixty-two percent of the entire sample of programs include occupational and career preparation as part, if not the major focus, of the curriculum. In contrast, only 3 percent of the programs place an exclusive emphasis on social problems and 6 percent on general or liberal studies.[11]

Would-be adult learners appear to be interested primarily in programs with a vocational thrust.[12] In this respect, they may be a more conservative clientele than the traditional college student. Colleges and universities, in turn, are moving increasingly toward programs which provide the nonresident student with a relatively conventional and/or occupational curriculum packaged in a manner which will facilitate progress toward a degree.

[11]Ibid, pp. 74–75.
[12]Abraham Carp, et al., "Adult Learning Interests and Experiences," *Planning Non-Traditional Programs,* pp. 18–19.

Models: Although no two external degree programs are packaged in precisely the same way, John R. Valley has suggested that there are some basic models. Valley's models, as modified by Cyril O. Houle, provide a useful framework for examining some of the approaches used in combining the different elements described above.[13]

In the administrative-facilitation model, a degree-granting agency establishes an organization and/or facilities to serve the needs of a nontraditional clientele but holds to its customary degree pattern. A traditional curriculum, utilizing conventional delivery systems, is typically offered at times and/or places accessible to the nonresident student. Houle cites university extension programs and evening schools as examples. According to the Association of University Evening Colleges, there are at least 146 programs of this sort.[14]

In the modes-of-learning model, a degree-granting institution establishes a new degree pattern of teaching and learning that adjusts to the capacities, circumstances, and interests of a different clientele. The most common example would be the special degree program designed for adults, as reflected in the British Open University.

A third type of external degree program is described by the assessment model, in which an agency, which may not itself offer formal instruction, awards a degree on the basis of examinations, credit for course work completed elsewhere, and/or credit for a variety of nonacademic learning experiences. In the Valley typology, these approaches are referred to as the examination, credit, and validation models, but more often than not they are found in combination under the more general rubric of the assessment model. A major example of this approach is the New York State Regents External Degree.

The fourth type of external degree program operative in the United States is the complex-systems model. In these programs, a degree-granting institution or agency employs a combination of approaches drawn from the various simple models to meet the needs

[13]John R. Valley, "External Degree Programs," *Explorations in Non-Traditional Study,* edited by Samuel B. Gould and K. Patricia Cross, (San Francisco: Jossey-Bass, 1972), pp. 95–128, and Houle, *The External Degree,* pp. 91–94. See also Leland Medsker, et al., *Extending Opportunities for a College Degree,* (Berkeley: Center for Research and Development in Higher Education, 1975), pp. 12–31, for a slightly different classification.

[14]W. A. Hoppe (ed.) *Policies and Practices in Evening Colleges, 1971,* (Metuchen, New Jersey: Scarecrow Press, 1972), cited in Houle, *The External Degree,* p. 89.

of a new clientele. The Empire State College in Saratoga Springs, New York, represents one such approach.

This typology of models is useful in defining the general nature and scope of the external degree movement and in classifying different programs into broad categories. The variety of practices in the field is such, however, that no examination of external degree models would be complete without some illustrations. The profiles which follow were selected, in part, to illustrate the application of the four basic models. It should be noted, however, that few programs fit precisely into the mold of a single model.

The Extended University of the University of California: Administrative Facilitation

The idea of an external degree program for the University of California was first introduced at an All-University Faculty Conference in early 1970 by President Charles A. Hitch. The favorable response to the idea prompted the President to appoint an all-university task force of faculty and administrators to consider the matter. For approximately eighteen months, the task force studied problems of degree programs for part-time students and sought to determine whether the University of California should expand its degree offerings in this area. The report of the task force, issued in November 1971, called for a "consortium of the campuses" to stimulate, coordinate, and serve as the degree-granting agency for programs for part-time students at the upper division and master's levels.[15]

The consortium was established in July 1972. Contrary to the task force report, it has worked with and through existing campus authorities in the development and implementation of extended degree programs. The period 1972–1975 was designated as a pilot phase, during which the university would experiment with new programs and procedures in preparation for a permanent set of changes in the university's educational and administrative policies.

In the fall of 1972, the Extended University enrolled its first 450

[15]Houle, *The External Degree,* pp. 107–8.

students in seven pilot programs at six of the university's nine campuses. As of June 1975, there are 23 programs at eight campuses (the San Diego campus is not participating), serving a student population of 1,600. Virtually all of these programs have been developed and approved through the traditional academic decision-making structures at the individual campuses. By the end of the pilot phase (spring 1975), the various programs had awarded 160 degrees.

Of the 23 programs in operation in 1975, 70 percent were professional master's degree programs, including offerings in business administration, public health, architecture, engineering, nursing, and education. Most of the baccalaureate programs involve newly designed curricula with a multi-disciplinary base. Although methods of instructional delivery vary from program to program, approximately 50 percent of the instruction occurs on one of the university campuses. Formats range from evening and weekend lectures and seminars to intensive term courses which meet for three to five sixteen-hour sessions during each quarter. The other 50 percent of the instruction (in some cases entire programs) occurs at 33 off-campus learning centers. Modes of delivery include video-taped lectures and classes with visiting faculty members. In one of the programs, offered at the Santa Cruz campus, faculty members conduct classes simultaneously in two separate locations which are linked by telephone.

Although resident students are allowed to enroll in many of the Extended University's courses, the regular student body is made up primarily of working adults. Because California has an elaborate network of community colleges, the Extended University does not offer instruction at the lower division level. Virtually all degree candidates must therefore have completed at least two years of undergraduate work to qualify for admission. Admissions standards generally conform to those of resident education programs but more emphasis is placed on work experience and employer recommendations, particularly in the professional masters degree programs. Approximately 10 percent of the students are 'special admits' who do not meet the formal academic requirements for enrollment but have demonstrated potential in their nonacademic pursuits. In some cases, students with nonacademically acquired knowledge or skills are eligible for credit by proficiency examination or assessment of work experience.

A recent statistical profile indicates that 53 percent of the students have personal incomes of over $10,000. Fifteen percent are members of minority groups but few of these are from the lower economic strata. The median age is between 30 to 35, although 33 percent are over 35. Almost all of the students maintain their nonacademic responsibilities while enrolled in the program. The attrition rate for regularly admitted students has been approximately 23 percent (18 percent for special admits), and most campuses report that they are performing academically at least as well as their resident counterparts.

At the present time, extended degree students are restricted to half-time enrollment, with fees reduced to approximately half of the normal resident tuition of $600 per year. Because methods of instruction are relatively conventional in nature, the cost of instruction is approximately the same as that of resident programs. The Extended University is funded by special state appropriations, with some assistance from the university's endowment. In addition, some of the individual campuses have received outside grants for new program development.

One of the major controversies with regard to external degree programs in California has been the apparent lack of coordination between the University of California and the California State University and College System (CSUC), which has also developed an external degree. There is now a joint committee of the two programs to promote cooperation and coordination. One of the first efforts at cooperation has been the establishment of a joint learning center at Ventura, which serves students in both external degree programs as well as the extension programs of both systems.

The University of California is optimistic about the future of the Extended University as a service to California's part-time student population and as a catalyst for policy and program innovations which will improve the system as a whole.

Britain's Open University:
New Modes of Learning [16]

The Open University was created in 1969, to serve the adult working population of Great Britain, with particular emphasis on reaching the blue-collar worker. There are no formal requirements for enrollment except that a potential applicant must be over twenty-one years of age and some attention is given to balancing enrollments by subject area, occupation, and locale. The demand in some subject areas exceeds the capacity of the program, and the rule of thumb in such cases has been "first-come, first-served."

The absence of traditional admissions requirements should not obscure the rigorous academic standards of the Open University, which were designed to conform to the standards of other British institutions.[17] The Open University offers two degrees: the Bachelor of Arts and the Bachelor of Arts with Honors, the former requiring six credits and the latter, eight. There are four levels of study, corresponding roughly to "years" in other universities. A student without credit exemptions for previous academic work must complete two foundation courses from among five broad areas: arts, mathematics, science, social science, and technology. Each course is 36 weeks in duration, including a one-week full-time summer session, and counts for one credit. At subsequent levels, the student develops an area of specialization and pursues a series of half- and one-credit courses in his major field. At present, there are almost 70 undergraduate course offerings, which have been developed by Open University faculty, educational technology specialists, and outside consultants.[18]

The core of the instructional delivery system are packages of printed materials mailed weekly, which also refer the student to outside readings. Evaluation takes place through written and practical exercises and tests. Some of these are scored by the students

[16]Ibid, pp. 34–38; "The Open University," *Group for Research and Innovation in Higher Education Newsletter* 2 (June 1973): 35–38; Malcolm Scully, "More Than Watching the Telly," *Chronicle of Higher Education,* May 5, 1975, p. 4; and Ruth Weinstock, "British Open University: Media Used in Context," *Planning for Higher Education* 4 (April 1975).

[17]Carnegie Commission on Higher Education, *New Students and New Places* (New York: McGraw-Hill, 1971), p. 113.

[18]Weinstock, "British Open University," p. 2.

themselves, and others are submitted to tutors for scoring and comment. University officials estimate that the average student spends 80 percent of his time working on correspondence materials and reading. The other 20 percent is devoted to radio and television broadcasts devised to supplement correspondence work and face-to-face contact with tutors and faculty members at required one-week summer sessions.

The university headquarters at Milton Keynes houses offices for a fulltime staff of some 450 academics, together with a library, laboratories, meeting rooms, a publications unit, and a data processing unit. In addition, there are numerous local study centers located in each of 13 regions throughout Great Britain. Each center is supervised by a counselor whose job it is to provide advice, lead discussions after broadcasts, and match students with tutors who visit the center at regular intervals to help students with special problems.

When the Open University opened in January, 1971, there were 43,000 applicants for 25,000 places. Since then the numbers have swelled to a total 1975 enrollment of 64,000. In the past year many of the foundation courses had to turn away four applicants for every one accepted. On the basis of current graduation rates, university officials predict that 60 percent of the university's first class will eventually receive degrees. Although the Open University is attracting increasing numbers of blue-collar workers, this category comprises only 10 percent of the present student body. Over 20 percent of the students are school teachers who have less than four-year certifications. Housewives make up the second largest group, followed by clerical workers, members of the professions, and technical workers.[19]

Across the Atlantic, more than 20 American institutions now offer Open University courses which make use of British materials.[20] Among the most carefully scrutinized of these experiments is the program being conducted at the Universities of Maryland and Houston and Rutgers University. Rodney Hartnett of ETS conducted a

---

[19]Scully, "More Than Watching the Telly," p. 4.
[20]Weinstock, "British Open University," p. 5.

detailed study following the completion of its first year of operation (1972–73).[21]

The initial experience, Hartnett found, challenges the assumption that small-scale Open University programs will achieve the same reduction in costs and/or faculty manhours as in Britain. On the other hand, Hartnett found predominantly positive attitudes among the faculty and adult learners who have been involved in the program. He concluded that the development of such programs in the United States should not be based on cost savings but on the conviction that they will be responsive to the needs of a significant number of potential students.[22]

The New York State Regents External Degree:
The Assessment Model

In September 1970, Ewald B. Nyquist, new Commissioner of Education and President of the University of the State of New York, announced in his inaugural address that the time had come to develop a mechanism for awarding a degree based on New York State's College Proficiency Examinations.[23] He proposed to the Board of Regents that "The University of the State of New York award undergraduate degrees to those who are able to demonstrate that they possess knowledge and abilities equivalent to those of a degree recipient from a New York State college or university, regardless of how the candidates had prepared themselves." The new program, he continued, would not compete with existing programs but would "serve those citizens who are, for whatever reason, unable to attend institutions of higher learning as resident students."[24]

---

[21]Rodney T. Hartnett, et. al., *The British Open University in the United States: Adaptation and Use at Three Universities* (Princeton: Educational Testing Service, 1974).

[22]Rodney T. Hartnett, "Adult Learners and New Faculty Roles," *ETS Findings,* 1, 3 (1974): 4.

[23]The University of the State of New York (not to be confused with the State University of New York), established by the legislature in 1784, is the oldest state educational agency in the United States. It includes all public and private colleges and universities, elementary and secondary schools, libraries, museums, historical societies, and other educational agencies in the state.

[24]Ewald B. Nyquist, *The Idea of the University in the State of New York* (Albany: State Department of Education, 1970), pp. 7–8, cited in Houle, *The External Degree,* p. 95.

With the financial assistance of the Carnegie Corporation and the Ford Foundation, the Regents External Degree Program began operation as a degree-granting agency, with no instructional program of its own, in 1971. The initial plan was to begin awarding an Associate of Arts degree in 1972, a Bachelor of Science in Business Administration in 1973, and an Associate of Applied Science in Nursing in 1973–74. The program now offers two additional associate degrees, a Bachelor of Science, and a Bachelor of Arts, and the Kellogg Foundation has recently provided a grant for the development of a baccalaureate degree in nursing.

The requirements for each degree and the ways in which they can be met are determined by faculty and administrators from New York colleges and universities, who serve in their capacity as faculty members of the University of the State of New York. There are five different approaches to earning credit for a degree: (1) college courses taken for credit from an accredited college or university; (2) proficiency examinations, including College Proficiency Examinations and Regents External Degree Examinations; (3) military education programs; (4) special assessment of knowledge or skills not testable by existing proficiency examinations; and (5) courses offered by nonacademic organizations which have been evaluated in terms of college credit.

There are no age, residence, or educational requirements for enrollment. A prospective student may obtain information about degree programs and requirements by mail and/or by consulting a volunteer counselor, often a full-time academic advisor at a college in his local area (New York State only). If he decides to enroll, he may then submit documentation of previous course-work and examinations for evaluation. Any credit awarded for previous work is entered on the student's status report, which serves as a record of his academic progress until completion of the degree. Following the determination of advanced standing, the student may proceed to earn additional credits via a combination of the mechanisms noted above.

The fees for a student enrolled in the Regents External Degree Program include a $50 enrollment fee, a $25 annual records maintenance fee, and a $10 graduation fee. Examination fees range from

$25–$50, and the cost of a special assessment ranges from $200 to $250. According to program literature, the average cost of degrees taken entirely by examination is between $250 and $700.

As of May 1975, the Regents External Degree Program has graduated 2,358 students, 86 percent of which have been associate of art recipients. A statistical profile of associate of art graduates as of October 1974 indicates student representation from 49 states. Ninety percent were employed full-time during their enrollment, and approximately 70 percent were in the armed services. Thirty-seven percent earned their degrees through a combination of college courses and proficiency exams, 23 percent through college courses alone, and approximately 18 percent through proficiency exams alone. Others earned their degrees through different combinations of courses, exams, and military schools. While current figures are not available on postgraduation activities, over half of the first 400 associate degree recipients went on to attend 88 different four-year colleges in 32 states.[25]

The Regents External Degree Program is performing a useful function for a clientele who are, for a variety of reasons, unable to obtain a degree via more traditional means. The Regents Program has recently expanded its services to this clientele by creating a "Credit Bank" which makes the program's credit evaluation services available to anyone, whether or not they wish to pursue a Regents External Degree.

Empire State College:

The Complex Systems Approach

In the fall of 1970, a small group of State University of New York (SUNY) administrators in the central office began to discuss the possibility of creating an innovative college within the SUNY system. University officials visited England in December of 1970 to study the British Open University, which was receiving a good deal of publicity at that time. A small planning group met in Albany in

---

[25]Beverly T. Watkins, "Goodbye Tradition," *Chronicle of Higher Education,* October 21, 1974, p. 5.

January 1971 to design what eventually became the Empire State College. The college enrolled its first students in fall 1971.

Although a separate college, Empire State College draws upon the resources of the entire SUNY system. The college has administrative offices at Saratoga Springs but maintains a network of learning centers and learning units throughout the state, where most student contact with the institution occurs. Each of the six centers is located in an urban setting and is administered by a dean and associate dean who are responsible for a physical plant of learning resources and for coordinating the work of the thirteen to sixteen faculty mentors. The learning units, of which there are 30, are smaller administrative entities consisting of one to three mentors and a coordinator. Many of these units are located on SUNY campuses.

The prospective student must be either a high school graduate (of any age), hold an equivalency certificate, or be able to demonstrate the capacity to do advanced work. Equally important for admissions, however, is the student's understanding of the values of the college, his awareness of how the program operates, and his willingness to undertake independent study.[26] Advanced standing may be awarded upon submission of a portfolio of prior learning and is granted on the basis of months earned toward the degree. A maximum of 26 months may be awarded toward a 32-month baccalaureate (ten months toward a 16-month associate degree), depending upon the level of congruence between the student's degree plan and the nature and content of his prior learning.

The college has no classes, no courses, and no formal grades. Learning experiences are planned by the student and his faculty mentor, who may be a full-time faculty member of the college or a faculty member at another SUNY campus with an adjunct relationship with Empire State. Each learning contract consists of a statement of activities which the student will pursue toward the goal of achieving a certain set of knowledge and/or skills, together with an agreement concerning the evaluation of that achievement. These learning activities may include one or a combination of the following: formal courses offered by colleges and other organizations; coopera-

[26]Houle, *The External Degree,* p. 98.

tive studies involving projects with other students; tutorials; organized programs of more or less self-contained resources (e.g., correspondence materials); direct experiences (travel, field work, etc.) which become the object of examination and reflection by the student; and independent study.

The college awards the Associate of Arts, Associate of Science, Bachelor of Arts, Bachelor of Science, and Bachelor of Professional Studies degrees. A student's degree program includes several learning contracts organized around a conceptual framework based on the student's interests, purposes, plans and aspirations. There are five basic frameworks or modes around which a degree program may be organized: disciplinary, interdisciplinary, problem-oriented, thematic, or vocational-professional.

Although the student has considerable flexibility in designing his degree program within one of these organizing frameworks, it must also fall within one of the general areas of study for which the college has developed a set of educational resources. There are nine such areas, ranging from the Arts to Mathematics, Science, and Technology. Finally, each degree program must define an area of concentration and a general learning component that supports that concentration and provides for a degree of breadth.

As the student nears the end of his program, usually before the start of his final contract, a faculty committee reviews his record to determine if the requirements of his degree program have been fulfilled. If so, the committee recommends that he be awarded the degree upon completion of his final contract.

As of April 1, 1974, 2,100 students were enrolled in Empire State College, ranging in age from 16 to 72. The college has deliberately avoided presenting aggregate data on its students, for it is felt that such data would obscure the highly individual nature of its students and their degree programs. Information about the college often takes the form of individual student profiles, selected to convey their diversity. A report written by a mentor at the Metropolitan New York Learning Center provides some useful illustrations.[27]

    [27]Bernard H. Stern, "College Without Walls: A Teacher's View," *Liberal Education* 59 (December 1973): 480–89.

Bernard Stern arranged learning contracts with 42 students during the period September 1972 to March 1973. This group ranged in age from 19 to 72. Many of the students had attended other colleges and were attracted to Empire State by the prospect of greater flexibility and the possibility of acceleration. Occupationally, the group consisted of six actors or actresses, six full-time students, three nurses, three waiters or waitresses, two teachers, two owners of bookshops, two nuns, two insurance agents, two electricians, and representatives from eleven other occupations.

Most of Stern's students pursued programs of study in literature, poetry, and general and critical writing. Illustrative of the contracts they arranged under Stern's guidance was a 35-year old dancer who adapted works of literature to dance and movement. A 28-year old housewife and mother of three explored literature for and by children, with special emphasis on the role of fantasy. A 42-year old school aide studied language arts programs in the "open classroom" and designed a language arts curriculum of her own. A 38-year old social worker wrote a body of poetry to be used for poetry therapy. While these examples represent the activity of only one mentor and a group of students concerned primarily with the arts, they convey some sense of the wide variety of needs and interests served by the Empire State College.

Problems and Prospects

To repeat an earlier statement, the objective of providing educational services to the part-time adult learner is by no means unique to the 1970s. It is probably true, however, that the validity of this objective has received greater currency in recent years. Nevertheless, the manner in which it is to be accomplished remains a subject of considerable debate. The concerns expressed by advocates and critics alike are worthy of note.

The primary concern is insuring academic quality.[28] Unless special precautions are taken, credit and degrees for off campus or part-time study can result in a spate of unplanned, low-quality programs con-

[28]Watkins, "Goodbye Tradition," p. 5.

trolled by entrepreneurs whose primary goal is a share of the educational dollar. The Commission on Nontraditional Study has been one of the more vociferous advocates of quality control among nontraditional programs. As expressed by Chairman Samuel B. Gould:

> The most careful monitoring of innovative adaptations and departures from the norm is necessary, not to discourage flexible and diverse approaches but to make certain that each person has a truly educative experience. An institution that chooses a nontraditional direction opens itself to extraordinary scrutiny and must ultimately be able to prove the worth of the way it has chosen.[29]

The definition and measurement of quality, however, is a matter of great complexity—even for traditional education. It may be, as Patricia Cross has suggested, that new approaches to learning cannot be judged by old standards.[30] Certainly at the experimental stage of innovation there should be an awareness that old standards may not apply. Hefferlin argues, however, that ultimately the best interests of education will be served by reassessing the old standards themselves. Indeed, the external degree movement might well provide the impetus for such an effort.[31]

Hefferlin observes that accrediting and regulatory agencies, from their beginnings, have focused on institutional structure and procedures—e.g., library holdings, teaching loads, faculty-student ratios, and organizational efficiency, as inferential measures of institutional quality.[32] If, indeed, such environmental criteria are adequate measures of the quality of the resident educational experience, they may prove inadequate to the task of assessing learning that occurs off campus. The solution, however, suggests Hefferlin, rests not with the application of separate standards, for this would threaten the credibility of both the accrediting process and of nontraditional programs. The solution, difficult though it may be, rests with the development of new methods of evaluation which will effectively measure the learning that occurs in both traditional and nontraditional programs.

[29]Houle, *The External Degree,* p. xi.
[30]Watkins, "Goodbye Tradition," p. 5.
[31]"Avoiding Cut-Rate Credits and Discount Degrees," *Planning Nontraditional Programs,* Cross, Valley, and Associates, pp. 148–74.
[32]Ibid, pp. 165–67.

The advocates of nontraditional study would do well to assume the initiative in this endeavor.[33]

A second concern in the external degree debate is the issue of cost —both to the institution and to the student. Initial enthusiasm for the external degree included an expectation that nontraditional programs would involve minimal capital investment in new facilities and reduce the number of faculty manhours from that required by resident instruction. Without denying the complexity or dearth of comparative data on instructional costs, the evidence available thus far would indicate that cost savings will not be nearly as significant as originally anticipated.

The British Open University appears to have achieved some important economies of scale, and many observers agree that there is a significant savings in instructional costs.[34] Medsker reported that annual costs per FTE student were, with rare exceptions, lower than comparable on campus programs in the 16 institutions studied.[35] As already noted, however, Hartnett found that the use of Open University materials on a smaller scale in the United States has not resulted in significant cost savings.[36] Stephen Bailey reports that Syracuse University's external degree in liberal studies is *more* expensive than on-campus programs.[37] Howard Bowen suggests that there is no reliable way to generalize about costs, but that high quality external degree programs are likely to be expensive.[38] The costs of planning, evaluation, hardware, software, and individualized guidance and instruction are likely to be high, at least at the outset. It is nevertheless possible, as illustrated by the British experience, that certain economies of scale may be achieved via multi-institutional efforts to share resources.

With regard to student costs, many institutions charge per-credit

[33]Ibid, pp. 165–70.

[34]Bruce Laidlow and Richard Layard. "Traditional Versus Open University Teaching Methods: A Cost Comparison," *Higher Education* 3 (1974): 439–68; and Leslie Wagner, "The Open University and the Costs of Expanding Higher Education," *Universities Quarterly* 27 (Autumn 1973) 394–406.

[35]Medsker, et. al., *Extending Opportunities for a College Degree*, pp. 254–55.

[36]Hartnett, et al., *The British Open University in the U.S.*, p. 93.

[37]Stephen K. Bailey, "Flexible Spare/Time Higher Education: Serpents in the Basket of Shiny Red Apples" (Paper delivered to the American Association for Higher Education, Chicago, March 1972), p. 5.

[38]Howard F. Bowen, "Financing the External Degree," *Journal of Higher Education* 54 (June 1973): 491.

tuition for external degree courses at the same rate as resident education. Other programs, particularly of the assessment variety, involve
substantially lower fees. The area in which external degree students
are not treated equitably, however, is that of financial aid. Although
the Higher Education Amendments of 1972 made part-time students
eligible for federal student aid, the American Council on Education
Committee on the Financing of Higher Education for Adult Students found that part-time students, on the whole, are "massively"
discriminated against in federal and state student and institutional
aid programs.[39] If an external degree student is not eligible for veterans or employee benefits, he is typically forced to finance his own
education. On the other hand, part-time students usually have lower
costs with respect to foregone income.

A third area of concern relates to the definition of an appropriate
clientele for external degree programs. Most external degree programs place considerable emphasis on the individual efforts of the
student. As Samuel Gould has suggested, "More rather than less
rigor is demanded of the external degree student; more rather than
less initiative is expected. A high degree of motivation is a fundamental requisite."[40] The mature, self-sufficient adult who has already
developed a set of basic learning skills is most likely to benefit from
the opportunities provided by external degree programs. In contrast,
the educationally and economically deprived are likely to experience
frustration and failure.

As previously noted, the British Open University, originally designed to bring higher education to the working class (blue collar
workers), has attracted a predominantly middle-class clientele, as
have all the other programs discussed herein. The task force which
designed the External Studies Program at the University of Pittsburgh determined from the start that the new program should not
attempt to serve the educationally and economically marginal student who was in need of remedial attention and nonexistent financial
aid. The message of these examples is that external degree programs

---

[39]*Financing Part-Time Students: The New Majority in Postsecondary Education* (Washington, D. C.: American Council on Education 1974), p. 3.
[40]Houle, *The External Degree,* p. xi.

do not, by any means, represent an effective solution to the problem of minority group access to postsecondary education.

Another potential clientele of external degree programs is the traditional college student who may be attracted for economic, intellectual, or other reasons to alternative programs. The prospect of attrition from traditional programs has generated some concern for the survival of the residential college and an effort to reexamine the value of the residential experience. It seems likely that some college-age students will be attracted to new learning formats. On the other hand, there is some evidence that others will reject the relative isolation and lack of structure characteristic of external degree programs.[41] In addition, the new clienteles served by external degree programs will undoubtedly bring about an increased demand for the instructional services of the residential college, though these services may differ somewhat from the traditional mold.

In spite of the many difficult problems that may never be totally resolved, the external degree movement has a strong potential for making a number of important contributions to postsecondary education. Perhaps most important is the prospect of serving a new clientele which, until recently, had been barred from gaining access to postsecondary education. Equally important, the external degree gives substance to the notion that learning can and should be a lifelong process.

The external degree has also forced the educational community to reassess a number of unproven assumptions and practices. The value of the residential experience is being reexamined, and the traditional procedures and criteria for accreditation are being challenged by new programs which emphasize *what* a student has learned rather than how, when, or where.

In the long run, cost savings may be possible through regional coordination and interinstitutional cooperation. There is also a great untapped potential for community involvement and for cooperation between academe, business, and industry.

Finally, the external degree provides a milieu for experimentation free of some of the structural constraints of traditional programs.

[41] Hartnett, "Adult Learners," p. 2.

Faculty involvement in such experiments may also cause new conceptions of the teaching-learning process to be carried back to the classroom.

The story of the external degree movement of the 1970s is still being written. While it does not seem likely that the demands for access which prompted the movement are likely to disappear, it remains to be seen whether the external degree, as it is currently taking shape, will prove adequate to the task of providing effective educational access to the adult student. The task of expanding access and maintaining quality under conditions of limited resources is a challenge to the educational community as a whole and to the land-grant tradition of service to new clienteles.

Chapter 16

THE PUBLIC INTEREST AND INSTITUTIONAL AUTONOMY

STANLEY O. IKENBERRY

LAND-GRANT universities have played a special role in the emergence of a system of American higher education. These institutions, more than others, began as a system in response to federal legislation. They signaled a joint commitment of the federal government and each state to support higher education. This early commitment developed broadly, becoming an extensive public sector of education that stimulated the demand for greater governmental coordination and control of American colleges and universities.

While land-grant universities guarded their autonomy and independence as zealously as any other class of institutions, their relationship to state and federal governments—representing the public interest—and their very character caused them to be the focus of a gradual evolution toward a more formalized, governmentally monitored system. If the Morrill Act of 1862 played an early and perhaps initiating role that helped shape the current system of American higher education, the Higher Education Amendments of 1972 and especially Section 1202, P.L. 93–318, which provides for what are now referred to as "1202 Commissions," is the latest and one of the more dramatic signals of government action that may define the American system of the future. It is the emergence of this governmental system—its historical and projected relations to interinstitutional cooperation and coordination and to institutional autonomy—to which this chapter is directed.

The early foundations of American higher education did not rest on governmental sponsorship or control although these were never totally absent. Until recent decades, American higher education was primarily a private enterprise. The absence of governmental coordination and control was coupled with the recognition that the effec-

tiveness if not the survival of the higher educational enterprise demanded coordination among institutions.

The Story of Nongovernmental Coordination

The early academic structure of American colleges and universities emerged largely through interinstitutional cooperative efforts.
Admissions standards, college credit as a measure of academic progress, the concept and substance of the general education curriculum,
the elective system, and the notion of a major and a minor grew in
the absence of governmental direction.

The American tradition of a nongovernmental system is exemplified by the development of regional accrediting associations
unique to higher education.[1] Accreditation emerged in the late nineteenth and early twentieth centuries as an institutionally devised
alternative to governmental coordination and control. It provided
peer evaluation of educational institutions and programs and some
degree of standardization essential to institutional survival.

The partitioning of the United States into six subdivisions for
purposes of general accreditation took place between 1885 and 1924,
beginning with New England and ending with the western regional
accrediting group. Although membership in the regional accrediting
association was always emphasized as voluntary, the price of ignoring the regional accrediting society quickly increased and became
more than most institutions were willing to pay. Many federal programs, for example, required regional accreditation as the threshold
for institutional eligibility for funding. Hence, voluntary associations
exercised a powerful coordinating influence.

In addition to the regional accrediting associations, a wide range
of voluntary professional accrediting societies emerged to monitor
the professions and, to a limited degree, the disciplines.[2] The Ameri-

[1]See William K. Selden, *Accreditation: A Struggle Over Standards in Higher Education* (New
York: Harper and Brothers, 1960); and Frank G. Dickey and Jerry W. Miller, *A Current
Perspective on Accreditation* (Washington, D.C.: ERIC Clearinghouse on Higher Education,
November 1972, Report No. 7).

[2]See G. Lester Anderson, *Trends in Education for the Professions* (Washington, D.C.: ERIC
Clearinghouse on Higher Education, 1974, Report No. 7).

can Chemical Society, the Association of American Medical Colleges, the American Psychological Association, and numerous other associations emerged over the years to accredit particular professional or academic areas. Similar to the regional accrediting associations, these societies were based on voluntary participation by institutions and their faculties, and in effect, they substituted peer review for state or federal certification of standards of quality.

Accreditation, both regionally and in the professions, is currently under intensive review with the emergence of new state and federal mechanisms and controls. The role of voluntary associations is being questioned. The most pressing of demands for proper accreditation monitoring is coming from the federal government because its default rate for guaranteed student loans has been much higher than is generally considered reasonable. Students in accredited institutions were eligible for such loans, but accreditation alone has proved insufficient to determine which students in which institutions are reasonable risks.[3] The differences in standards of the regional accrediting associations has also become difficult to deal with as the higher educational system has become truly national. A consequence of this situation has been that in January 1975 a super-accreditation structure called the Council on Postsecondary Accreditation was created.[4] Once again, the public interest had redressed the balance of institutional autonomy and institutional accountability.

There has also been an unmeasurable but significant impact from the several associations that bring together administrators and faculty members for purposes of discussing common problems and issues. The American Council on Education, the National Association of State Universities and Land-Grant Colleges, the American Association of State Colleges and Universities, the Association of American Colleges, the American Association of Community and Junior Colleges, the American Association of University Professors, the American Association for Higher Education, and the multitude of professional associations of professors, discipline by discipline,

[3]See Harold Orlans, *Private Accreditation and Public Eligibility* (Lexington, Massachusetts: Lexington Books, D. C. Heath and Company, 1975).
[4]Ibid., p. 27.

professional field by field, suggest the complex network that, over the years, has knit together what is now called a system.

The philanthropic foundations have deliberately attempted to strengthen this voluntary system. The Carnegie Commission, for example, was instrumental in the establishment of the Teachers' Insurance and Annuity Association (TIAA) at the end of the first World War. This association made it possible for a professor to take his pension with him from one institution to another, a level of coordination presently unmatched in many other segments of American society.

The pressures for interinstitutional collaboration continue to remain strong. The Carnegie Commission on Higher Education, for example, recommended in 1971 "that colleges and universities continue to seek ways of sharing facilities, courses, and specialized programs through cooperative arrangements; that existing consortia make continuous efforts toward increasing the effectiveness of their cooperative programs; and that institutions—especially small colleges—that are not now members of consortia carefully consider possibilities for forming consortia with neighboring institutions."[5]

While other examples of the extent and variety of interinstitutional cooperation and the impact of these efforts on the development of the American higher education system could be cited, it is sufficient to note that American colleges and universities and their faculties and administrators have, of necessity, developed a strong tradition of institutionally initiated coordination, more so than their sister institutions in other nations.

The dominance of nongovernmental coordination and cooperation, however, has yielded to more and more pressures for greater governmental involvement. Writing in 1960, Algo Henderson commented that "Washington has little to say about higher education . . . [and] the state departments of education have only a minor role in the supervision of the colleges and the universities."[6]

Henderson continued to describe the American system of higher education of that time rather precisely when he wrote, "In a system

[5]The Carnegie Commission on Higher Education, *New Students and New Places, Policies for the Future Growth and Development of American Higher Education* (New York: McGraw-Hill, October 1971), pp. 93–94.

[6]Algo D. Henderson, *Policies and Practices in Higher Education,* p. 267.

of higher education that is composed of as many diverse and complex elements as is that of the United States, there are many problems of competition, cooperation, and coordination. It is a much simpler situation in most other countries, because there the usual pattern of organization is either to have all institutions operated by the state or to have all of them strongly directed or influenced by a central ministry of education. But this is not our pattern."[7]

With the passage of more than a decade, it is now clear that the pattern of which Henderson spoke has changed. Stephen K. Bailey, writing in the mid-seventies, described the considerable array of "edifices, privileges, and encouragements" presently furnished to postsecondary institutions by the government. "The protections and dispensations range all the way from tax exemptions and direct appropriations to student loans, risk guarantees, contract enforcement, campus security, fair personnel practices, (and) support for basic and applied research."[8]

Toward Formal Coordination

The United States is moving more rapidly than is generally acknowledged toward a quasi-governmental system of higher education. While the Carnegie Commission continued to recommend that "the United States should not move in the direction of a single national system of higher education as have many nations,"[9] nearly every state has taken substantial steps over the last 15 years to formalize a state system of higher education. Federal involvement, as suggested in the formation of state commissions called for in the 1972 Higher Education Amendments and as reflected in the enforcement of federal policies through the grant or denial of federal funds, is more and more in evidence.

The pressures toward more formalized systems of coordination and control, in preference to the traditional voluntary approaches, have come from many directions. Much of the movement stemmed

[7]Ibid., p. 267.
[8]Stephen K. Bailey, "Education and the State," *Education and the State,* edited by John F. Hughes (Washington, D.C.: American Council on Education, 1975), pp. 3–4.
[9]The Carnegie Commission on Higher Education, *The Capitol and the Campus* (New York: McGraw-Hill, April 1971), p. 1.

directly or indirectly from the phenomenal post-World War II growth of American higher education. The total degree credit enrollment, for example, increased from approximately 1.5 million students in 1940 to approximately 7.7 million students in 1970 and to nearly 10 million students in 1975.

Approximately 1,000 new colleges and universities were founded in the United States during the 1950s and 1960s. To be dramatic about it, one new college came into being each week over a period of twenty years. Some two-thirds of these new institutions were two-year community colleges, adding a new and major dimension to the higher education complex in many states.

It is significant that 55 percent of the 1,000 new institutions were sponsored and controlled by public agencies, thus further shifting the balance toward the public—or governmental—sector.[10] By 1960, 60 percent of all students were enrolled in public institutions, and by 1970 the proportion of enrollments in the public sector had increased to 75 percent. All indicators suggest a continued expansion of public responsibility for higher education, either through direct sponsorship or through indirect assistance to institutions and to students. Robert Berdahl summarized these forces well when he commented:

> This growth in the number and types of institutions and in the richness of their offerings reflected the tremendous postwar growth in student numbers and in turn led to a huge increase in state expenditures on higher education. Whereas, in 1900, for example, only about 4 percent of U.S. college-age population attended college, after 1945 the proportion mounted steadily to one-half, and this at a time when the "baby boom" was vastly increasingly the basic pool from which this group was drawn . . . State expenditures on higher education rose from 500 million in 1950 to about 5 billion in 1967, and, unless federal aid increases massively, they should reach 10 billion by 1980. Constituting about 7 percent of all state expenditures in 1950, higher education now consumes about 15 percent. Clearly, higher education has become a major concern of state governments.[11]

---

[10]*New Academic Institutions* (Washington, D. C.: American Council on Education, 1971), p. 1.

[11]Robert O. Berdahl, *Statewide Coordination of Higher Education* (Washington, D. C.: American Council on Education, 1971), pp. 28–29.

The Carnegie Council on Policy Studies has recently spoken to what the council calls "Unfinished Business, 1975–1980." This policy statement is directed to the federal role with major attention to financial assistance in a variety of forms and to the variety of implications. The first recommendation is as follows: *The Council recommends that the federal government's share of total public financial support of postsecondary education gradually be increased to 50 percent.* [12] Both the state and federal role and power will continue to grow.

It was obvious in 1960, and is now even more obvious that the institutionally initiated efforts to coordinate the massive and expensive system of American higher education, amazing as these have been in the past, are inadequate for the future. It was inevitable that governmental efforts would emerge to develop new structures and new mechanisms for coordination of higher education. Perhaps it was equally inevitable that these new mechanisms would be met with institutional resistance.

The very character of many state universities and land-grant colleges made it difficult for them to accept the need for greater governmental coordination of higher education. Land-grant universities and their programs tend to operate statewide, in contrast to more regionally or locally oriented institutions. On the whole, they tend to be comprehensive universities in terms of breadth of program. They tend to serve students from all geographic areas of the state. Their programs of cooperative extension and research are not only statewide in character but are carried out in a national and international context. These diverse roles have brought many land-grant universities into apparent conflict and competition with other universities and colleges that wished to serve a specific constituency or geographic area of the state and do so without the intrusion of the land-grant university. Land-grant universities, in turn, were frequently concerned that their traditional roles not be reshaped and redefined by statewide coordinating agencies.

[12]The Carnegie Council on Policy Studies in Higher Education, *The Federal Role in Postsecondary Education* (San Francisco: Jossey-Bass, 1975). See chapter 2, specifically page 14.

Framework for Governmental Coordination

Nearly every state now has a formalized, governmentally defined system of higher education. Many such coordination mechanisms were fashioned in a climate of public frustration stemming from the apparent failure of institutionally initiated approaches to coordination. Patterns vary from state to state, and the implications of a given pattern to quality education and economy of operations has yet to be conclusively demonstrated. The demands for better planning and for economy grew as the decade of the 60s progressed. The response was the introduction of state coordinating boards, and in some states 'super' boards. At stake for institutions were the traditions of institutional autonomy and governance and the prospect of a loss of control over institutional programs. Berdahl, commenting on these strains, observed that "many academics are trying to protect too much, and many persons in state government are trying to claim too much."[13]

Others commented on the development of heavy-handed regulatory councils over higher education. The Carnegie Commission suggested that "the new coordinating systems serve best when they concentrate on planning and consultation, rather than on routine administrative tasks, bureaucratic controls, and detailed regulation. They should provide enlightened guidance and not stifling delay and restraint. Routine regulation and control are neither needed nor compatible with the statesmanlike planning and advice that are so essential."[14]

This same view was reinforced in the commission report on *Governance of Higher Education: Six Priority Problems*. What is needed, the commission argued, is an understanding between the universities and their benefactors that recognizes both the right of the public to set priorities and the need of institutions for intellectual, academic, and administrative independence.

The 1971 study commission chaired by Frank Newman also expressed concern that government may have overreacted. "At present what discussion there is about governance at the state level is focused

[13]Berdahl, *Statewide Coordination,* p. 5.
[14]Carnegie Commission, *Capitol and Campus,* p. 2.

on extending and consolidating multi-campus systems and achieving greater coordination of both public and private colleges. We believe serious study should be given to the opposite point of view. What gains (and risks) would there be in breaking up large systems? What are the advantages of pluralism of several systems within a state? What can be done about reversing the trend to central control within systems?"[15]

Autonomy of institutions of higher education neither can be nor should be complete. This reality has long since been recognized and accepted not only by land-grant institutions, but by all institutions, including the traditionally independent private sector. Effective programs of education, research, and service, however, are the ultimate ends. This is where the public interest is ultimately served. It is possible for institutional autonomy to be infringed upon to the degree that there is, in fact, a measurable loss in the effectiveness of the programs of institutions.

In retrospect, it is now clear that land-grant colleges and universities and other public as well as private institutions could have guarded essential institutional independence more effectively and served the public interest more constructively had they understood and helped the public understand the distinctions between planning and coordination on the one hand and governance and institutional management on the other. Failure to do so has created confusion of coordinating and governing functions in many states.

There has been a rapid increase, for example, in the number of consolidated governing boards or 'super boards' established to both govern and coordinate total state systems of higher education. While consolidated governing boards were earlier utilized only in relatively small states such as New Hampshire and Maine, and more recently in Utah and West Virginia, the introduction of the consolidated governing board system in Wisconsin and North Carolina departs from this earlier pattern.

If the counsel of the Carnegie Commission and others is to be taken seriously, institutions must demonstrate to policy makers and

[15]Report on Higher Education (Newman Report), (Washington, D. C.: U. S. Department of Health, Education, and Welfare, March 1971), p. 72.

to the public at large that a separation of powers of coordination and governance will protect the public interest and at the same time enhance institutional effectiveness. The distinction has become much more important now that the federal government has entered the arena in a major way.

Several frameworks for future coordination of higher education systems which do distinguish between public and institutional prerogatives have been proposed. The Carnegie Commission guidelines, for example, suggested the following areas as appropriate for the exercise of strong state influence and even control:

- Number of places available in state institutions as a total and in specific programs where there are clear manpower needs (e.g., medicine)
- Number and location of new campuses
- Minimum and maximum size of institutions by type
- General admissions policy (i.e., whether open door or selective)
- General level of institution budgets, including construction budgets
- General level of salaries
- Accounting practices
- General functions of institutions
- Major new endeavors
- Effective use of resources
- Continued effective operation of institutions within the general law.[16]

Direct state control should stop short of governance of large, complex systems of institutions. For example, budget control should be limited to a postaudit; the hiring, firing, and assignment of faculty and staff and the terms of appointment should be within the internal control of the institution.

The Carnegie Commission did recommend that certain powers be reserved to the institution, including the appointment and promotion of faculty members and administrators; determination of courses of instruction and content of courses; selection and content of individual research projects and freedom to publish and otherwise dissemi-

[16]Carnegie Commission, *Capitol and Campus,* p. 105.

nate research results; freedom of inquiry; and freedom of speech, assembly, and other constitutional freedoms so central to the educational process.

Extra-Institutional Coordinating Forces

Three types of agencies and activities not heretofore dealt with as significant extra-institutional forces shaping the higher education system are regional development agencies involving several states, the Education Commission of the States, and an accelerating move toward regional planning of higher education within states. The most notable and visible of the regional development agencies are the Southern Regional Education Board (SREB) and the Western Interstate Commission for Higher Education (WICHE). Both are legally established bodies provided for in state statutes whose activities transcend state boundaries; but they are not national. The Education Commission of the States is an organization serving each of its member states at the level of their state governments in helping legislators and executive officers formulate policies for basic as well as higher education. The point is that these organizations have established new dimensions of interaction among institutions and among states. They do not govern, they do not coordinate, and they have no direct authority over institutions or other legal bodies, but they very definitely influence developments in higher education and expand resources available for instruction, research, and service. Regional planning is not yet highly developed, but represents a further advance in state educational planning in that it does not treat a state as a monolith.

The Southern Regional Education Board was founded in 1948 and is the oldest of the multi-state agencies. Its membership of fifteen states includes all states in the Southeast and Arkansas, Oklahoma, and Texas. The board's purpose is to further the social and economic advancement of the South by helping the states to widen educational opportunities in the region and particularly to broaden opportunities in advanced programs. Its programs of consultation, research, planning, and student interchange are extensive. Recently the cooperation of institutions in the region was advanced by the development of *The Academic Common Market.* President Godwin has stated the market "will operate as a mechanism through which the states and institutions voluntarily participate in a joint allocation of functions to avoid unnecessary duplication of programs and to assure availability and access to as many programs as are necessary in meeting the educational needs of the region's constituencies."[17] Institutions in twelve of the member states share 118 programs. As examples, Alabama has made arrangements for its residents to have access to 54 of these programs; South Carolina residents have access to 42. Representative program titles are as follows: biomedical engineering, criminal justice and criminology, electromagnetic theory, food systems administration, neurosciences, polymer science, seed technology, and wood and paper science.

The Western Interstate Commission for Higher Education was established in 1951. Thirteen of the most western states including Hawaii and Alaska are members. The commission has purposes not unlike the southern regional board: it seeks to increase educational opportunities for western youth, to help colleges and universities to improve programs and management, and to respond to changing regional needs. It works to expand the supply of specialized manpower in the west and has been particularly active in health fields. WICHE has no control over states or institutions. It operates as a service agency by gathering and reporting facts relevant to higher education, and serving as a clearinghouse for other information. It is also an administrative and fiscal agency for interstate arrangements for educational services. Through conferences and like activities it works to achieve an educational consensus on many matters relevant to education in the West.[18] Since the late 1960s, WICHE, through its National Center for Higher Education Management Systems (NCHEMS), is helping to improve institutional planning and management systems. The influence and activity of NCHEMS is national in scope. The initial activities of NCHEMS were with information systems per se, but the emphasis is shifting according to the

---

[17] *The Academic Common Market* (Atlanta: Southern Regional Education Board, 1974–75), p. 3.
[18] *Annual Report* (Boulder, Colo.: Western Interstate Commission for Higher Education, 1974).

director's 1974 annual report to evaluation, analysis and use of data, implementation of existing information-producing procedures, and the information requirements of statewide agencies.[19]

These regional boards and commissions have been remarkably successful. Their small staffs are supported by assessments of the member states, but the agencies also receive funding from a variety of outside sources including federal agencies. This funding permits them to make studies, conduct conferences, and publish materials that make them a significant force both unifying and progressive for all of American higher education. They operate without authority or control of institutions, but their influence is considerable. An interesting feature of the agencies just described is the mix of prosperous and highly populated states and less populated states. Advantages of agency activity flow to both classes, but the less advantaged states have been very well served.

The Education Commission of the States was established in 1966 with 22 states and territories as members. Today it has 47 members and a staff of 225. Its original and continuing purpose was and is "to forge an alliance between state officials and educators . . . so that they may mutually examine educational problems and arrive at mutually agreeable solutions."[20] The commission rests on a compact, i.e., an agreement of the states to work together on matters of moment in the field of education—preschool through graduate studies. Each state names seven commissioners, one of whom is the state's governor and two of whom are members of the state's legislature. A significant feature of the commission and its activity is that it has placed politically responsible persons and educators together in a forum and it has placed education in the mainstream of national policy making. It is generally agreed that the commission idea has worked and is working. While its formation was viewed with some skepticism, it appears to be an organization whose time had come. The commission has a low profile in any advocacy or lobbying role, but its service is immense, particularly as an objective fact gatherer

[19] *Director's Annual Report* (Boulder, Colo.: National Center for Higher Education Management Systems at WICHE, 1974).

[20] Justus Hope, "Focusing on the States," *American Education* 9 & 10 (December 1973): 4–9.

and as a preparer of a variety of materials basic to education policy formation at state and national levels. It can anticipate emerging educational issues and problems and prepare policy makers for such. Again, the Education Commission of the States represents an organization of no authority over institutions or states, but of considerable influence. As such, the regional agencies and the commission contribute to the developing concept of a national system of higher education.

Intrastate Regionalism in Postsecondary Education

Intrastate regional coordination of postsecondary education is a newly developing form of coordination. It has arisen from two separate but parallel trends of coordination interest: the movement from attention to the individual institution to a statewide system of postsecondary education and an increased interest by institutions themselves in voluntary collective activities. These two trends merge in the regionalization of postsecondary education.[21]

Regionalism differs from consortia in that the former, by definition, is accomplished through acts of an agency with official state level authority, whereas the latter are initiated by voluntary institutional action. Regionalism usually emerges as a geographic configuration of postsecondary educational resources joined by state legislative or administration action in a coordinated planning effort to solve certain institutional and regional educational problems. This type of planning seems to be motivated by four factors: (1) public demands for greater accountability for use of resources has led to increased efforts to end wasteful program duplication and achieve greater efficiency in the use of resources; (2) new educational technologies, such as closed circuit and video tape recorded television, have enhanced capabilities to share resources; (3) postsecondary education has been more widely accepted as a complex of services provided by a broad range of auspices to serve "the learning society"; (4) individual cam-

[21]S. V. Martorana and W. Gary McGuire, *Regionalism and Statewide Coordination of Postsecondary Education: A Preliminary Report of a Continuing Study* (University Park: Center for the Study of Higher Education, The Pennsylvania State University, in press).

puses are being pressured to meet the needs of a more diverse student constituency; and, (5) state funding of private and proprietary institutions through direct of indirect means is increasing.

Two preliminary studies of regionalization activities have shown that it is a widespread phenomena. In 1974 the Education Commission of the States identified formal interrelationships between consortia and coordinating agencies in 30 states.[22] Martorana and McGuire have identified 43 regionalization programs in 31 states.

Among the most active states in the development of intrastate regional alliances are New York, Illinois, Pennsylvania, and Virginia. The Illinois Higher Education Cooperation Act of 1972 provides an annual appropriation of $350,000 to fund interinstitutional cooperative efforts. The provisions of the act are administered by the Illinois Board of Higher Education which supported over 75 cooperative projects with funds provided by the act.[23]

Regionalism in Pennsylvania has gained formal recognition by the State Board of Education and the Department of Education. In April 1973, *A Design for Regionalization of Higher Education* was published as the state's regionalization plan. The plan divided the state into ten planning regions. Regional planning councils, including representatives of all the postsecondary educational institutions in the region, have been formed. The Department of Education has established a position for a special assistant for regional planning council coordination.

Both the Illinois and Pennsylvania regionalization plans include a variety of postsecondary education programs. Regionalization in effect in Virginia is limited to one type—continuing education. The 1973 legislation provides for the establishment of six regional consortia for the coordination of continuing education offerings. Member institutions in each region are required to eliminate duplicate offerings and to provide cooperative programs for the people of the region. Regional councils involve all private and public colleges offering significant off-campus continuing edu-

[22]Fritz H. Grupy and Anthony Murphy, "Survey of Statewide Agency/Consortia Relationships," *Higher Education In the States* 4 (1974): 173–84.
[23]*Progress Through Cooperation: A Report on the Illinois Higher Education Cooperation Act* (Springfield: Illinois Board of Higher Education, June 1974).

cation programs.[24] Regionalism can increase the effectiveness of statewide coordination of postsecondary educational resources and at the same time retain some measure of institutional autonomy. Regional councils allow the views of institutions to be heard early in the planning process. Regional consortia can report data on a regional basis to state agencies and facilitate consideration of the impact of the programs and enrollment in one institution upon others. The complexity of higher education today requires a systematic approach to coordination. The close participation by institutions in the policy development process through regionalism will make the systems approach more tolerable.

Reference was earlier made to the "1202 Commissions" provided for in the Higher Education Amendments of 1972. It is only now in 1975 that the 1202 provision of the amendments is being implemented. There is not yet a history to indicate how these commissions will behave, but they could become a significant force in the continuing quest for rational balance between the enforcement of public interest and preservation of institutional interests.

The federal government's call for 1202 commissions in the fifty states was a call for comprehensive planning. The essence of Section 1202 is embodied in this paragraph.

> Any state which desires to receive assistance under section 1203 of Title X shall establish a State Commission or designate an existing state agency or state commission (to be known as the State Commission) which is broadly and equitably representative of the general public and public and private nonprofit and proprietary institutions of postsecondary education in the state including community colleges (as defined in Table X), junior colleges, postsecondary vocational schools, area vocational schools, technical institutes, four-year institutions of higher education and branches thereof.
>
> Section 1203 provides for federal grants to any commission . . . to enable it to expand the scope of the studies and planning required in Title X through comprehensive inventories of, and studies with respect to, all public and private postsecondary educational resources

---

[24]*Coordination of Continuing Higher Education in Virginia: A State Plan for Regional Consortia for Continuing Higher Education* (Richmond: State Council of Higher Education for Virginia) mimeographed.

in the state, including planning, necessary for such resources to be better coordinated, improved, expanded or altered so that all persons within the state who desire, and who can benefit from, postsecondary education may have an opportunity to do so.

The 1202 Commissions were simply another step in the trend manifested since 1945 to achieve improved systems for planning and coordination. The 1202 Commissions do not fill a void; they extend the public interest through federal mandates. The federal interest and interaction has been a growing one for the last quarter of a century and has by no means climaxed. As a source of funds for categorical research, the federal purse has been wide open. Training grants, facilities grants, and more currently grants-scholarships and loans to students have been significant. While a few major universities have been the primary recipients of the federal largess, all institutions are now making their pleas louder and louder. Congress has been made aware of the entire postsecondary complex of educational endeavor, including the proprietary sector which is far from silent. Sections 1202 and 1203 of the 1972 amendments provide the potential framework for the total complex of postsecondary education to be coordinated; whether this potential will in fact be realized is far from apparent.

With federal efforts as with improved statewide planning and coordination of higher education, the broader goal is effectiveness of higher education programs in the United States. Effectiveness, as well as fine-tuned efficiency, must be the ultimate concern of both institutions and public policy makers. Maintenance of an appropriate balance between the public interest and institutional autonomy and academic freedom is possible only if there is mutual understanding of the need for such balance and mutual commitment by both the public and the institutions to make the system work.

Chapter 17

GOVERNANCE AND CONTROL OF
TOMORROW'S UNIVERSITY: WHOSE VALUES?

G. LESTER ANDERSON and KENNETH P. MORTIMER

DESPITE the challenge to higher education for the future that has been set forth in this volume, it must be acknowledged that land-grant universities have been successful in this century. In accomplishing their purposes as historically defined, they have been more than effective, they have been spectacularly successful. The success is evident in the "green revolution" as symbolized by the awarding of the Nobel Peace Prize to Norman E. Borlaug, a graduate of the University of Minnesota's College of Agriculture. It is also evident in the unqualified distinction of land-grant universities in the basic disciplines. The University of California (Berkeley), for example, is a land-grant university whose quality of research and scholarship may be rivaled but not exceeded. Wisconsin, Cornell, Minnesota, Purdue, Illinois, Michigan State, Penn State, Massachusetts Institute of Technology—land-grant universities all—are distinguished institutions.

Contrary to man-on-the-street wisdom, there is no evidence that land-grant institutions or other universities of the land are inefficient in their use of resources or that on the basis of legitimate measures of academic production they are found wanting. Their administrators are men of affairs, and so are their senior professors. They could and often do operate with confidence in government, business, industry, and international affairs. Three university presidents have been presidents of these United States. Land-grant university boards of trustees are composed of men and women who have well served government and labor, business and industry, and the professions. These universities command the loyalties of the men and women of entire states: the people of Wisconsin or Minnesota, for example, have no greater pride than that they accord to their land-grant universities.

If the land-grant universities are such successes, if they are so well-managed and esteemed, why raise issues about their governance? The answer lies in current trends that have implications of great magnitude for higher education as a system as well as for individual institutions. These trends may be summarized as the increased intervention by external agents and societal affairs into university life. Land-grant universities, as well as other public agencies and institutions, are experiencing a marked decrease in their ability to control the direction of their own development.

It is important to look at the elements involved in the current status of governance and control of public universities, including those of a land-grant character. This treatment, while necessarily limited in scope, will reflect the crucial nature of the debate over national, state, and local higher education policy.[1]

Statewide Coordination

The state rather than the federal government historically has the major responsibility for postsecondary education in America. In recent years this state responsibility has been extended beyond chartering and financing activities. Today they have established mechanisms—some elaborate—that make them a significant factor in almost day-by-day governance of public higher education. As of 1971, only three states—Delaware, Indiana, and Vermont—had no state agency for coordinating higher education.[2] In 1973, twenty-five states had statewide governing boards with regulatory authority over higher education, and twenty-five states had some form of coordinating board.

Coordinating boards are usually created by statute. Some of these agencies have specifically defined responsibilities; some have delegated authority; others have advisory functions only. The particular mix of advisory and regulatory responsibilities varies from state to state; but according to the Carnegie Commission, the boards in thirteen of the twenty-five states are primarily advisory in nature; the

[1]For a more complete discussion, see Kenneth P. Mortimer, *Accountability in Higher Education* (Washington, D.C.: American Association for Higher Education, 1972).

[2]Carnegie Commission on Higher Education, *The Capitol and the Campus* (New York: McGraw-Hill, 1971), pp. 122–24.

remaining twelve are regulatory.[3] Coordinating agencies seldom control hiring and firing of the institution's personnel or control the budget at the operational level.

Statewide governing boards operate very much like boards of trustees for individual institutions. The Carnegie Commission has taken the position that a single governing board is unlikely to be the most appropriate form of coordination except for small states with relatively little private higher education, very few public institutions, and a generally simple postsecondary system.[4] They make this recommendation because the administrative concerns of such a board can too easily displace planning functions.

Coordinating agencies are established to achieve a variety of functions and purposes. Because land-grant universities are not only pervasive in the states but have, with other state universities, a comprehensive role, they affect land-grant universities significantly. Among the purposes or functioning of these boards are:

1. Avoiding wasteful duplication in programs and harmful competition for resources.
2. Fostering greater efficiency in the use of scarce resources.
3. Aiding the orderly growth of higher education facilities within the state and the location of new campuses.
4. Assisting in developing state policy on admissions of students.
5. Gathering data for policy determination.
6. Ensuring diversity within the state system.
7. Providing a communication agency between and among colleges and universities, the state government and the public.
8. Fostering and enhancing excellence in the development of programs and the entire higher education network in the state.

There appears to be a slight trend away from coordinating boards towards statewide governing boards. If this trend develops more fully or rapidly, the implications for governance in state universities will be significant. Glenny and his colleagues believe this trend indicates a characteristic search for simplistic solutions to complex prob-

[3]Ibid., p. 25.
[4]Ibid., p. 26.

lems and a resurgence of the idea that a single all-powerful board should be charged with full responsibility for all that happens in colleges and universities.[5] Those who favor the governing board structure tend to argue that its regulatory powers put it into a position to exercise firmer standards of accountability and efficiency from the institutions within the state. They might do well to consider that "the danger of creating a board with insufficient power is that the public's interest will not be adequately protected; in creating a board with too much power, that the necessary autonomy and initiative of the institutions will be threatened."[6] Since we have held to the point of view that for more than one hundred years the development of state universities and land-grant colleges has been spectacularly successful, these trends to impose greater external governance must be continuously assessed.

Perhaps the most important dilemma raised by the existence of state coordinating and governing boards is the necessity to define and defend institutional autonomy and to distinguish such autonomy from intellectual freedom. The real issue with respect to institutional autonomy *vis-à-vis* intellectual freedom is not whether the state or coordinating boards will intervene but whether the inevitable tension between accountability and autonomy will be confined to the proper topics and expressed through a mechanism which is sensitive to both the public and institutional interests. The best of the land-grant and other state universities have in part achieved their greatness because of the high degree of autonomy they have experienced. Such universities as California, Michigan and Michigan State, Minnesota and Wisconsin are often cited for their quality and the relationships of this quality to their status as constitutionally created. They have again historically enjoyed a freedom from controls and interference by the transient governments of states that has seemed to bear a causal relationship to this quality. It should be noted that Cornell and the Massachusetts Institute of Technology, with the status and authority of private universities, are nonetheless land-grant institu-

[5]Lyman Glenny, et al., *Guidelines for Statewide Coordination of Higher Education* (Berkeley: Center for Research and Development in Higher Education, 1973).
[6]Ibid., p. 8.

tions. And the superb quality of these two institutions is not to be contradicted.

As the Carnegie Commission (April 1971), summing up the need for accountability and the dangers of the situation, said:

> Under no circumstances can institutional independence be considered absolute. Not even its strongest advocates can seriously question the legitimacy of requiring some degree of public accountability from educational institutions receiving public support. . . . The technique used to achieve public accountability of educational institutions must be balanced against the need of educational institutions for that degree of institutional independence which is essential for their continued vitality.[7]

The commission argues that the following are basic freedoms which should be protected from external control for all institutions:

> Appointment and promotion of faculty members and administrators
> Determination of courses of instruction and content of courses
> Selection of individual students
> Awarding individual degrees
> Selection and conduct of individual research projects and freedom to publish and otherwise disseminate research results
> Freedom of inquiry
> Freedom of speech, assembly, and other constitutional freedoms[8]

Land-grant and other public universities have been, in recent years, particularly susceptible to increased conflict over the definition of basic intellectual freedoms. Witness the California oath controversy and more recent sustained assaults upon the autonomy of the University of California by a conservative state government. The latter threat will be more explicitly noted later. Whether or not the public universities are able to maintain their independence while achieving accountability will be one of the crucial issues of the seventies and eighties, for such a balance is difficult to define and is likely to change over time.

---

[7] Carnegie Commission on Higher Education, *Capitol and Campus,* p. 104.
[8] Ibid., p. 106.

The Executive Branch of Federal and State Governments

The executive branches of the federal and state governments—i.e., their executive bureaucracies—all are increasing their control over public and private higher education, with land-grant and other state universities seemingly as vulnerable as the states' colleges.

In referring to the federal government's interest in higher education, Glenny wrote:

> The federal interests in higher education are highly specialized ones, with their own priorities. . . . Imbalances have been created in the educational programs by the concentration of federal funds on research and graduate training in the sciences. The project system of support through which funds are granted directly to university scientists has tended to draw the primary loyalty of faculty members from their institutions to agencies providing research funds.
>
> Each federal grant and contract carries with it controlling rules and conditions. Moreover, each also allows other federal laws to be applied to the recipient institution. . . . These legal constrictions apply to the operation of the whole institution, however small the grant received, and also private companies that construct campus buildings and provide major services.[9]

The demands of affirmative action programs on personnel policies and practices is the most obvious example of current federal intervention in higher education. While the elimination of sex or racial discrimination is justifiable without qualification, the maintenance of scholarly quality and integrity in state universities has, in the opinion of many university administrators, not been fully protected. The rulings and surveillance of and by federal officials have at times been unrealistic, confusing, or inconsistent—and hence threatening. The federal impact on postsecondary funding patterns, which is of even more recent consequence, will be discussed later.

Although it is quite difficult to document the full nature of gubernatorial control over public higher education in many states, sophisticated observers of higher education know that the governor can be

[9]Lyman Glenny, "The Anonymous Leaders of Higher Education," *The Journal of Higher Education* 43 (January 1972): 16.

an influential force. Two examples illustrate this fact very clearly.

Former Governor Reagan's influence had, without doubt, debilitating effects on the budget of the University of California system. According to Wood:

> In Governor Reagan's reign, he has twice reduced significantly the legislature's appropriations for university faculty salaries. Once he did nothing to change what he, himself, called a 'punitive' act by the legislature to forego the faculty cost of living increase; and this year, putting the blame on recession, he has disallowed any faculty salary increases again.[10]

This journalist raises three very important questions. The first is whether the governor politicized unduly the nine state campuses of the university for his own political advantage and to the detriment of the university. The second is whether the governor wielded his control over the university's budget in a punitive manner. Finally, and most important, is whether Governor Reagan was on a course that could ruin what many consider to be the finest public university system in the country. Regardless of one's views on that matter, few in California would argue that Governor Reagan's influence on the development of the University of California was anything but substantial. Reagan is no longer governor, but his course could well be repeated by governors in California and elsewhere.

In Wisconsin, Governor Patrick J. Lucey was the man most responsible for legislation which forced the University of Wisconsin into a merger with the former state colleges. Apparently:

> [Governor Lucey] championed the merger and pushed it through the legislature in spite of the opposition of the University of Wisconsin's president, both Boards of Regents, the University of Wisconsin Faculty Organization, and relative public indifference. . . . When he was through, Madison Campus and its twelve campuses were joined with the nine Wisconsin State Universities (formerly normal schools) and their four branches. The weak coordinating council for higher educa-

---

[10]John W. Wood, "Dollars Versus Scholars: The Reaganization of U.C." *College and University Business* 51 (November 1971): 50.

tion had been eliminated, the Boards of Regents had become a single body, and a central administration had been established above all campuses.[11]

Again, one may argue that there were a variety of sources which led to that merger; but few in Wisconsin or otherwise would disclaim Governor Lucey's strong influence in completing the merger.

In addition to increased control or influence on the part of the governor, the executive branch and the executive bureaucracies have gained increased control over higher education in the states. In Pennsylvania, for example, the legislature passed a bill in the fall of 1972 significantly expanding the duties and authority of the State Board of Education and the Secretary of Education over public higher education. These increases in the duties of the board include:

- Annual review of the budget of publicly financed higher education with authority to recommend approval or disapproval of the budget to the General Assembly
- Approval or disapproval of any additional branches or campuses of public institutions in the state
- Approval or disapproval of any new professional schools or upper division programs by community colleges
- Review of long-range plans from all public and private institutions in the state
- Adoption and periodic review of a master plan for higher education which defines the role for each type of institution in the state
- Recommendation of enrollment levels for each institution and a method of governance of the entire system
- Providing formulas for the distribution of state funds among the institutions
- Providing for the orderly development of the system
- Making all reasonable rules and regulations necessary to carry out the purposes of the act.

Pennsylvania's past and present roles in higher education can be

[11]Jane Show, "Madison Versus the Merger," *College and University Business* 54 (April 1973): 39.

instructive. The fourteen state colleges and university (former teachers colleges), since their purchase[12] in the earlier years of this century, have been dominated by the state. But Penn State, the land-grant university, has had high autonomy. It was joined by the University of Pittsburgh and Temple University in the 1960s as designated 'state-related' institutions. The autonomy of these three universities has been markedly eroded in recent years.

Other examples of state bureaucracies which have gained considerable influence upon higher education include state budget offices; state civil service systems, which can control nonacademic employees; and a state building commission or department of public works, which may design, build, and accept for the state all academic and in some cases nonacademic buildings. A number of states, approximately twenty-six, have state planning offices which have been formed to provide research and analyses, encourage improved planning, and improve the coordination of the total program of the state government. Finally, twenty or so states have scholarship and loan commissions which may have control over the distribution of several million dollars of state and, at times, federal funds.

Land-grant institutions have become deeply enmeshed in a complex and confusing network of controls and guidelines handed down by federal and state bureaucracies. As the absolute number of dollars devoted to higher education has increased, so has executive interest in controlling their expenditure. The full course of external controls has not yet been run: the situation is still open and the ultimate consequences for autonomy and control and, obviously, quality is unknown.

State Legislatures

State legislatures are also taking an increased interest in specifying higher education. Some legislatures have formalized standards of faculty and student behavior. The Carnegie Commission on Higher

---

[12]William Toombs and Stephan D. Millman, *Pennsylvania's "State-Owned" Institutions: Some Dimensions of Degree Output*—Report No. 20 (University Park, Pa.: Center for the Study of Higher Education, The Pennsylvania State University, 1973).

Education reports that twenty-nine of the fifty states enacted legislation in 1969–70 regarding campus unrest, the control of firearms,
antidisturbance regulations, and other legislation including penalties
for campus unrest and criminal offenses, and the curtailment of
student financial aid.[13]

Many state legislatures have shown an interest in fixing faculty
teaching loads. The Michigan legislature just a few years ago attempted to legislate the number of hours professors should spend in
the classroom, but the courts subsequently ruled that this violated
the constitutional autonomy of the University of Michigan, Michigan State and Wayne State Universities. Similar legislation has been
passed in New York, Florida, and Washington and narrowly de-
feated in Illinois and Arizona. In Pennsylvania, the legislature attached a rider to the appropriations bills requiring reports on faculty
activities in those institutions receiving state funds. When the reports
were rendered, institutions were accused of submitting dishonest
reports.

After a review of legislative actions relative to higher education,
O'Neil concluded:

> A composite prediction now emerges: Regardless of the level of recur-
> rence of student protest, legislative regulation of academic life is likely
> to persist up to the point it is checked by the courts. All factors seem
> to point towards continued regulation as well as continued oversight.
> As these pressures intensify, the need for protective measures will
> increase correspondingly.[14]

He has suggested that this protection may take the form of litigation,
lobbying, constitutional amendments, and, in the long run, greater
realliance on alternative sources of funding. This last will probably
be the most difficult to achieve.

---

[13]Carnegie Commission on Higher Education, *Dissent and Disruption* (New York: McGraw-
Hill, 1971), p. 165.

[14]Robert M. O'Neil, *The Courts, Government and Higher Education* (Washington, D.C.:
Committee for Economic Development, 1972), p. 9.

The Courts and Higher Education

There has been a flood of litigation in the courts relative to court-campus relations in the last five or more years, especially since May 1970. O'Neil has referred to the Kent-Cambodia crisis as the catalytic force in a major realignment in court-campus relations.

> Within the past two or three years, the federal courts have become forums for the litigation of a broad range of issues that one would not have thought justifiable a decade ago: legality of dormitory room searches; confidentiality of student files and records of student organizations; recognition and status of student political groups; administrative control over campus newspapers and other publications; access of insiders and outsiders to campus facilities for meetings and rallies; denial of enrollment in or credit for particular courses as well as degree programs; withdrawal of student government positions or offices from alleged campus wrongdoers; and other comparable issues. Nor were the issues noted in this list approached lightly; while the majority of cases went against the plaintiffs, a surprising number held that the university had abridged constitutional liberties of students, faculty or staff members, or of outsiders seeking access to the campus.[15]

Increased resort to the courts in future years seems likely for a number of reasons. Student plaintiffs have received a remarkably high degree of success in the courts, legal services are becoming increasingly more available, the courts are gradually becoming more accustomed to handling academic matters, and courts are becoming more accessible to aggrieved members of the academic community.

The influence of the courts over higher education, especially in its internal decision-making structures, is likely to increase. O'Neil says the American university has already become, in its administrative aspects, a quasi-judicial institution. In the process of increasing the subjection of academic decisions to the scrutiny of the courts, many internal decision-making processes have been discredited and repudiated. In response, many colleges and universities have tended to judicialize their internal procedures. Campus tribunals in many insti-

---

[15]Ibid., pp. 11–12.

tutions do now in fact observe due process and have adopted court standards for internal dispute settlement. There appears to be an increasing trend to appoint lawyers as presidents of institutions and in middle-level nonlegal posts.[16] University constituencies are more often represented by counsel than has been the case in the past. Finally, formal procedures are likely to be mandated in a growing number of states by the application of general administrative procedures statutes.

Collective Bargaining

The increase in executive, legislative, and judicial control over higher education has been accompanied by a spurt of collective bargaining in the late sixties and early seventies. The first contracts with faculties at two-year colleges were signed in the mid-1960s; the first contracts with faculties at four-year colleges were signed in 1969 at Central Michigan University, the City University of New York, and Southeastern Massachusetts University. Since that recent beginning, collective bargaining has grown to the extent that as of January 1975, the faculty at 243 institutions, covering 357 campuses, had chosen bargaining agents. Approximately 309 (86 per cent) of these campuses were in the public sector and 211 (59 per cent) were two-year colleges.

Land-grant universities where faculties have chosen bargaining agents include the Universities of Delaware, Hawaii, and Rhode Island; Rutgers; and the teaching assistants at the University of Wisconsin. There is substantial organizing activity at a number of other land-grant universities including the Universities of Massachusetts, Minnesota, and California and The Pennsylvania State University. The faculty at the University of Massachusetts at Amherst voted to reject collective bargaining. Bargaining with faculty in public institutions normally is governed under the regulation of state labor laws for public employees. Approximately twenty-three states now have legislation which either specifically guarantees faculty the right to organize and requires the administration to recognize duly

[16]At this writing, the presidents of Harvard, Yale, and Michigan are lawyers.

chosen bargaining agents or has been so interpreted. Approximately eighty per cent of the campuses with collective bargaining agents are located in nine states: New York, Michigan, Massachusetts, Pennsylvania, New Jersey, Wisconsin, Washington, Illinois, and Minnesota.

Public employee legislation of a comprehensive sort does three things for the faculty at an institution. The law normally guarantees the faculty the right to organize and protects them in the exercise of this right by prohibiting administrations from punishing faculty for exercising this right. Second, the law requires management to bargain in good faith. That does not mean that either party has to agree to a proposal but merely that under labor relations statutes the administration and faculty both have to listen to proposals and counterproposals and eventually sign a legally binding agreement. Third, the labor relations statutes in a number of states such as New York and Pennsylvania set up public employee labor relations boards to administer the provisions of the act. These boards are responsible for defining unfair labor practices, determining or adjudicating the membership of bargaining units, and performing other normal labor relations activities.

The impact that collective bargaining will have on institutions is as yet undetermined. The nature of bargaining and the institutional context under which it occurs are so complex as to make predictions about its future hazardous.

Garbarino has identified three basic types of unionism:[17]

Defensive unionism occurs in single-campus institutions. The traditional mechanisms of faculty participation in governance, such as senates and councils, have evolved into unions often with the same leaders as formerly were in the senate. Under defensive unionism the form of governance may shift slightly but the substance of faculty-administrative relations does not. Under defensive unionism it is likely that existing senates and councils will coexist with the union. This particular type of unionism appears to be occurring at one land-grant university, Rutgers, and would probably be the dominant

---

[17]Joseph W. Garbarino, "Emerging Patterns of Faculty Bargaining," *Academics at the Bargaining Table,* ed. James P. Begin (New Brunswick, N.J.: Institute of Management and Labor Relations, Rutgers University, 1973), pp. 1–15.

model at a number of others—e.g., Berkeley, Madison, and Minnesota.

Constitutional unionism occurs in those institutions in which the tradition of faculty participation in governance is weak or nonexistent. The bargaining session tends to develop into a constitutional convention in which governance procedures are developed and put into a legally binding contract. The most prevalent examples of constitutional unionism exist in the Pennsylvania State College and University system and the Massachusetts State Colleges.[18]

Typical contracts in Massachusetts such as those at Boston State and Worcester State Colleges tend to include existing governance arrangements, such as councils and committees, into the contract. In this regard, these contracts are distinctly different from the defensive unionism mentioned earlier.

The third major type of unionism which appears to Garbarino to be occurring in the country is called *reform unionism*. This type tends to occur at large, complex, multicampus systems like the City University of New York, the State University of New York, and the University of Hawaii. (The latter institution is a land-grant university.) The University of Hawaii's system includes a main campus at Manoa, a four-year institution at Hilo, and six two-year campuses in other locations in the Hawaiian Islands. The State University of New York is a twenty-nine-campus unit consisting of university centers, four-year colleges, medical centers, two-year technical and agricultural colleges, and a maritime academy. The City University of New York is a twenty-campus unit including a number of four-year and two-year institutions plus a graduate center—all in the same bargaining unit. The activities in these large and complex systems should be known and studied by officers in all land-grant and state universities. These institutions may become prototypes for the future of the majority of land-grant and state universities as is noted below.

In their book, *Professors, Unions, and American Higher Education* (1973), Ladd and Lipset point out the nature of the diversity within

18Donald E. Walters, "Collective Bargaining in Higher Education," *AGB Reports* 15 (March 1973): 2–8.

such multi-campus systems and the effect this has had on collective
bargaining elections.[19] The simple point is that faculty in two-year
colleges and universities perceive a different set of problems and vote
differently in collective bargaining elections than do the faculty in the
major university centers within a multi-campus system.

In the second University of Hawaii election, only 67 per cent of
the faculty on the main campus voted as contrasted with 82 per cent
of the faculty on the six two-year campuses and 78 per cent of the
faculty on the four-year campus at Hilo. Fifty-five per cent of the
faculty on the main campus who voted in the second election supported the AAUP, whereas 85 per cent of the faculty who voted on
the two-year campuses supported the American Federation of
Teachers.[20] In the first City University of New York election to
represent full-time faculty, 75 per cent of the faculty in the graduate
centers and 65 per cent of the faculty in the four older senior colleges
were in favor of the Legislative Conference in the second or run-off
election. Sixty-seven per cent of the faculty in the community colleges in this election favored the AFT.[21] This and other evidence
indicates that in these types of collective bargaining units conflict
within the faculty will be intense. In those cases where the faculty
from the two-year colleges control the union, there is likely to be, and
indeed there is, evidence that these faculties try to redress some of
the inequities they see between their own institutions and the four-
year and graduate centers within the system. The implications of
these developments as they relate to ultimate faculty authority and
power and the mission and processes of public university education
and research can be of major significance.

It is apparent that the contracts being negotiated in higher education differ substantially among institutions. A variety of factors can
enter into this variability. Up to July 1974, Massachusetts law had
been interpreted as prohibiting negotiations on salary. In other
states, such as Rhode Island, there are few limits placed upon the
scope of negotiable items. Other laws are more specific about the
definition of bargainability.

[19]Everett Carll Ladd, Jr. and Seymour Martin Lipset, *Professors, Unions, and American
Higher Education* (Berkeley: Carnegie Commission on Higher Education, 1973), pp. 47–52.
[20]Ibid., p. 51.
[21]Ibid., p. 50.

Three types of contracts are apparent in higher education:

First is a limited contract which tends to be concerned only with wages, hours, and working conditions.[22] Such contracts as those at Central Michigan and Rutgers (a land-grant university) are examples.

Other contracts are substantially broader in scope because they cover more issues. The ways in which those issues are covered, however, are such that perhaps only the process of the matter is handled. For example, a number of contracts handle workload by simply stating that workload "shall at all times be reasonable." Workload in land-grant and other state universities is a complicated and controversial matter and is closely related to mission and the balance of responsibilities of research, teaching and service.

The third type of contract deals with process and substance. The Pennsylvania State College contract, for example, specifies not only that faculty will be evaluated, but the manner in which they will be evaluated and what criteria will be used. In other words, the contract deals with the substance of the matter of faculty evaluation. This activity has spilled over to make Pennsylvania's state-related universities, including the land-grant Penn State, sensitive to both faculty and academic administrator evaluations. If administration is to evaluate faculty, faculty hold they should at least have a part in administrator evaluations.

The impact of unionization will vary with such circumstances as the type of unionism involved in the institution and the type of contract that has been negotiated. This variability adds to the difficulty of predicting the impact that unionization will have on colleges and universities. Nevertheless there do appear to be some significant possibilities.

It seems certain that collective bargaining will tend to formalize faculty-administrative relations to a greater extent than has been the case. As has been pointed out in another context, bureaucratization of university life is proceeding apace and collective bargaining is adding to this trend. Several institutions have created new positions to handle bargaining, such as a vice-president for industrial relations

---

[22]Neil S. Bucklew, "Collective Bargaining and Policymaking," *Current Issues in Higher Education* 1974, ed. Dyckman Vermilye (San Francisco: Jossey-Bass, 1974), pp. 36–41.

or personnel resources. Other institutions are appointing faculty grievance officers and making changes in their personnel administration systems. The unionization of faculty is affecting not only unionized institutions but also is affecting all institutions. For any land-grant or other state university to ignore unionism would seem to be folly.

Second, it is likely that collective bargaining will further the view that academic administration is a profession with its own set of distinct skills. Because of this, the scholar-administrator may become an endangered species.[23] Administrators will have to be trained in personnel policies and procedures, and the opportunities for faculty members to serve as short-term administrators will be less frequent. An administrative assignment may require a significant change in a faculty member's career. Speculation is that few faculty members will want to take such a significant turn from their traditional roles.

Third, under collective bargaining there is likely to be more direct contact between representatives of the faculty and boards of trustees. In multicampus systems this contact most often will be between representatives of the faculty and the agencies of state government as already has occurred in New York and Pennsylvania. One can speculate about the adverse effect this will have on administrative authority. It is difficult, however, to predict that the authority relationships of the administration will be adversely affected in every case. In multicampus systems, where the contract is negotiated directly between a system-wide faculty representative and an agency of the state government, campus administrators may well be relegated to the role of administering a contract negotiated in a central office. In such situations, the functions of administrators will be quite different from those cases where they can initiate action or negotiate their own binding agreements. It is likely that collective bargaining, to be consistent with our earlier remarks, will require different kinds of administrative skills from those currently needed. Administrators will surely have to have a more substantive concern for legal and bureaucratic skills and to be sensitive to concepts of due process.

[23]Garbarino, "Faculty Bargaining."

Finally, more serious thought must be given to the eventual role of students in collective bargaining than has heretofore been considered. In a number of community colleges, including Chicago City College and Philadelphia Community Colleges, students have intervened legally against faculty strikes. Students are involved in the bargaining process at Boston, Worcester, Fitchburg, and Salem State Colleges in Massachusetts and at Long Island University. If an institution negotiates a contract that will result in increased tuition costs, it is predictable that students will intervene at some point.

The inattentive administrators may conclude that since the major collective bargaining and unionization activity has occurred in other than land-grant and other state universities, they need have no concern. If so, they miss the point. Major changes in any one or more sectors of higher education in faculty-administrative-exterior authority relations will exert influence for these relations in all sectors. All higher education administrators, if they are not now so, must become attentive.

Fiscal Factors

Several factors inherent in national demographic data portend certain changes in the postsecondary education milieu. First, for all save perhaps a few exceptional institutions, the great age of expansion is almost over. Adjusting to slow growth or no growth in enrollment is and will be the order of the day in the late seventies and in the decade of the eighties.

Second, many observers, including Glenny, have predicted that, with the exception of a few states, the proportion of the state budget going to higher education will be no greater in 1980 than in the next year or so.[24] This projection reflects the general opinion that higher education has suffered a relative decline in importance in the public mind when compared to other social services. Health care, crime

[24]Lyman Glenny, "Diversification and Quality Control," *Higher Education: Myths, Realities and Possibilities,* Winfred L. Godwin and Peter B. Mann, eds. (Atlanta: Southern Regional Education Board, 1972), pp. 4–5.

control, ecology, and the lower schools are emerging as funding high priorities in many state legislatures.

It is clear that private higher education will receive increased funding from state legislatures over the next several years. Plans such as the Bundy Plan in New York and the McConnell Plan in Illinois will become more common in an effort to rescue private higher education from its current financial nadir. In the face of increased legislative scrutiny of budgets, it is difficult to conclude anything except that these gains for private higher education will have significant effects on funding public higher education systems, including land-grant universities.

Those observers who have been close to the changes in state funding patterns have tended to look to the federal government as a savior for higher education's financial doldrums. While it is not likely that the federal government will increase substantially its support for higher education, a more basic problem is a change in the form that federal financial support might take. Federal assistance through students has been actively practiced for some time. There is currently much discussion of an almost complete shift in the funding pattern from direct institutional grants to grants made directly to students: i.e., the market model of funding.

Immediately following World War II, the G.I. Bill provided direct financial support to students and reimbursed institutions for educational service to veterans. Loans to students and work-study programs have been expanded sharply with the Education Amendments of 1972, extending and strengthening many of these features.

Leslie has reviewed the major trend towards government funding of higher education through students that has emerged.[25] As he sees it, the reports of the Carnegie Commission and the Newman Task Force, which emphasize equality of opportunity, have encouraged emphasis on state voucher programs and influenced the federal higher education bill of 1972, which is essentially a plan for a national voucher system. In its recommendations, the commission

---

[25]Larry L. Leslie, *The Trend Toward Government Financing of Higher Education Through Students: Can the Market Model be Applied?* (University Park, Pa.: Center for the Study of Higher Education, The Pennsylvania State University, 1973).

favored federal pressures upon states to follow the federal funding pattern of student vouchers, by urging states to allocate matching monies equal to the amount of nonfederal grants to those EOP students who have both federal and nonfederal grants. The federal government, in the form of the Higher Education Amendments of 1972, has furthered this intrusion into state higher education affairs by requiring statewide planning and formation of a state higher education commission before certain funds can be received from the federal government. The federal requirements for state commissions, called 1202 Commissions, have now been effected but their structures and modes of operation are not yet stabilized.

Leslie points out that the goals of such programs as grants-in-aid to students are to improve efficiency in higher education and to redistribute income in order to equalize education opportunity. Both of these goals are economic solutions which do not take full cognizance of the complex nature of higher education as a *social* institution. He concludes the following:

> A market system as a guiding framework for higher education would tend to exclude any activity not related to producing the goods or services being purchased. Evidence of this can easily be noted by reflecting on the nature of proprietary schools, which are the best existing examples of a market system in higher education.[26]

The point of all this is that the American political systems are engaged in a debate about the fundamental problem of who should pay for higher education. There seems to be a redirection from support of low-cost tuition to an assumption that students benefit most from higher education and should therefore assume a greater share of its cost. The major question that remains is whether or not a system approaching full-cost tuition and direct funding of students will result in significant redirection of the financial sources from which land-grant universities receive sustenance. The question is: Will students be diverted from land-grant institutions if they have funds to go elsewhere? There is evidence

[26]Ibid., pp. 15–16.

that they may.[27] There almost certainly will be strong pressures on colleges and universities to become more consumer-oriented in response to the marketplace.

One further aspect of the financial situation deserves mention. The cutback on research funds by the federal government, if continued, can have devastating results on the research efforts of all colleges and universities. The land-grant universities are particularly vulnerable. As of this writing, one can only speculate that this is an aberration introduced by a temporary shift in political forces. The future of research on the great scale of the 1960s depends on a reversal of federal research policy.

The overwhelming evidence is that external agencies such as executive bureaucracies, governors, legislatures, the courts, the federal government, and those in favor of collective bargaining will increase their attempts to direct, regulate, and/or control higher education.

Many of these trends are not only inevitable; they are rational. All bear credence to the accelerating significance of the work of universities. If universities did not count, few would care. Yet, all the trends mentioned above have a high potential for interrupting or limiting or even eliminating the autonomy which universities have not only enjoyed but have believed essential to their proper functioning. Surely, it would be tragic if the power of the professoriate were greatly diminished. The genius of the university during its nearly 1000 years of history in the West is that, while it was of the state and of the culture, it was also outside the state and the culture. In its earliest days, it was self-governing; it was also a sanctuary.

In our time, professionalism and decision making by professionals is perhaps the single most important descriptor of university governance. The achievement of this state is the theme of *The Academic Revolution* by Jencks and Riesman.[28] These authors advance the concept that the first half of this century represented a shift in the control of universities from high-placed administrative officers and

[27]Larry L. Leslie and Jonathan D. Fife, "The College Student Grant Study," *The Journal of Higher Education* 45 (December 1974).

[28]Cristopher Jencks and David Reisman, *The Academic Revolution* (Garden City, N.Y.: Anchor Books, 1969).

boards of trustees to the professoriate. This condition appears to be directly proportional to the amount of prestige within an institution. The land-grant universities are, by and large, institutions of high prestige and great faculty authority and influence in institutional decision. They—the professoriate, by and large—decide who the institutions will educate (admission decisions), who will educate them (personnel decisions), what shall be the content of their education (curriculum decisions), who shall graduate (quality control decisions), and what they as scholars shall do by way of research (program decisions).

This very professionalism has made the university too important to be ignored, too potent not to be watched, and too expensive to be unaccountable in the use of its resources.

Yet autonomy must be sustained, conditions of the marketplace dare not dominate the decision-making process, and government bureaucrats should not control. While all decisions regarding such an important social instrument as universities are ultimately political, the normative operations of politics as expressed through elective processes, i.e., through legislatures and governors, are scarcely the most effective instruments for university governance.

A blueprint for future university governance structures cannot be prepared at this time. It seems that new governance patterns quite different from those of the past are sure to emerge. One can expect a major shift in authority relationships to occur as faculty unionize. The powers of governors and legislatures and their instrumentations relevant to universities are sure to accrue great power in the near future. But as this power is used, a backlash may occur and a new form of political decision making may be adopted or invented.

Clark Kerr has projected universities as quasi-public utilities. As the private sector of higher education is more and more the recipient directly and indirectly of tax money, the supervision, control, and a demand for accountability for the private sector is almost sure to follow. What may then develop is a commission type of regulation and control for all on higher education—public and private—as is now normative for such bodies as stock exchanges, aviation, telephone companies, the insurance industry, and so on. Under such regulation, private universities would become quasi-public utilities in terms of state governance and control and in response and account-ability to the public weal. If this occurs for the now private universi-ties, the public sector of higher education may then also become a quasi-public utility to an even greater degree. Regulatory agencies at state and national levels may be created to deal with these quasi-public university utilities.

Another form for societal participation in governance may be some pattern analogous to that now found in public authorities, e.g., a port authority, a transportation authority, or a state power author-ity. Strangely, no one seems to have been watching the development of such authorities in higher education matters over the last two decades. The majority of buildings erected for public higher educa-tion institutions in Pennsylvania since World War II have been built by the General State Authority. Interactive with the State University of New York, not a part of it nor a part of the normal state bureau-cratic structure, are the state dormitory authority, the state univer-sity construction fund, the state university research corporation, the scholar incentive scholarship program, and faculty-student associa-tions on each campus. The Board of Regents of New York and its operating arm—the state department of education—are constitu-tionally created and enjoy an autonomy from intervention by gover-nors and their bureaucracies and by legislators that in many respects makes the Board of Regents a fourth branch of government. The Board of Regents of New York is now a unique institution. It might become a pattern for other states as statewide boards of control become not only commonplace but mature.

It might be a very useful exercise to develop a rather complete university authority model, utilizing what is known about analogous authorities operational at both state and national levels. We know a fair amount about the Tennessee Valley Authority operating at a regional level and we have recently witnessed the creation of a postal authority at the national level. Whether or not these two authorities become models for 'university public authorities' is problematic, but new patterns of state, regional, national, and federal interactions with the institutions of higher learning are inevitable.

Let us hope, however, that whatever evolves will recognize the special competence and the special role of the professoriate in the governance of higher education. What is ultimately at stake in any significant shifts in power and authority relative to universities are the goals of the institution and the means to accomplish them. For example, the goals of land-grant universities are far more inclusive than conventional collegiate instruction. If, however, a market model for financing universities should come to have major recognition, the land-grant university might well be forced to modify its goals or reorder its priorities. In complex systems of which the land-grant university is one component (Wisconsin, New York, Georgia, Florida, Hawaii, and others) such developments as full faculty unionization or control from a single board through a single system chief administrator might well weaken the unique mission and modes of fulfillment of the land-grant sector.

This volume has not challenged the traditional character of land-grant universities. It supports the idea of the land-grant university and esteems its values. It asks for an extension of this idea and these values into new areas of service to the people of the states.

CONTRIBUTORS

G. LESTER ANDERSON is Director of the Center for the Study of Higher Education and Professor of Higher Education in the College of Education, The Pennsylvania State University.

HENRY R. FORTMANN is Assistant Director of the Agricultural Experiment Station and Professor of Agronomy, The Pennsylvania State University. He is also Northeast Regional Coordinator for the Association of Agricultural Experiment Station Directors.

RENEE C. FRIEDMAN is Staff Associate at the Center for the Study of Higher Education, The Pennsylvania State University.

ROBERT S. FRIEDMAN is Professor and Head of the Department of Political Science, The Pennsylvania State University.

MAXWELL H. GOLDBERG is Project Director, The Converse College Center for Humanities—South Carolina Committee for the Humanities, Project on Greater Spartanburg in Transition and Andrew J. R. Helmus Distinguished Professor of Humanities and Literature, Converse College.

RALPH K. HUITT is Executive Director, National Association of State Universities and Land-Grant Colleges.

STANLEY O. IKENBERRY is Senior Vice President for University Development and Relations and Professor of Higher Education, The Pennsylvania State University.

THOMAS B. KING is Associate Director of the Cooperative Extension Service and Professor of Animal Science, The Pennsylvania State University.

OTIS E. LANCASTER is George Westinghouse Professor of Engineering, The Pennsylvania State University.

LARRY L. LESLIE is Research Associate in the Center for the Study of Higher Education and Professor and Chairman of Higher Education, The Pennsylvania State University.

DAVID MADSEN is Professor of the History of Education, the University of Washington.

KENNETH P. MORTIMER is Research Associate in the Center for the Study of Higher Education and Professor of Higher Education, The Pennsylvania State University.

DAVID C. NICHOLS is Associate Director of the National Advisory Council on Education Professions Development, Washington, D.C.

JEROME K. PASTO is Associate Dean for Resident Instruction, College of Agriculture, The Pennsylvania State University.

SAMUEL D. PROCTOR is Professor of Education in the Graduate School of Education, Rutgers University.

RICHARD D. SCHEIN is Professor of Botany, The Pennsylvania State University.

WILLIAM TOOMBS is Research Associate in the Center for the Study of Higher Education and Associate Professor of Higher Education, The Pennsylvania State University.

THEODORE R. VALLANCE is Associate Dean for Resident and Graduate Instruction, College of Human Development, The Pennsylvania State University.

Appendix

IN the opening chapter we stated that the distinctions between land-grant universities and non land-grant state universities had become blurred over the last century. Both sets of institutions hold membership in the National Association of State Universities and Land-Grant Colleges, 130 in all. Yet the origins of the land-grant institutions are of more than historical interest. These origins represent a value commitment by the American people and the federal government. This is attested to by the act of 1890 that brought 14 institutions into the land-grant category—institutions that were then for black students and that are predominantly still so. Then, again, Congress created Federal City College in 1966 as a land-grant college. Finally, by the educational amendments of 1972, the University of Guam, founded in 1952, and the University of the Virgin Islands, founded in 1962, were made land-grant universities. In lieu of land or scrip, these three universities received a federal endowment— Guam and the Virgin Islands received $3,000,000 each and Federal City received $7,800,000. The original commitment of the land-grant institutions now permeate the whole of the public university complex. The theme of this volume is that these commitments can be reviewed, broadened, and enriched as these universities move into the last quarter of this century and into the next century.

Table 1 lists the members of the National Association of State Universities and Land-Grant Colleges, identifying land-grant insitutions by an asterisk.

Table 2 lists the land-grant institutions with dates relevant to their founding, land-grant designation, and opening to students. The table also reports enrollments for 1960, 1970, and 1974.

Table 3 lists those land-grant institutions that shared in land or scrip as provided by the Morrill Act of 1862 and gives the current status of the disposition of the land or scrip. Four institutions, Guam, Federal City, Hawaii, and the Virgin Islands received cash appropriations instead of land and scrip. Only three of the 1890 institutions, Alcorn A and M, South Carolina State, and Virginia State shared in the grants of 1862. None of the other eleven 1890 institutions appear in Table 3; apparently they received nothing.

Data for the appendix were provided by the National Association of State Universities and Land-Grant Colleges, but the arrangement in the tables and errors, if there be any, are the responsibility of the editor.

G. Lester Anderson
June 27, 1975

TABLE 1
Members:

National Association of State Universities and Land-Grant Colleges*

ALABAMA
>*Alabama A & M University
>*Auburn University
>University of Alabama

ALASKA
>*University of Alaska

ARIZONA
>Arizona State University
>*University of Arizona

ARKANSAS
>*University of Arkansas
>*University of Arkansas, Pine Bluff

CALIFORNIA
>*University of California System
>University of California, Berkeley
>University of California, Davis
>University of California, Irvine
>University of California, Los Angeles
>University of California, Riverside
>University of California, San Diego
>University of California, Santa Barbara

COLORADO
>*Colorado State University
>University of Colorado

CONNECTICUT
>*Connecticut Agricultural Experiment Station
>*University of Connecticut

DELAWARE
>*Delaware State College
>*University of Delaware

DISTRICT OF COLUMBIA
>*Federal City College

FLORIDA
>*Florida A & M University
>Florida State University
>*University of Florida

GEORGIA
*Fort Valley State College
Georgia Institute of Technology
*University of Georgia

GUAM
*University of Guam

HAWAII
*University of Hawaii

IDAHO
*University of Idaho

ILLINOIS
Southern Illinois University
*University of Illinois
University of Illinois, Chicago Circle
University of Illinois, Urbana-Champaign

INDIANA
Indiana University
Indiana University, Bloomington
*Purdue University

IOWA
*Iowa State University
University of Iowa

KANSAS
*Kansas State University
University of Kansas

KENTUCKY
*Kentucky State University
*University of Kentucky

LOUISIANA
*Louisiana State University
Louisiana State University, Baton Rouge
*Southern University

MAINE
*University of Maine
University of Maine, Orono

MARYLAND
*University of Maryland
University of Maryland, College Park
*University of Maryland, Eastern Shore

AND THEIR CONTINUING CHALLENGE

MASSACHUSETTS
*Massachusetts Institute of Technology
*University of Massachusetts
University of Massachusetts, Amherst

MICHIGAN
*Michigan State University
University of Michigan
Wayne State University

MINNESOTA
*University of Minnesota

MISSISSIPPI
*Alcorn A & M College
*Mississippi State University
University of Mississippi

MISSOURI
*Lincoln University
*University of Missouri
University of Missouri, Columbia

MONTANA
*Montana State University
University of Montana

NEBRASKA
*University of Nebraska
University of Nebraska, Lincoln

NEVADA
*University of Nevada, Reno

NEW HAMPSHIRE
*University of New Hampshire

NEW JERSEY
*Rutgers, The State University

NEW MEXICO
*New Mexico State University
University of New Mexico

NEW YORK
City University of New York
*Cornell University
State University of New York
State University of New York, Albany
State University of New York, Binghamton
State University of New York, Buffalo
State University of New York, Stony Brook

NORTH CAROLINA
*North Carolina A & T State University
*North Carolina State University
University of North Carolina
University of North Carolina, Chapel Hill

NORTH DAKOTA
*North Dakota State University
University of North Dakota

OHIO
Kent State University
Miami University
*Ohio State University

OKLAHOMA
*Langston University
*Oklahoma State University
University of Oklahoma

OREGON
*Oregon State University
University of Oregon

PENNSYLVANIA
*Pennsylvania State University
Temple University
University of Pittsburgh

PUERTO RICO
*University of Puerto Rico

RHODE ISLAND
*University of Rhode Island

SOUTH CAROLINA
*Clemson University
*South Carolina State College
University of South Carolina

SOUTH DAKOTA
*South Dakota State University
University of South Dakota

TENNESSEE
*Tennessee State University
*University of Tennessee
University of Tennessee, Knoxville

TEXAS
*Prairie View A & M University
*Texas A & M University System

 Texas Southern University
 Texas Tech University
 University of Houston
 University of Texas System
 University of Texas, Austin

UTAH
 University of Utah
 *Utah State University

VERMONT
 *University of Vermont

VIRGIN ISLANDS
 *College of the Virgin Islands

VIRGINIA
 University of Virginia
 *Virginia Polytechnic Institute & State University
 *Virginia State College

WASHINGTON
 University of Washington
 *Washington State University

WEST VIRGINIA
 *West Virginia University

WISCONSIN
 *University of Wisconsin System
 University of Wisconsin, Madison
 University of Wisconsin, Milwaukee

WYOMING
 *University of Wyoming

TABLE 2

Institution	Date State Accepted Morrill Act	Date College was Authorized	Date College Opened to Students	Enrollments		
				1960	1970	1974
Alabama A & M University	1891	1873	1875	1,265	2,129	4,046
Auburn University	1867	1872	1872	7,333	15,217	19,155
University of Alaska	1929	1922	1922	781	8,770	11,548
University of Arizona	1910	1885	1891	11,772	26,123	29,241
University of Arkansas	1864	1871	1872	5,086	17,053	25,498
University of Arkansas, Pine Bluff	1891	1873	1882	1,436	3,353	2,241
University of California	1866	1868	1869	42,617	147,279	122,606
Colorado State University	1879	1877	1879	5,305	17,045	18,133
University of Connecticut	1862	1881	1881	8,774	20,028	23,024
Delaware State College	1891	1891	1892	336	1,393	2,058
University of Delaware	1867	1867	1869	2,494	15,730	18,486
Federal City College		1966	1968		5,646	7,783
Florida A & M University	1891	1887	1887	2,574	5,024	4,871
University of Florida	1870	1870	1884	11,353	23,958	23,332
Fort Valley State College	1890	1891	1891	787	2,338	1,807
University of Georgia	1886	1785	1801	8,190	21,181	23,146
University of Guam	1972	1952			2,349	
University of Hawaii		1907	1908	7,738	32,969	46,502
University of Idaho	1890	1889	1892	3,658	7,007	7,676
University of Illinois	1867	1867	1868	24,442	58,002	61,168

Institution	Date State Accepted Morrill Act	Date College was Authorized	Date College Opened to Students	Enrollments		
				1960	1970	1974
Purdue University	1865	1869	1874	13,173	38,314	39,098
Iowa State University	1862	1858	1859	9,252	19,620	20,412
Kansas State University	1863	1863	1863	6,507	13,847	16,422
Kentucky State University	1893	1866	1887	611	1,754	2,174
University of Kentucky	1863	1879	1880	8,045	28,235	34,297
Louisiana State University	1869	1874	1874	10,974	35,031	43,479
Southern University	1892	1880	1881	4,344	9,722	12,226
University of Maine	1863	1865	1868	3,668	22,576	25,696
University of Maryland	1864	1856	1859	19,130	52,225	56,464
University of Massachusetts	1863	1863	1867	5,424	24,989	31,976
Massachusetts Institute of Technology	1863	1861	1865	6,270	7,557	8,050
Michigan State University	1863	1855	1857	20,930	44,092	46,794
University of Minnesota	1863	1851	1851	26,538	68,709	68,899
Alcorn A & M College	1892	1871	1872	822	2,520	2,386
Mississippi State University	1866	1878	1880	4,272	9,605	11,664
Lincoln University	1891	1866	1866	1,364	2,411	2,537
University of Missouri	1863	1839	1841	12,203	48,896	52,062
Montana State College	1889	1839	1893	3,404	8,230	8,425
University of Nebraska	1867	1869	1871	7,969	34,895	22,428
University of Nevada, Reno	1866	1873	1874	3,704	6,709	7,085[a]
University of New Hampshire	1863	1866	1868	3,370	15,169	16,254
Rutgers, the State University	1863	1766	1771	14,426	32,600	44,750

Institution	Date State Accepted Morrill Act	Date College was Authorized	Date College Opened to Students	Enrollments		
				1960	1970	1974
New Mexico State University	1898	1889	1890	2,654	10,065	12,639
Cornell University	1863	1865	1868	10,705	19,600	16,208
N. Carolina A & T State Univ.	1891	1891	1891	1,998	3,797	4,937
N. Carolina State University	1866	1887	1889	7,959	14,408	16,609
N. Dakota State University	1889	1890	1891	3,300	7,471	8,034
Ohio State University	1864	1870	1873	20,487	50,547	57,790
Langston University	1890	1897	1898	591	1,109	1,153
Oklahoma State University	1890	1890	1891	9,566	20,793	21,431
Oregon State University	1868	1865	1865	6,923	15,361	15,915
Pennsylvania State University	1863	1855	1859	19,109	55,403	64,777
University of Puerto Rico	—	1903	1903	13,153	42,516	47,533[b]
University of Rhode Island	1863	1888	1890	3,150	15,066	16,385
Clemson University	1868	1869	1893	3,649	7,888	10,586
S. Carolina State College	1868	1895	1896	1,388	2,148	3,152
S. Dakota State University	1889	1881	1884	2,926	6,791	6,590
Tennessee State University	1868	1912	1912	2,963	4,404	4,977
University of Tennessee	1868	1794	1794	10,040	38,500	45,440
Texas A & M University	1866	1871	1876	6,376	14,316	21,368
Prairie View A & M University	1891	1876	1876	2,320	4,575	4,870
Utah State University	1888	1888	1890	4,957	9,091	9,850
University of Vermont	1862	1791	1801	3,097	9,214	10,475
College of the Virgin Islands	1972	1962			1,446	617
Virginia State College	1870	1867	1868	2,409	3,178	4,176

Institution	Date State Accepted Morrill Act	Date College was Authorized	Date College Opened to Students	Enrollments		
				1960	1970	1974
Virginia Polytechnic Institute and State University	1870	1872	1872	4,826	12,014	17,470
Washington State University	1889	1890	1892	5,981	14,667	15,694
West Virginia University	1863	1867	1868	5,957	19,858	20,975
University of Wisconsin	1863	1848	1849	24,311	70,582	142,852
University of Wyoming	1889	1886	1887	3,501	8,800	9,629

[a]Enrollment figures given are for Fall 1973 since 1974 figures were not available.
[b]Enrollment figures given are for Fall 1972 since 1973 and 1974 figures were not available.

TABLE 3

Institution	Land Acres Received	Acres. Rec. in Scrip	Sale Price for Land or Scrip	1862 Land Grant Endowment Fund	Income from Fund	Acres Unsold	Value of Unsold Acres
Auburn University	—	240,000	$216,000	$253,500	$20,529	—	—
University of Alaska	123,000	—	—	16,256	275	26,561	undetermined
University of Arizona	150,000	—	—	71,585	29,351	149,405	$489,200
University of Arkansas	—	150,000	135,000	133,000	6,633	—	—
University of California	150,000	—	732,233	990,632	29,642	280	undetermined
Colorado State University	91,600	—	185,956	722,909	30,507	30,000	undetermined
University of Connecticut	—	180,000	135,000	135,000	6,799	—	—
University of Delaware	—	90,000	83,000	84,426	2,505	—	—
Federal City College	—	—	7,800,000[a]	—	—	—	—
University of Florida	—	90,000	80,000	157,385	7,750	—	—
University of Georgia	—	270,000	242,202	242,202	6,535	—	—
University of Guam	—	—	3,000,000[a]	—	—	—	—
University of Hawaii	—	—	6,000,000	—	—	—	—
University of Idaho	90,000	—	129,615	2,591,443	72,707	38,185	381,850
University of Illinois	—	480,000	648,442	649,013	32,451	—	—
Purdue University	—	390,000	212,238	340,000	7,996	—	—
Iowa State University	240,000	—	686,817	589,754	20,086	—	—
Kansas State University	97,682	—	491,746	672,064	18,147	—	—
Kentucky State College	—	—	—	20,925	1,256	—	—
University of Kentucky	—	330,000	164,746	144,075	8,645	—	—
Louisiana State University	—	210,000	182,630	182,313	9,115	—	—
University of Maine	—	210,000	116,356	118,300	5,915	—	—

Institution	Land Acres Received	Acres rec. in Scrip	Sale Price for Land or Scrip	1862 Land Grant Endowment Fund	Income from Fund	Acres Unsold	Value of Unsold Acres
University of Maryland	—	210,000	112,504	132,400	3,310	—	—
University of Massachusetts	—	360,000	236,287	146,000	7,300	—	—
Massachusetts Institute of Technology	—	—	—	73,000	3,650	—	—
Michigan State University	240,000	—	991,673	1,059,379	74,175	—	—
University of Minnesota	120,000	—	579,430	45,701,377	1,283,018	25,524	127,619
Alcorn A & M College	—	210,000	—	96,296	12,592	—	—
Mississippi State University	—	—	188,928	98,575	5,914	18,235	72,940
University of Missouri	330,000	—	363,441	545,406	22,916	63,337	633,778
Montana State College	140,000	—	533,148	1,130,447	60,807	3,844	116,630
University of Nebraska	90,800	—	560,072	705,992	34,224	—	—
University of Nevada	90,800	—	107,363	134,282	4,445	—	—
University of New Hampshire	—	150,000	80,000	80,000	4,800	—	—
Rutgers, the State University	—	210,000	115,945	116,000	5,800	—	—
New Mexico State University	250,000	—	—	1,311,737	155,739	210,445	631,335
Cornell University	—	989,920	688,576[b]	688,576	34,429	—	—
N. Carolina State University	—	270,000	135,000	125,000	7,500	—	—
N. Dakota State University	130,000	—	455,924	2,275,828	89,190	13,172	131,718
Ohio State University	—	629,920	340,906	524,177	31,451	—	—
Oklahoma State University	350,000	—	835,637[c]	—	—	—	—
Oregon State University	90,000	—	202,113	246,865	6,746	182	182
Pennsylvania St. University	—	780,000	439,186	500,000	25,000	—	—
University of Rhode Island	—	120,000	50,000	50,000	2,164	—	—

Institution	Land Acres Received	Acres Rec. in Scrip	Sale Price for Land or Scrip	1862 Land Grant Endowment Fund	Income from Fund	Acres Unsold	Value of Unsold Acres
Clemson University	—	180,000	130,500	95,900	5,754	—	—
S. Carolina State College	160,000	—	—	95,000	5,754	—	—
S. Dakota State University	—	300,000	128,804	1,305,864	92,069	88,364	883,640
University of Tennessee	—	180,000	271,875	400,000	10,870	—	—
Texas A & M University	200,000	—	174,000	209,000	27,620	—	—
Utah State University	—	150,000	194,136	385,520	27,343	31,528	157,638
University of Vermont	—	—	122,626	122,000	7,320	—	—
University of the Virgin Islands	—	—	3,000,000[a]	—	—	—	—
Virginia State College	—	300,000	—	173,892	6,470	—	—
Virginia Polytechnic Ins. and State University	—	—	285,000	344,312	13,722	—	—
Washington State University	90,000	150,000	247,608	7,027,608	227,211	64,276	2,571,040
West Virginia University	—	—	90,000	126,900	3,622	—	—
University of Wisconsin	240,000	—	303,594	303,595	7,399	—	—
University of Wyoming	90,000	—	73,355	478,512	38,536	73,529	735,292

[a]Direct cash appropriation instead of land or scrip.
[b]Scrip bought by Mr. Cornell yielding later through resale $5,460,038 for institution.
[c]$103,482 in cash and $732,155 in deferred payments on lands sold.